AF326541

THE FULL POWER PLAN

UNLOCK NATURE'S FORMULA
FOR OPTIMAL BODYMIND VITALITY

THE FULL POWER PLAN

ERNEST J. BRAKE

"After 40 years in medicine and community health outreach in Canada and internationally, I've witnessed countless 'miracles' when patients embrace lifestyle medicine. Dr. Brake brilliantly consolidates these principles into a powerful resource for health and wellness—the first line of defence against disease. I highly recommend The FULL POWER Plan." *- Dr. Sidney Kettner, MD, Family Physician, Former Leader in the Complete Health Improvement Program (CHIP), Creston, British Columbia, Canada.*

"As a family physician on the front lines, I have met many people with chronic health conditions who long to be healthy. Unfortunately, they often have lost their health because of unwitting self-sabotage, lacking the understanding of what it truly takes. Through years of sweat and tears, Ernest J. Brake has gone the extra mile to come alongside and help many in the throws of fighting for their health. He is well-positioned to lead you to success as he powerfully brings together the time-honored principles that undergird personal growth and optimal health." *- Greg Steinke, MD, MPH, President and Medical Director of LifeMed Clinic, Chattanooga Tennessee, United States, and Author of 30 Days to Natural Blood Pressure Control.*

"Thanks Dr. Brake for this breathe of fresh air. Instead of tackling our broken health care system with the same stale old ideas; spending cuts, more taxes, or privatization you have empowered us with an exciting, personalized program full of creativity. You have not only made us part of the solution, you have made it a powerful life changing experience." *- Phil Brewer, Founder and President, Silver Hills Guesthouse, Lifestyle Makeover Coach, Lumby, British Columbia, Canada.*

www.ernestjbrake.com

ISBN: 978-1-0688040-2-1 (paperback)
ISBN: 978-1-0688040-0-7 (ebook)
ISBN: 978-1-0688040-1-4 (hardcover)
ISBN: 978-1-0688040-3-8 (audiobook)

Ordering Information:
Special discounts are available on quantity purchases by corporations, associations, and others. For details, contact Ernest J. Brake at ejbrake@fulllpower1.com.

TABLE OF CONTENTS

PART 3

Launch Your Plan—Phase 2:

Restructuring the Habits of the Bodymind

APPENDICES

CHAPTER 1

MIDNIGHT TO DAYLIGHT

FINDING THE PATH TO OPTIMAL VITALITY

The very good news is there is quite a number of internal circumstances [...] under your voluntary control. If you decide to change them (and be warned that none of these changes come without real effort), your level of happiness is likely to increase lastingly.

Dr. Martin Seligman

Usually, darkness was my friend. But hitchhiking after midnight felt eerie this time. Earlier that night 10 of us were squeezed around a table made for five at the Green Dory Tavern in Halifax, Nova Scotia, Canada. The happy young women sat on the guys' laps as we all sang exuberantly, "Farewell to Nova Scotia," pounding the table with our beer glasses to the beat of the band. Later, we continued the party at a private home, rocking into the night with more beer, pot, and pizza.

Now, party over, and all alone, the sound of my steps echoed through the dark, silent street of a middle-class neighborhood. As the alcohol wore off, so did the false bravado. A foreign feeling crept over me—a strange hollowness. The fun I had at the party should have made me happy. But it didn't. Now, with no distractions but my thoughts, I was forced to admit that the flirting and joking was a mask that prevented any real connection. I continued down the silent street feeling as empty as the road I was on.

Tomorrow, I would need to shake it off and attend morning classes at Dalhousie University. But I knew from my track record, I wouldn't wake up in time. I never did. My addiction to nightlife was killing my educational dreams. My long-term goal of earning a bachelor's degree in arts and science was fading away. And now my mind and body were wasting away on the streets of Halifax.

I kicked a rock into the curb. "What's wrong with me?" I muttered. "I'm better than this. If I keep this up, I'll be a burned-out failure. This is not the me I want to be."

I felt like a worn-out Ferrari, built to be slick and powerful, but with warning lights flashing, "Systems are breaking down!" I had potential to be something better. I desperately knew it. But at 19, I was enchained by self-sabotaging behaviors.

My inner voice, made audible by the silence of the night, forced me to confront a sobering question: "How long are you going to continue wasting your life away?"

"I don't know," I said.

The voice spoke again: "How long are you going to let your lifestyle steal your future?"

As if in an act of defiance against the darkness, I squared my shoulders, eyed the nearest house silhouetted in the moonlight, and said, "I can do better than this."

The house sat there, unconvinced.

But I was determined. This time I shouted. "I can do better!"

The house wasn't any more convinced.

But I sure was.

THE DARE TO DREAM

I gazed at the moonlit sky and dared to dream of walking on stage, donning cap and gown, to shake hands with the president of Dalhousie University. He would smile proudly as he handed me my bachelor's degree—my key to opening doors into the fields of psychology, journalism, and technology.

I dared to dream of finding an authentic community of friends that went beyond a night of partying. I dared to dream of finding that special woman with whom I could venture out to make the world a better place. I dared to dream of owning a sleek physique well into old age.

Inspired by that vision of a bright future, an inexpressible longing came over me. It was a hunger to turn my drifting life into one of purpose and power. I ached for that future. To fuel those dreams, I determined to find the key to that secret door to profound personal growth. Intuitively, I knew that door hinged on two vital components: a sharp mind and a healthy body.

But doubts crept in. "How is this even possible? Can I really change? Maybe it's not meant for me."

The inner voice spoke again. "Others have it. Why not you?"

Yes. Others have it. But how do they get it? How does the athlete make it to the top? I know they train hard. But their success seems to come from something more than physical fitness. What motivational power are they tapping into to keep pushing forward? How do I get that?

What makes certain older men and women look so young and vibrant when I'm wearing out at 19? How does the tradesman, entrepreneur, or scientist reach success? They must have something I don't have. It's more than money or luck. What is it? How does the successful parent or teacher inspire greatness in the child? How does the addict conquer their demons?

What laws of the mind could I follow that would light my path to success? What laws of the body would strengthen me for the journey?

Deep down, I was hoping for a magic silver bullet that would restore me to peak vitality and help me achieve life mastery. I had a lot to learn.

FAST FORWARD THREE DECADES

It's 30 years later, and I am walking down that street again, now bustling with traffic in the midday sun. This time I walk hand in hand with my loving wife of 25 years, June. She gives me a listening ear as I reflect on my journey since that post-midnight walk three decades before. I did earn a bachelor's degree—plus a master's and a doctorate.

Along the way, I became a passenger train porter, journalist-turned-editor of a university newspaper, pastor, lifestyle medicine researcher, seminar speaker, health outreach director and trainer, strategic planner, and C-Suite executive administrator with a corner office.

I organized hundreds of personal-growth events, ran half marathons, sledded down glaciers, wrote songs, made friends, and traveled the world—sometimes as a tourist, many times as a speaker, always as a curious learner.

But June says my greatest accomplishment is being a loving husband and wonderful dad to our late special-needs son, Michael. She hugs me and whispers in my ear, "I have the world in my arms."

Everything I dreamed of on that dark night 30 years before had come true. And then some. I live in an inspiring home, mortgage-free, with the love of my life, in the most beautiful part of Vancouver Island, British Columbia, Canada. I have the physical energy to accomplish meaningful goals with no need of pills. I have a purpose that eagerly awakes me in the morning, and an inner sense of peace and confidence I had never thought possible.

I cherish a deep sense of gratitude for the life I lead.

THE GOLDEN FORMULA

I was hoping for a silver bullet. But what I uncovered was a golden formula—the secrets to long-lasting vitality for the body and mind. While lacking a standardized definition, "vitality" is often associated with the ideal condition of the body, mind, and heart. Because of its balanced focus on physical, mental, and emotional strength, "vitality" was the perfect word to describe my lofty goal of optimal personal development.

The ingredients of the final formula came together over three decades of passionate research in areas of personal growth and health. It included collaboration with healthcare professionals (doctors, nurses, psychologists, therapists, and personal trainers) in diverse health- and self-improvement programs. It involved the observation of thousands of participants, including myself, in which clear patterns emerged regarding what really generates vitality. The search felt like an adventure in discovering and unlocking a treasure chest that yielded its gems one by one.

Ultimately, this book is written for seekers of bodymind vitality—the most precious of all treasures.

My search was guided by four key assumptions:

They are:

1. **Long-Term/Short-Term:** Long-term health is infinitely more valuable than short-term fixes.
2. **Body/Mind:** The body and mind are intricately connected and act as one. So much so they can truly be combined into one word— "bodymind."[1] Long-term health, therefore, is best achieved by taking into account the complex interdependence of every body part including the brain.
3. **Causes vs. Symptoms:** Tracing back to, and treating, the root cause of an illness—physical, mental, or emotional—is more therapeutic than symptom management. By strengthening the body's defenses, we may prevent illnesses before they develop.
4. **Feeling and Doing:** We have the power to improve how we feel (the diagnosis) by changing what we do (the prescription).

With these foundational concepts as guides, the ingredients of the golden formula emerged as a set of principles that linked two wellness concepts together: personal growth and optimal health. Without the one, we'll never really have the other.

For the purposes of this book, personal growth, synonymous with personal development, means "becoming more effective at what we were born to do." Optimal health means "the most effective functioning of the body-mind." Combining the two concepts led to this insight: By leveraging the potential of the bodymind, we become more effective at what we were born to do. Thus, we capture the essence of life satisfaction.

As I discovered (and you will discover, too, if you haven't already), optimal health is critical to personal growth. And personal growth is critical to optimal health. By using a unique blend of evidence-based principles, the golden formula becomes the driver of both.

This set of principles became a supremely effective formula for helping people find levels of health—both mental and physical—they never thought possible. I watched as these principles enabled individuals to reach their full potential in all aspects of life without pills or surgery. It seemed they were a prescription from Doctor Mother Nature herself. So, I dubbed them "nature's formula for bodymind vitality."

I was so blown away by the profound transformational effect of this formula, I felt compelled—called, even—to leave my executive role so that I could share these gems with the world. I offer them to you so you can launch your journey toward the strongest and finest version of yourself.

Nature's formula for bodymind vitality is encapsulated in the acronym, FULL POWER. Hence, "The FULL POWER Plan":

F - Find Your Superpower
U - Unleash Healthy Spirituality
L - Lovify Your Life
L - Launch Your Plan

P - Prioritize High-Octane Fuel
O - Omit What Is Harmful
W - Water Up
E - Exercise Outdoors
R - Rest Up

Any one of these nine principles has proven to enhance some aspect of life and longevity. Now imagine combining all nine into one package. The resulting synergy becomes truly life-changing for the vitality seeker.

In the coming pages, we will discover how these interlocking principles encompass nine sets of behaviors that provide the best conditions for our bodymind to heal itself and set us on the path to deeply satisfying personal growth.

The formula has two parts: "FULL" and "POWER." The "POWER" principles rely on the "FULL" principles. The "FULL" principles rely on the "POWER" principles. Together, the FULL POWER principles build up every system of the bodymind—the immune system, cardiovascular system, respiratory system, digestive system, nervous system, renal system, endocrine system, musculoskeletal system, etc.

As a result, the FULL POWER principles, as the science shows, reduce the risk of—and in some cases, reverse—chronic diseases like heart disease, stroke, cancer, asthma, inflammation, autoimmune disease, obesity, diabetes, digestive diseases, infections, high blood pressure, liver diseases, and kidney diseases. The principles also fight depression, anxiety, and low self-esteem—so necessary for life satisfaction.

To oversimplify the therapeutic impact of the FULL POWER formula, consider the cause-and-effect sequence illustrated by a set of falling dominos. The pattern goes like this: there is a symptom (pain, illness, weakness, or disease) illustrated by the last falling domino. That symptom is the effect of contributing causes, the preceding dominos. Those contributing causes are the effect of previous causes, ultimately going back to the root causes. The premise of this book is that the root causes of bodymind weakness are deficiencies in one or more of the FULL POWER principles, the first dominos.

The goal, therefore, is to fill up on each of the FULL POWER principles as if they are tanks of fuel. By implementing the principles one by one, we write our own prescription for bodymind vitality. Weight loss, for example, is just one of the hundreds of positive outcomes of FULL POWER.

However, I and many others have found the FULL POWER Plan does more than make us healthier. It awakens the champion within. It renews our hopes and refuels our dreams.

MY ROLE AS AUTHOR

At first, I thought a book such as this might better be written by a motivational psychologist because it opens our eyes to the feel-good benefits and strategies for achieving mental well-being. Then, I thought a medical doctor might be a better fit because it offers strategies for achieving physical well-being.

But this book reaches far beyond the scope of any one field of expertise. The aim of this book is very ambitious. It needs to be. The goal is nothing short of putting into your hands the finest tools for life mastery. This means that, as a curator of knowledge, I will draw upon every field of expertise necessary to help you reach your goal of optimal bodymind vitality.

The best analogy to describe the role of the author of a book such as this is to think of the general contractor you hire to build your dream home. The general contractor is the only one who has a comprehensive understanding of the process that leads to the finishing of the house. He knows what specialist to bring in at the right time. When needed, he calls in the architect, excavator, carpenter, plumber, electrician, drywaller, roofer, or painter. Each specialist is under his supervision as they contribute their part to the grand project.

In essence, I play the role of a general contractor. My aim, guided by the values and principles introduced above, is to help you build your dream bodymind. Throughout these chapters, I will use my experience as a strategic planner, researcher, personal counselor, and community health outreach trainer to call upon the right specialist at the right time—psychologists, nutrition scientists, research doctors, therapists, neuroscientists, clinicians, cardiologists, trainers, and other experts as needed—to help you reach optimal bodymind vitality.

I imagine that if you were to put Caldwell Esselstyn, T. Colin Campbell, Michael Greger, John Gottman, Nadine Burke Harris, Jim Kwik, Gabor Maté, Bruce Perry, Oprah Winfrey, Tony Robbins, Roger Seheult, Matthew Walker, Phil Brewer, Brené Brown, James Clear, Hans Diehl, and representatives from Harvard Medical School, Mayo Clinic, and Loma Linda University Medical Centre into one room, and ask them to collaborate on a book that would help you reach optimal bodymind vitality using natural means, this is the book they would write.

HOW THIS BOOK IS ORGANIZED

This book is divided into three parts. The first two parts correspond to the two parts of FULL POWER—the FULL chapters and the POWER chapters. The FULL chapters are primarily about strengthening the mind. The POWER chapters are primarily about strengthening the body.

PART 1, the four FULL chapters, explores the personal growth and mental aspects foundational to optimal vitality. In the realm of mental well-being, the FULL chapters address feelings of lostness, anxiety, depression, and low self-confidence. Consequently, they bolster life satisfaction, motivation, confidence, serenity, belonging, and a zest for life. In the FULL principles, you will discover the four most important contributors to lifelong mental health.

PART 1 lays the mental groundwork for PART 2.

PART 2, the POWER chapters, largely draws from and contributes to the field of "lifestyle medicine." Lifestyle medicine is an evidence-based practice that prescribes lifestyle change as medicine to prevent, treat—and, in some cases, reverse—chronic conditions and optimize bodymind vitality.[2] These chapters take on the physical and physiological aspects of health at the level of first causes. In the realm of physical well-being, the five

POWER principles fight obesity, fatigue, weakness, chronic disease, and chronic pain, and do it by serving as a roadmap for weight loss, strength, flexibility, alertness, and energy.

The "POW" chapters highlight what we put into our bodymind. The "ER" chapters highlight what we do with our bodymind.

Each chapter begins with a story introducing a FULL POWER principle,[3] followed by the science behind the principle and its crucial role in optimal vitality. Then, practical suggestions are offered. Most chapters include a checklist to help you to evaluate yourself, based on the previous seven days, on how well you are living out the principle discussed in that chapter.

Scoring yourself on the Vitality Self-Assessment (see Appendix) and using the end-of-chapter checklists in Parts 1 and 2 are the best preparation for PART 3.

PART 3 shows how you may transform this book into an action plan. It activates your "prescription" for bodymind vitality. It uses a dashboard to assist you in implementing a system of habits grounded in the FULL POWER principles.

Together, these chapters outline the FULL POWER Plan, a treasure trove of gems designed by nature to create a better life and, ultimately, a better world. For the most exciting results, journey through this book with a partner or with others in a group.

THE JOURNEY TOWARD THE NEW YOU

Perhaps you are wondering, as I did, whether this kind of transformation is realistic. Maybe you fear that life's circumstances have locked you in, making it impossible to change. As you will see in the following chapters, there are reasons for hope. Each principle allows for baby steps that begin to unlock your potential—even in limited circumstances. Then, when you are ready to take more steps, the chapter tips and checklists will identify them for you.

After you turn your newfound knowledge into action, you will feel a difference in your body and mind within the first week. Between the first and 10th month, depending on your situation, the habits inspired by the FULL POWER principles become the foundation of your new identity as a life champion. You will literally be a different person. Or perhaps more accurately, you will have found your true self.

For some, "near miracles" happen. But it's simply the remarkable science of cause and effect. Almost every enthusiastic participant sees a noticeable difference in the mirror within the first month. That's when others take notice, and say, "You look 10 years younger," or "You seem more confident. What did you do?"

Let's begin our journey in the next chapter with the first principle of FULL POWER. It's about superpowers—how I found mine, and why you need to find yours.

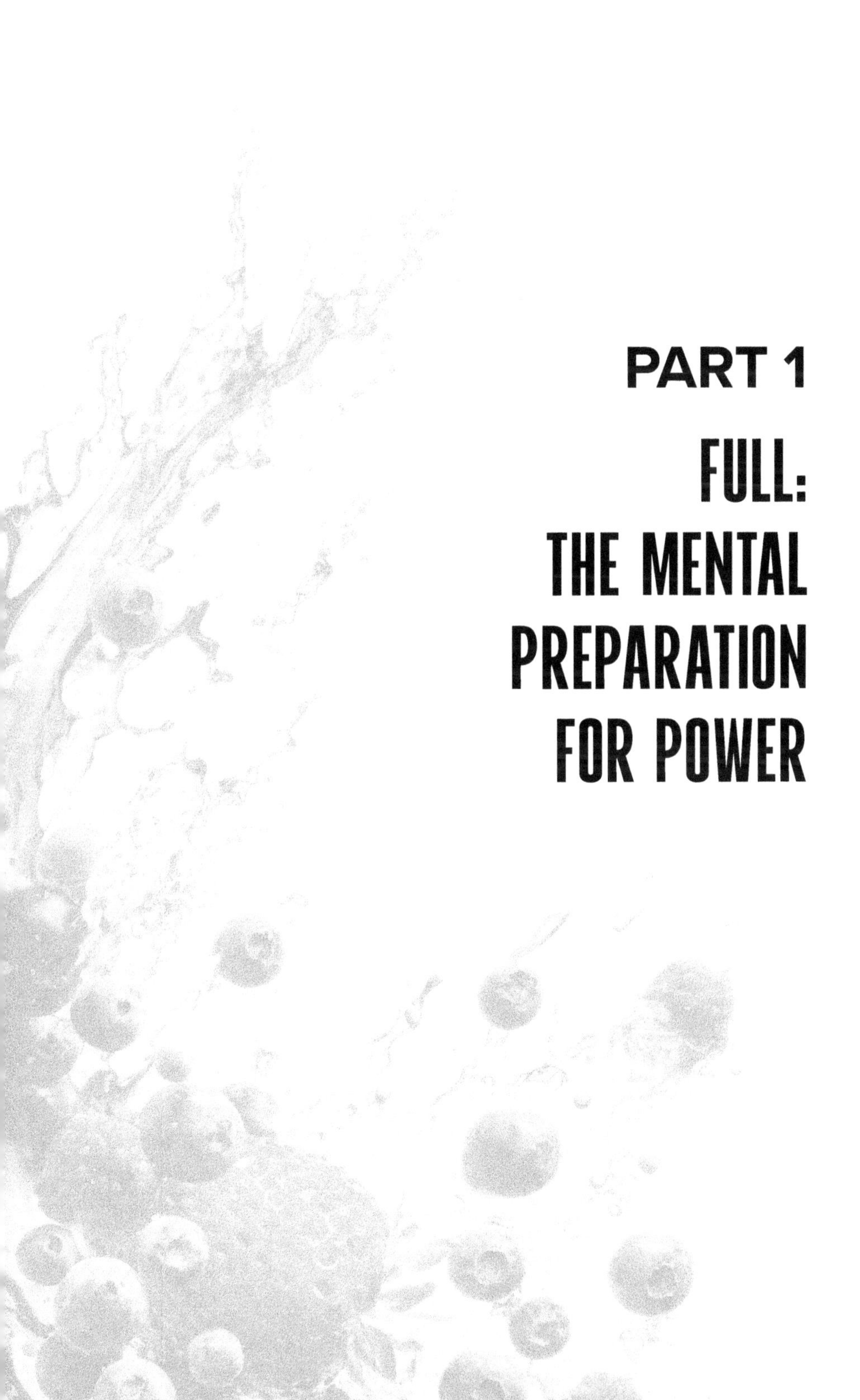

PART 1

FULL:
THE MENTAL PREPARATION FOR POWER

CHAPTER 2

FIND YOUR SUPERPOWER

*Some people discover their purpose. Others create their
purpose by discovering their superpower.*

Ernest J. Brake

If something didn't change, Dylan would be fired. It wouldn't be pretty.

When I visited him in his office, his speech was tired and monotone. His shoulders were slumped, and he had put on weight. He confessed he was underperforming. He knew he wasn't meeting deadlines, especially with his paperwork. He did things that weren't required, such as helping new employees in other departments, because he was so unhappy and unfulfilled with his assigned duties. What made it worse was knowing his co-workers were talking about him behind his back because he wasn't doing the job he was hired to do.

I felt bad for him because he was super smart, kind, and conscientious. He could organize any event and had the natural ability to put people at ease. But clearly his skills weren't being appreciated or utilized in his current job.

My wife commented that "a fish out of water doesn't always look his best." Dylan was like a poor fish out of water—flopping on the ground, pumping its gills as it gasps for life—like millions of others. Dylan didn't say it, but I think, deep in his soul, he was beginning to doubt his worth.

Keeping with the fish analogy, if a fish feels judged by its inability to walk on land, it will swim through its whole life believing it's stupid.

One of the tragic truths in the world today is that too many people are judged by something they were never meant to do or by a job they were never meant to have. Not only does this often-unintended judgment squelch the spirit of a person, it deprives the world of great leaders. The world loses out on a scientist, technician, teacher, business innovator, artist, philanthropist, or healer because they were never given the environment to blossom.

Two weeks after my visit with Dylan, he was fired. And it wasn't pretty. Six months later, he told me that getting fired forced him to go on a search, not just to find a job, but to find his purpose. Now he is at a job that suits his strengths. He loves knowing that he is making a positive difference. He said getting fired was the best thing that ever happened to him.

Some aren't as fortunate as Dylan. When discussing his 2022 book, *Friends, Lovers, and the Big Terrible Thing*, the late Matthew Perry, who played Chandler Bing in the smash hit TV sitcom, *Friends*, said that when he reached star status, he thought the fame and fortune would bring happiness. It didn't. Even with a net worth of over $100 million he was still searching for it.[4]

Pop singer Lady Gaga sang about trying to "fill that void" in her song, "Shallow," with Bradley Cooper from the movie A Star Is Born. Lil Wayne sang "I Feel Like Dying" at the peak of his popularity in 2007. Linda Perry of 4 Non-Blondes sang of searching for some elusive "destination" in "What's Up" (1992). Bono, lead singer of the rock group U2, sang "I Still Haven't Found What I'm Looking For" (1987). Going back still further, Neil Diamond sang that he felt lost and couldn't explain it in "I Am, I Said," in 1971.

FIRST PRINCIPLE OF BODYMIND VITALITY – FIND YOUR SUPERPOWER

Themes of emptiness, alienation, and discontent are so pervasive in music and movies, it's hard not to miss the cry of the culture. Once our basic human needs for food, shelter, and safety are met, filling this void is a major step in personal growth.

Here's how it worked for me.

I was a "fish out of water" hitchhiking down that lonely road in Halifax. I felt that alienation stirring again as a young college student after arriving at Burman University in Lacombe, Alberta, Canada.

Having been accepted at Burman, I left my home, family, friends, and my VIA Rail Canada porter job in Nova Scotia to fly to a strange new place 3,000 miles away in search of a new adventure. It was August—just before the start of the new school year.

In my dorm room, as I sat facing the empty bed wondering who my roommate would be, I began to doubt whether it was the right decision to make such a big move. Lady Gaga, Lil Wayne, Bono, Linda Perry, and Neil Diamond were singing about me. I was still trying to "fill that void" and "hadn't found what I was looking for." If you had asked me then what I was looking for, I would have given a simple yet deeply personal answer that most might have given: happiness.

But I didn't know how to find it.

I picked up a book a friend had given me as a gift and began reading.

It contained an ancient story called The Parable of the Talents. I had never heard of it before. It was about a boss who gave money to three of his employees to take care of his business while he was away. When he returned, he asked his employees how they used his money. Two of the employees invested it and doubled their investment. The other employee clung onto his, afraid he would lose it.

What caught my attention was the boss's reaction to the two productive employees. He not only promoted them but said, "Come share in my happiness."

That word, "happiness," jumped out at me. That's just what I was craving. What a coincidence that the thoughts in my head were addressed by the words on the page.

What was this parable teaching about happiness? The first clue was that happiness came from being a good manager over the things they'd been given. What things? I flipped back to the beginning of the parable and noticed the boss gave "talents" to each of them—a metaphor for special skills, strengths, competencies, or natural abilities.

In other words, a talent is a superpower. The parable was saying that if I used my talents, I'd find happiness. So, I needed to figure out what I was good at.

THE HUNT FOR TALENTS

I tried to think of a time when somebody gave me a compliment. My reasoning was that if I received a compliment, it meant somebody was recognizing something that was potentially a talent.

The first memory that jumped into my mind was of a phone conversation with my girlfriend when I was a teen. I had given her a golden ring made of four interlocking bands. She had removed the ring to do some baking and it fell apart.

Over the phone, I gave her step-by-step instructions on how to reassemble the ring. When she was able to assemble it, she thanked me and said, "Hey, you're a good teacher."

After I hung up the phone, my mother, who had overheard our phone conversation, said, "You would make a good teacher. I just heard you give step-by-step instructions on how to put the ring together, and you didn't even have it in front of you. You did it all from your head."

I shrugged. "Anybody could do that."

"I can't," she replied.

We all are unique. Most of us just don't know how we're unique. Until somebody tells us.

Ever the scientist, I needed to put "teaching as a talent" to the test. How? I recalled a time my grandmother said I'd make a good writer. She said this because when my parents went out for the evening and I babysat, I'd write up a "noncompliance report" because my three younger siblings were, um, noncompliant. My grandmother pointed out that to express myself in writing was natural for me. So, maybe writing was a talent.

The parable said using one's talents would lead to happiness. I put the three compliments together and resolved to experiment with teaching through writing. It turned out to be a great strategy.

DEVELOPING MY TALENT

I rushed to the administration building looking for Eric Rajah, the sponsor of student activities and the future cofounder of A Better World, a humanitarian organization. I asked him whether he knew of anybody on campus who needed any writing done.

"The campus newspaper is looking for writers," he said. He gave me directions to the sponsor of the Aurora Newspaper.

When I arrived at her office, I discovered she was an English professor, Dr. Beverly Matiko. I asked whether she needed any writing done.

"Can you write an article for the first issue of the paper? Choose any subject you'd like so long as it is helpful and uplifting to the students."

I wrote an article, "Snobs," sharing lessons I had learned at Dalhousie University on how humility works better than arrogance in college life. It was published in the paper, and I was asked to write more.

A few months later, she asked me to join her journalism class and write as a college journalist. It was intimidating, but she encouraged me to dive in. That year I wrote many articles for the newspaper. I enjoyed interviewing people, including the new university president, Malcolm Graham, which made the front page accompanied by a huge photo of me shaking his hand. Truly a proud moment. Along the journey, I found myself becoming more confident, no longer aimless, and no longer feeling empty inside. I felt useful and motivated. I had a purpose. It felt good.

So good, in fact, I had the confidence to do something I had never done before. During the summer break, an ad on the community bulletin board caught my eye. A mother was looking for a math tutor for her seventh-grade son. I was good at math—at least seventh-grade math—and needed some extra cash. Ordinarily, I wouldn't have given it much notice. But now, having some success under my belt from the newspaper, I stepped out of my comfort zone again and answered the ad.

I enjoyed teaching young Mark, and he took the lessons well. Mark's mother was proud of her son's summer accomplishment. After the summer was over, I couldn't help thinking, "I just made a difference in someone's life. I even got paid for it. Hmmm…maybe teaching is what I was made to do."

PROGRESS UP THE LADDER

A year later, Dr. Matiko asked me to succeed Bret Dobbin as the editor of the newspaper. I had seen how hard Bret worked and knew I could not measure up to his abilities. But Bret shared how he did it and how he knew it would be a rewarding challenge.

With the guidance of Professor Matiko, and help from friends, June and Bruce, I built on Bret's foundation as the editor of the *Aurora Newspaper* at Burman University. The position came with the added responsibility of being a member of the Student Association, an organization run by students to enhance university life. It greatly expanded my world.

As the editor, I dreamed of the impact a college paper could make. With my team, I devised strategies to increase circulation and ways to recruit students who wanted to build school spirit through their writing. I brainstormed editorial topics that would stimulate thinking on educational success, life satisfaction, ethics, mental and social health in the context of a university setting. I wanted to create appreciation for our professors by featuring a professor bio in each issue, complete with a cartoon caricature drawn by local artist Bob Mumford. I conceived of photo ideas to accompany each news article and was thankful that our yearbook editor/photographer, Colin Hill, was willing to take the photos. My mind continued to bubble with exciting ideas.

DISCOVERING NEW TALENTS

Executing those ideas, though, was another story. To meet the ever-increasing challenge, I learned skills that went beyond teaching, reporting, and writing. It was now about familiarizing myself with college resources and department personnel. It was about connecting with fellow students who were intrinsically motivated to use their writing and artistic talents and giving them opportunities and resources to apply their talents toward something meaningful. I still used my teaching and writing skills when younger students needed help. But I was developing another talent I didn't know I had: leadership.

I made lots of mistakes. But I was assured by professors and students that the paper was making a difference in campus life. Students and faculty alike enjoyed being informed and feeling part of a community. When challenges arose, my new sense of purpose strengthened me to push through.

One afternoon, I woke up in history class. I had spent the entire night working with June and Bruce, putting the final touches on the paper. The interviews, writing, organizing, photography, photo-mechanical transfers, typing, editing, cutting, pasting, and layout work were done. It was now at the printers at Lacombe Globe and would roll off the presses, ready for distribution in two days. I am not sure what the history lesson was that day, but I was filled with satisfaction of work well done.

That's when I recalled the parable of the talents. And it dawned on me. I had put my talent to work and found happiness. The principle worked.

FLOW

My mind and heart were engaged—so much so that I found myself losing track of time when working on the paper. The famous researcher, Mihaly Csikszentmihalyi, calls that "flow."

In his 1990 classic, *Flow: The Psychology of Optimal Experience*, Csikszentmihalyi gives eight steps toward enhancing enjoyment in life. Flow happens when you:

1. confront a task you have a chance of completing;
2. have the ability to concentrate on the task;
3. have a clear goal;
4. receive immediate feedback;
5. act with deep and effortless involvement that removes from awareness the worries and frustrations of everyday life;
6. are allowed to exercise control over your actions;
7. find that your concern for self disappears, yet paradoxically the sense of self emerges stronger after the flow experience is over;
8. have an altered experience of time; hours pass in minutes and minutes stretch out to hours.[5]

I was experiencing all of them. My feelings, thoughts, and actions were in harmony and aligned to achieve a meaningful goal. Life had meaning. Even though I was tired at times, I felt strong, energetic, enthusiastic, confident, and motivated.

I had finally discovered what turned out to be the first component, the first "biohack" of bodymind vitality: I found my superpower—the talent cluster of teaching, writing, and leadership. And it led me to fulfill a higher purpose—to enhance campus spirit and create a sense of community.

I learned to organize, collaborate, and prioritize. I reactivated my dormant artistic talent from childhood. My sense of purpose grew from the experiences and feedback I received from applying my ever-growing set of inter-related skills. It led me on an adventure. It became my passion. It gave me a reason to get up in the morning.

The invaluable insights I gained from my newspaper experience turned out to be universal principles for success. Here's what I learned:

1. When talent usage increases, happiness increases. So does success.
2. My superpower isn't about me. It's about others. That discovery led to a general definition of purpose: an emotionally satisfying intention to focus your superpower on empowering others. John Stuart Mill, 19th-century English philosopher and political economist, reflected that lesson when he wrote, "Those only are happy…who have their minds fixed on some object other than their own happiness… Aiming thus at something else, they find happiness by the way."[6]
3. Mentors are as vital to growth as water is to a plant. (Thank you, Dr. Matiko.)
4. A supportive team makes any endeavor easier and fun. (Thank you, June, now my dear wife ☺, and Bruce, my close friend.)
5. Success is achieved by standing on the shoulders of those who have gone before. (Thank you, Bret.)
6. A supportive environment is essential—one that gives opportunities and allows for failure without judgment, and therefore, growth without measure. (Thank you, Burman University.)
7. Fulfilling a higher purpose often leads to more social connections, which are, in themselves, empowering and emotionally healing—so necessary for pensive introverts.
8. A sense of purpose makes it easier to say no to distractions and temptations.
9. A sense of purpose motivates healthier life choices, like exercise and more nutritious eating.[7]

Toward the end of the second year, I was sitting in the office of one of the university administrators. We were reflecting on the success of the paper when he said, "I didn't think you would have the stick-to-it-iveness."

I didn't expect that, but I understood why he said it. The previous year, he had likely seen me on campus acting foolish, aimless, and awkward. But when I tapped into a talent-driven purpose, he saw someone with reliability, endurance, and confidence. That's the power of a purpose. It comes from finding your superpower.

You can surprise people too. Find your superpower and fulfill your purpose.

HEALTH BENEFITS OF POSSESSING PURPOSE

According to research done by *National Geographic* journalist Dan Buettner, a sense of purpose is worth up to seven years of extra life expectancy."[8]

It's not just more years of life. It's more life in your years.

One of the healthiest, happiest, and longest-living groups in the world are those people who live on the Japanese island of Okinawa. When Buettner interviewed them, they said they attributed their health and longevity to "ikigai." Loosely translated, ikigai (*ee – key – guy*) is "life's purpose" or "reason for being." It's why you want to get up in the morning to start your day.

To the happy centenarians of Okinawa, ikigai is a combination of four things:

- doing what you love
- doing what you are good at
- doing something that fills a need in the world
- doing something for which you are rewarded

If you find that one activity, project, job, talent expression, mission, or side hustle that combines all four of these factors, you've got your ikigai. The ancient parable of the talents helped me find my ikigai by inspiring me to figure out what I was good at. Loved ones helped me zero in on what it was. Gallup's Dean Jones nailed it when he said that knowing your talents "shows you where to invest your time and efforts."[9] Knowing where to invest our time and efforts is a stepping stone to the optimized life.

A purpose-driven life influences physical well-being, showcasing the interconnectedness of mind and body. According to UC Berkley's *Greater Good Magazine*, which provides science-based insights for a meaningful life, fulfilling your purpose reduces stress.[10] It fuels optimism and turns challenges into opportunities for growth. It makes us masters, not slaves, of circumstance.

A sense of purpose stimulates motivation to engage in more preventative behaviors, including cholesterol tests and cancer screenings.[11]

Without a sense of purpose, we are like a Ferrari without the fuel. The potential is there, but motive power is gone. It's as if the brain is thinking, "If you've got nothing significant for me to work on, I might as well start shutting down." Many humans look alive, but there is a sense in which they are really shut down for lack of purpose. As they grow older, they experience a decrease in functionality along with increased cognitive and memory impairments.

But older adults who report a greater sense of purpose experience less functional decline (like weakened grip strength). They also have less cognitive and memory impairment, and lower risk of Alzheimer's disease.[12]

SURPRISING BY-PRODUCT OF PURPOSE

While working on the newspaper, I was not focused on being healthy. But when it came time to eat, I was choosy because I wanted a clear mind and energy to do the work I loved doing. Plus, I was too happily busy to give junk food a second thought. Nor did I have the time to linger longer at the table being tempted by a second helping. The ability to resist junk food turned out to be a powerful by-product of being caught up in purposeful activity. (We'll talk more about this topic in Chapters 7 and 8 when we tackle how to avoid what is harmful.)

Likewise, in Dylan's "good fortune" of losing his job, the same principle was at work helping him shed his excess weight. When he found a job that supported his life's purpose, not only did he find the confidence to take on more challenges, but he also found it easier to bypass the doughnut shop. Temptations lost their power because he was too busy dancing his way toward a glorious purpose.

YOU HAVE A SUPERPOWER

At times, people experience life as a meaningless round of boring activities. With tears in their eyes, they may shake their head and look at the ground, and say to themselves, "Why am I stuck in this rut? What's wrong with me?"

If that person is you or someone you love, here is what you or they need to hear: "Listen very closely. There is nothing wrong with you. You are having a normal human reaction to not using your superpower toward a purpose. And because of that, you may feel empty inside. But know this: You are a masterpiece yet to be unveiled."

Even if you don't have much control over your situation, knowing your strengths makes you alert to opportune moments of growth. Dr. Matiko and other mentors wanted me to see beyond a limited view of myself to new horizons. Without that vision of what could be, my aimless life would have contributed to depression. But because I aimed my superpower at a noble purpose, I felt fully alive.

STEPS TO FINDING YOUR SUPERPOWER AND FULFILLING YOUR PURPOSE

To zero in on your life's purpose, identify your top strengths. It could be working with your hands, working with people, working with your mind, or any combination of these or other things. Whatever your talent-driven purpose is, it will be your foundation for optimal vitality.

Here are some steps:

Step 1 – Assess Yourself

Learn your score on the "Find Your Superpower – Fulfill Your Purpose" checklist at the end of this chapter. This is the first ingredient of nature's prescription for optimal vitality. Clarifying your higher purpose supplies the critical motive power for the other principles of FULL POWER. For example, don't even think of trying to lose weight unless you have a captivating purpose in life. Otherwise, the weight lost from a short-term spurt of motivation will find its way back. More on this in succeeding chapters.

Step 2 – Answer Guiding Questions for Finding Your Superpower and Fulfilling Your Purpose

If you are not sure of your superpower or your purpose, ask yourself these questions:

1. What do people compliment me on the most?
2. Do these compliments identify a talent I could put to work?
3. What am I naturally good at that others find hard to do?
4. What activities make me lose track of time?
5. What projects/hobbies do I look forward to doing after I've finished eating?
6. What dream can I not help but think about every day?

7. What inspires me?

8. Who inspires me?

9. What is the version of myself for which I am willing to pay a high price to reach?

10. What abilities do I have that make hard work fun?

11. What do I do that gives me energy?

12. What would I persist in doing even if I failed at it for the first 50 attempts?

13. If I were guaranteed success, what would I try?

14. What is that thing that makes my day incomplete if I don't work on it?

15. When I look at the needs in the world, what makes my heart ache?

16. What kind of people am I best qualified to serve?

17. What kind of people do I want to serve?

18. What do these people need that I am able to give them?

19. What did I do the last time I felt both powerful and useful?

20. What lights me up inside?

21. What topic of conversation keeps me talking late into the night?

Once you have a clearer understanding of your superpower and purpose, you'll be able to complete this sentence:

"I _________________________ so people can_____________________________ ."

Here are some examples:

1. I fix bicycles so people can ride safely.

2. I give hospitality so strangers can know they belong.

3. I organize conventions so professionals can achieve excellence in their field.

4. I heal so people can live without pain.

5. I raise children so they can be happy, responsible citizens.

6. I cook healthy meals so people can be energized.

7. I feed hungry children so they can know they are loved.
8. I teach FULL POWER principles so people can experience optimal vitality.

Step 3 – Act

Take action. Find somebody to benefit from your strengths. Activating your top strengths is like plugging into a continual power source. Even though it may be hard work, using your superpower feels energizing rather than draining. That's why it's a superpower. It's like an eagle when she flies. Feel the call to use that power in service to others. It will contribute to a life of joy. Both for you and for others.

LIKE DISCOVERING A TREASURE

Finding your superpower is like discovering a treasure. That's because it unlocks a world of empowerment so crucial to personal growth. Here are some of the benefits people experience when they find their superpower and fulfill their purpose:

Shields Against Depression: Feeling a sense of purpose is your armor against the darkness of depression. It fuels motivation and ignites confidence, reducing the likelihood of experiencing feelings of hopelessness.

Awakens the Fire Within: When you discover your purpose, you stoke the fires of excitement within your soul. With a clear sense of direction, you become a force of nature, charging toward your goals with a zest for life. It feels powerful.

Elevates Self-Worth: Pursuing meaningful goals tied to your purpose elevates your self-esteem. As you conquer milestones in alignment with your life's mission, you not only supercharge your self-confidence but also elevate your standing in the eyes of society.

Forges Unbreakable Resilience: Armed with purpose, you transform into a resilient warrior, capable of facing life's fiercest battles. Your sense of purpose fuels your spirit, enabling you to triumph over adversity and conquer any obstacle that dares cross your path. You become a dragon-slayer.

Radiates Vitality: Your purpose doesn't just invigorate your spirit; it breathes life into your physical being. Dan Buettner's discoveries of the Blue Zones[13] showed us that those with a strong sense of purpose live longer and enjoy robust health. Purpose also propels you to embrace healthier habits, motivating you to embrace exercise and a nourishing diet to fuel your journey.

Nurtures Profound Connections: Enriching the lives of others with your superpower weaves threads of connection that bind hearts. Aligning with kindred spirits who resonate with your mission fosters more meaningful relationships. It cultivates empathy and compassion that deepen friendships.

The most profound sense of purpose and zest for life is fueled by your superpower. Your superpower is your destiny.

Complete the checklist below to gauge your sense of purpose.

In the next chapter, you'll take another step in claiming your destiny. You'll discover the surprising but powerful principle of bodymind strength: healthy spirituality.

CHECKLIST FOR
"FIND YOUR SUPERPOWER – FULFILL YOUR PURPOSE"

	To what degree am I living a life of purpose? On a scale of 0-10, answer these questions, based on the last seven days. The cumulative sum of all nine end-of-chapter checklists will result in a total out of 100.	
1	My daily activities were driven by a sense of purpose.	
2	I daily used at least one of my top strengths or talents.	
3	I daily found myself in a state of flow, completely absorbed in what I was doing.	
4	I minimized distractions so I could focus on what was important.	
5	I used the part of the day when I'm at my best for the most crucial part of my work (unless it's a day off).	
6	I learned something that helped me, or will help me, accomplish my purpose.	
7	I regularly had a positive impact on someone.	
8	My work or activities contributed to life satisfaction.	
9	I had projects to work on each day that I loved more than eating (unless it's a day off).	
10	My sense of purpose strengthened me to resist harmful habits.	
	Total out of 100	
	Divide by 10 for average out of 10	

CHAPTER 3

UNLEASH HEALTHY SPIRITUALITY

*It appears that people who pay attention to their
spiritual side have lower rates of cardiovascular disease,
depression, stress, and suicide, and their immune
systems seem to work better.*

Dan Buettner, National Geographic

I stumbled down the stairs into my pitch-black bedroom. It was 3:30 a.m. The night had been like most of my Saturday nights, filled with partying. I was too restless to sleep.

Instead, I wrote in my journal:

Went to another party. But after it was all over, I had that empty feeling again.

It's only an hour later, yet the fun is a distant echo. It's haunting. The fun feeling disappears so quickly. Now that I'm by myself, I feel nothing but emptiness, unfulfillment, and insecurity. It's like living next door to despair. What does it all mean? No wonder I want to be with people all the time. It's to distract me from the awful emptiness.

My pleasure-seeking lifestyle isn't working for me. It gives the illusion of happiness for a while, but it falls as flat as a cardboard cutout. There has to be something else.

A few days later, Nicole, a girl from my study group at Dalhousie University, said she derived a sense of fulfillment from having a spiritual life. I gazed at her in disbelief. Admitting to being "spiritual" or "religious"—I didn't know the difference—was like saying you believed in fairy tales. I felt sorry for anyone who was victim of the magical thinking that religious leaders try to impose on a vulnerable population.

Imagine my surprise when the next time I saw Nicole, she invited me to a party with her religious friends. I tried to imagine what they would do at parties. Do they gather around and read prayers from a book? Do they sit on the floor with their hands on their knees and chant "om" all night? And most importantly, do they serve food?

I was pretty sure that whatever they did wouldn't be fun. But I was curious, and nothing else was going on that evening, so I went, dragging my friend, Bruce, with me.

At the party, there were no drugs, alcohol, loud music, or dancing. But there was live—although tame—guitar music, games, conversation, and laughter. And, yes, food…lots of food.

Besides the potato chips, cheezies, pretzels, three types of cookies, and soft drinks, what caught my attention was a passionate debate about spirituality around the buffet table. A group of freshmen and sophomores, finger food in hand, stood around the table discussing arguments for and against the existence of God.

Okay, I admit, I was the one who started the debate. I wanted to see how religious people responded when someone challenged their worldview. I may have alluded to fairy tales when a pre-med student said something about belief in a higher power.

Kathy and Maryanne said their life experience didn't reflect my contention that their beliefs were fanciful and devoid of verifiable fact. But no matter how I challenged their claims and arguments, they listened with interest and respect. I was surprised by how fun they were to talk to.

Rylan was different.

At a lanky six feet two inches, Rylan had a way of looking down on you that made you feel not only shorter, but lesser. Not long after joining our conversation, he told me to my face, in front of others, "Unless you change your ways, you're going straight to hell." He gave me a slight grin. "And it's a hundred times hotter than the hottest fire you have ever experienced."

Amazed at his audacity, I deadpanned, "I appreciate your concern about my future well-being. Where's hell so I can be sure to avoid it? It sounds like the weather there isn't so great."

He didn't crack a smile. Nor could he pinpoint hell on a map. But he did give me inside knowledge about hell being a mystical fire that burns souls, particularly mine.

I shook my head and headed back to the living room to load up another plate of salt and vinegar potato chips. There I found myself in other conversations about our classes, professors, and hockey.

Except for Rylan, it was a friendly atmosphere. Everyone was approachable, kind, and seemed to genuinely care for one another.

Later, as Bruce was dropping me off at home, I commented on the people at the party. I needed to debrief. "Except for their weird beliefs," I said, "they seem to have their heads screwed on right."

That quip drove us into a conversation about what made Nicole and her friends so different.

Bruce shut off the engine. "I liked how humble yet confident they were."

"All except for Rylan," I added.

Bruce laughed. "There always has to be one in the crowd, doesn't there?"

"Yes. But, you know, all the rest? They weren't putting each other down. They were at peace with us even though we don't believe like them."

"It's like there's no competition."

"That's it," I said. "There's no social competition among Nicole's friends. With our friends, we're always jostling to see who can be the coolest, strongest, smartest, drunkest, sexiest, or craziest. It's like we're all compelled to prove something to the world. Maybe we're just compensating for an insecurity deep within us. Maybe we strive for supremacy just to feel accepted. But Nicole and her friends…they weren't like that."

"You're right," Bruce said. "They seem to be happy with who they are."

I recalled the post-party emptiness I had written about a few nights before. The contrast between that party and this party was striking.

"Yeah. There's a certain vitality about them that is attractive. You know, Bruce, I think I'd like more of that."

Years later, I read an article about *The Big Bang Theory* actress, and Jeopardy host, Mayim Bialik. When Bialik was a new mom, she left a new moms' group meeting in tears because the other moms had been so competitive with each other.

"I instantly felt out of place," she said. The women at this moms' group were encouraged to "brag" about every aspect of motherhood: "How fast their labor was, how precocious their babies were with pooping, rolling over, sitting up, smiling…everything was a competition."

"These were not my people," she said. "I never went to any such moms' group again."[14]

So, I wasn't the only one to notice that kind of socially competitive atmosphere. While I loved competition in sports, grandstanding among friends suddenly seemed lame. Like Bialik, I instantly felt out of place in my little world. Nicole showed me something better.

But I had questions. What did Nicole have that contributed to that something better? It couldn't have been her religion, I mused. I couldn't reconcile the peace I felt in Nicole's world with the contempt I felt for religion. How could deluded people be so smart? How could people who believe in fairy tales be so mature? How could a religious snob like Rylan belong to a community that was so loving and lovable?

At the root of those questions was this one: What accounted for the contrast between Nicole's world and mine? Whatever it was, it became a candidate for an ingredient in the formula for bodymind vitality.

From then on, I was more observant of Nicole. She always received high grades on her tests and always had fun going out of her way to help others without being condescending. When I asked her about her accomplishments and liveliness, I prepared myself for a tactful lecture on how religion makes the difference.

Nicole paused a long time and finally answered, "It's those quiet moments between me and God. That's what makes all the difference in my life. Yes, my religion helps. But it only helps in that it strengthens my spiritual life.

And it's my spirituality that energizes me, motivates me, helps me see the world with compassionate eyes, and makes me feel strong."

As delightful as those things sounded, I could not understand how "quiet moments" had anything to do with making someone feel strong. Unless my mind was engaged by the wonders of nature, the only thing "quiet moments" did for me was remind me of my emptiness.

As always, I had much to learn.

Four discoveries brought clarity and opened my mind to a new world of possibilities:

1. **The Spirituality Spectrum:** a definition of spirituality that wasn't necessarily tied to religion.
2. **The Distinction:** the contrast between toxic spirituality and healthy spirituality.
3. **The Support:** evidence showing spirituality's link with bodymind vitality.
4. **Suggestions:** tips to boost healthy spirituality.

My discussions with Nicole and her friends piqued my curiosity about the relationship between spirituality and vitality. Eager to explore further, I embarked on a quest to seek out evidence for this connection. However, before delving into the research, it became clear that I needed to establish an understanding of what spirituality really was.

Over the years, I developed a map of sorts that would have been incredibly helpful back then to help me through this exploration. I call it the Spirituality Spectrum. It can act as a compass to navigate the various dimensions, practices, and beliefs in connection to spirituality.

1. THE SPIRITUALITY SPECTRUM

As I researched, I learned that religion was a system of values, beliefs, and practices embodied by a faith tradition that included a set of propositions about how the world works. There were positives. But as I looked at history, I couldn't help but see an ugly side to religion. The Rylans of history, when they were powerful enough, could judge, persecute, or kill you based on whether your beliefs aligned with their approved set of propositions. No wonder John Lennon alluded to religion as a force that gets in the way of world peace in his song "Imagine."

However, there was also a health-giving side to religion. Science, history, and Nicole seemed to show that, at least in some cases, it contributed to people's well-being. These confusingly contrasting faces of religion presented two hurdles on my road to understanding:

1.   How do I make sense of the contrasting faces of religion?
2.   What's the relationship between religion and spirituality?

Regarding the first hurdle, there was only one way I could make sense of the contrasting faces, or influences, of religion around the world. That was to evaluate religion according to its influence on health and well-being—that of both the individual and society. In other words, if religion makes you healthier in mind and body, it is beneficial; if not, it is detrimental.

Regarding the second hurdle, the only way I could clarify religion's relationship to spirituality was to subordinate the narrower term, religion, to the broader term, spirituality. In other words, religion is one expression of spirituality. Additionally, I would use healthy spirituality—the kind that boosts the health of mind and body—as the measuring stick to evaluate religion.

Many times, I stopped using the word "religion" altogether and just used "spirituality."

As Nicole put it, spirituality—not religion—was the secret to her vitality. Her religion helped only to the degree that it strengthened her spiritual life. Otherwise, her religion would have had little value.

That concept necessitated a definition of healthy spirituality that was useful and inclusive of all people regardless of their culture or where they were on their journey of life.

I dug into the books at the university library and found none of the science experts in the field could agree on the definition of spirituality, healthy or not. Spirituality was a term attached to a wide range of mindsets, attitudes, and practices that covered everything from personal growth to inner peace to trust in a supreme being. It was confusing.

I eventually found that the research basically separated spirituality into two broad categories, or two camps:

1. One that is focused on personal growth and fulfillment.
2. One that centered around the belief in some form of higher power or powers.

Incorporating Nicole's insight and consolidating countless other definitions of spirituality I put together this definition of healthy spirituality:

Healthy spirituality, broadly defined, is a sense that there is something valuable beyond the self and material world, that, when coupled with a wisdom-inspired mindfulness, nurtures the body, mind, and heart. It is deeply personal and different for each person. It may or may not need religion.

Happy with this definition, I was then able to divide the two broad categories of spirituality into five distinct subcategories of spirituality as observed around the world. The five subcategories are represented by five concentric circles (below) and comprise the Spirituality Spectrum.

Each of the five concentric circles represents a distinct expression of spirituality. As one moves out from the center of the circle there is an ever-increasing level of religious inclination and belief in transcendence. The three inner circles represent a spirituality that focuses on personal growth and fulfillment, whereas the two outer rings represent a spirituality that focuses on some kind of higher power. The outer rings seem to generate more intense disagreement than the inner rings.

Here are the titles and summaries of each concentric circle:

1. **Me**: The innermost circle represents things to do with personal development—such as the search for meaning, fulfillment, authenticity, creativity, and developing personal potential.
2. **Me and Nature**: The second circle represents things to do with one's relationship with nature—such as walks in the forest, mountains, desert, or beach, and appreciating the grand in nature.
3. **Me and Others**: The third circle represents the self as it relates to others—such as service to humanity or deep relationships.
4. **Me and the Universe**: The fourth circle represents beliefs about one's relationship with the universe as a higher power.
5. **Me and the Creator**: The fifth and outer circle represents beliefs about one's relationship with a creator God, as an exclusive higher power.

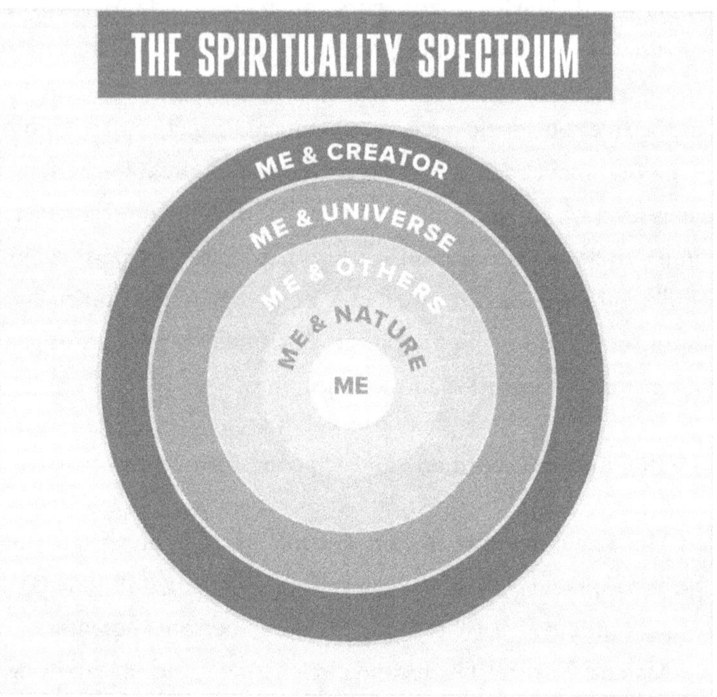

The Spirituality Spectrum

Next, I filled in the concentric circles with things people say are spiritual for them. It became easy to see that one person's spirituality can be un-recognizable by another. Here is how I filled in the spirituality spectrum, starting from the innermost circle. Notice which of each nurtures your bodymind:

Me

1. striving for authenticity
2. appreciating art and music
3. the quest to clarify beliefs about life and death
4. the quest to clarify beliefs about good and evil

5. developing a good character: humility, love, joy, peace, reliability, self-control, compassion, courage, self-sacrifice
6. being creative
7. listening to my conscience
8. clarifying deepest values, purpose, vision, and goals
9. being aware of deepest emotions
10. being inspired
11. experiencing "flow"
12. expressing gratitude
13. practicing optimism
14. monitoring motives
15. strengthening motivation
16. cultivating peacefulness deep within
17. seeking fulfillment and personal growth
18. meditating
19. feeling of being alive
20. searching for wisdom
21. conquering the lower self to live out the higher self
22. playing music
23. intuition

Me & Nature

1. connecting with nature (forests, fields, mountains, rivers, oceans, beaches, deserts, etc.)
2. learning from nature (observing the laws of cause and effect in plants, animals, climates)
3. watching or being with animals
4. the stewardship of environment
5. experiencing awe (being humbled by the beauty, danger, and power of nature)

Me & Others

1. experiencing and practicing love
2. feeling compassion
3. forgiving others
4. asking for forgiveness
5. connecting deeply with fellow human beings
6. cherishing a soulmate
7. gleaning wisdom from others
8. experiencing unity (tight band, sports team, choir, social club, religious participation, etc.)
9. contributing to the world through acts of service
10. philanthropy

Me & the Universe

1. feeling the call of destiny
2. experiencing oneness
3. feeling supported by the universe
4. valuing serendipity
5. being inspired by something bigger than the self
6. honoring universal law
7. experiencing transcendence

Me & the Creator

1. trust in divine power
2. a sense that a higher power is showing a higher path of life
3. feeling the call of providence
4. contemplating on values, vision, and goals as perceived as given by God
5. cultivating an awareness of God's presence

6. making efforts to connect with the creator
7. participating in the practices of a monotheistic belief system
8. being inspired by a loving creator
9. praying/talking to God as to a friend
10. attending a religious service
11. meditating on inspiring texts
12. experiencing mental growth through faith in God
13. loving God and experiencing God's love
14. growing in understanding of God's worldview
15. respecting others as an equal part of God's creation
16. listening to, or playing, music that brings a feeling of connection with God

Such a list is never complete or perfectly representative of all that people consider spiritual. Some may be surprised at what others find spiritual. What this construct did for me as a beginner "happiness seeker" was to show that I was on a spiritual journey even though I was an atheist. Also, locating myself on the spirituality spectrum helped me see other options to explore in my quest for optimal vitality.

Whatever those options were, I needed some way to determine whether they were helpful or harmful. That consideration led to my conclusions in the next section.

2. THE DISTINCTION: THE CONTRAST BETWEEN TOXIC SPIRITUALITY AND HEALTHY SPIRITUALITY

As stated previously, what became evident from my research and personal experience was that spirituality seemed to be expressed in two opposite ways. If I could reduce all the research and observations into one simple double axiom it would be this:

Healthy spirituality is characterized by the power of love.

Toxic spirituality is characterized by the love of power.

Expanding on the contrast, I built a list of words and phrases that are associated with each side of spirituality no matter where one was on the spirituality map. The collection bolstered the case for incorporating "healthy spirituality" into the formula for bodymind vitality.

Healthy Spirituality

1. increases compassion
2. strives for authenticity
3. builds character by fostering inner peace, humility, integrity, forgiveness, acceptance, kindness, gratitude, and connection
4. strengthens self-control
5. builds unity, empathy, and community
6. allows freedom of choice

Toxic Spirituality

1. fosters judgmentalism
2. desires control
3. focuses on external behaviors of self and others
4. imposes beliefs on others with little regard for their internal needs
5. is driven by fear, guilt, or angst

It seemed that both sides of spirituality could show up in any faith tradition and in any ring on the spirituality spectrum. The benefits of spirituality come through much more strongly with the kind of spirituality that seemed evident in Nicole's life. That kind of spirituality was distinct from the judgmental, dogmatic spirituality exhibited by Rylan, which was, at least from my perspective, toxic. For all his so-called "concern" for my "soul," Rylan simply wasn't healthy to be around.

I had many opportunities to confirm the usefulness of this double axiom after I became a pastor at the age of 25. As a pastor, I had many group discussions and private conversations confirming that spirituality had the power to either contribute to mental health or to destroy it. Depending on how you practiced it, spirituality could create joy, peace, and purpose, or it could induce feelings of guilt, fear, or suffocating.

On the dark side, some of these private conversations were with aging parents—usually fathers—agonizing over lost relationships with their adult children. Often, with heads bowed in remorse, they shared how they raised their children in an atmosphere of religious dogmatism focusing on external behaviors.

Now, they lived with the regret of having driven away their loved ones. The misguided religious conscientiousness of the parent did not, according to our definition above, "nurture the body, mind, and spirit" of the child. It suffocated the child until they were strong enough to break free. Such is the tragedy of toxic spirituality. In no way did it contribute to optimal vitality. As a matter of fact, that kind of spirituality was antagonistic to health.

On the bright side, some of these parents were awakened to the real meaning of unconditional love as taught by their very own faith tradition. Empowered by a newfound faith-inspired humility, they were able to reunite with their children, bringing a joy to the parent-child relationship they had never before experienced. Healed relationships—such is the power of healthy spirituality. (More on the vitality-boosting benefits of healthy relationships in the next chapter.)

The confusion surrounding the expression of spirituality became such an issue I felt compelled to develop a spiritual healthiness assessment to help people find clarity on whether their spirituality is healthy. Here are some guidelines I found useful.

Spiritual Healthiness Assessment

1. My spirituality reduces my stress.
2. My spirituality gives me wisdom and clarity in making important decisions.
3. My spirituality contributes to my sense of purpose and meaning.
4. My spirituality enhances the quality of my relationships.
5. My spirituality makes me a compassionate person.
6. My spirituality motivates me to respect my body.
7. My spirituality clears my conscience.
8. My spirituality strengthens my character.
9. My spirituality contributes to my self-care.
10. My spirituality dispels feelings of shame.

Notice that each of the statements represents principles that link spirituality to vitality—health of the bodymind.

Let's anchor this relationship with a deeper scientific understanding.

3. THE SUPPORT: EVIDENCE SHOWING SPIRITUALITY'S LINK WITH VITALITY

The World Health Organization reported that "depression is a leading cause of disability around the world and contributes greatly to the global burden of disease."[15] Clearly, many forms of medical treatment for depression have proven beneficial. Yet, despite their having exhausted the various treatments for depression, many people have discovered additional reasons for hope. Extending beyond pharmaceutical treatments, the therapeutic nature of spirituality for the treatment of depression was what intrigued me.

My research led me to the work of Dr. Lisa Miller, director of the Spirituality Mind Body Institute at Columbia University in New York and author of *The Awakened Brain: The New Science of Spirituality and Our Quest for an Inspired Life*. Dr. Miller and her team were intensely engaged in tackling the challenge of how to prevent depression. She explained how her team took magnetic resonance imagining (MRI) scans of the brains of those who were depressed and those who were not depressed. In preparation for the study, each participant reported on how important spirituality was to them.[16]

When the results came back, the brains of those who reported high spirituality were healthier and more robust than the brains of those who reported low spirituality. It was surprising that spirituality showed up in the very structures of the brain. Miller reported that "the high-spiritual brain was thicker and stronger in the exactly the same regions that weaken and wither in depressed brains."[17]

Dr. Miller's research showed that spirituality "was a vital, though overlooked, component of healing."[18] She wrote, "Spirituality appeared to protect against mental suffering" and to enhance "overall health."[19] Additionally, teens with high levels of spirituality were up to "75 percent less likely to experience clinical depression."[20]

Here is her conclusion: "For spiritually aware people across faith traditions—and including those without a faith tradition—the brain appeared able to protect itself from the long-standing neurological structures of depression."[21] It was interesting that people of all faith traditions benefit from healthy spirituality, and that even spiritual people without a faith tradition could benefit.

Dr. Miller's research reinforced the significance of including spirituality in the formula for optimal vitality.

Ever the pragmatist, though, I wondered about the practical application of spirituality in real-world situations. Would institutions, for example, see the potential of spirituality in their day-to-day operations?

Yes.

The prevalence of depression has created a crisis for the U.S. military, among other organizations. The military is encountering a situation where young individuals are joining its ranks with relatively low levels of maturity and higher levels of dysfunction and depression. Their deficiency poses increased difficulties for the military in terms of effectively training them for their assigned duties.

The solution?

Spirituality.

It came in the form of a program called the "Spiritual Readiness Initiative." In partnership with Dr. Miller, "the [U.S.] military is leading the way in a data-driven approach using the science in the awakened brain to address the plague that has attacked our young adults – the diseases of despair."[22]

The military developed an "Army Field Manual (FM) 7-22" to initiate the "Introduction to Spiritual Readiness." Its goal is to teach spiritual readiness practices that "define the essence of a person, enable one to build inner strength, make meaning of experiences, behave ethically, persevere through challenges, and be resilient when faced with adversity." What caught my attention was that the U.S. military considered spirituality as a contributor to those noble goals. Despite earlier reservations, I concluded, "If spirituality can do all that, it is a necessary ingredient in the formula for optimal bodymind vitality."

At the other end of the age spectrum were the findings of Dan Buettner, celebrated National Geographic Fellow. He set out to find the healthiest, most long-lived people in the world. With a team of medical researchers, anthropologists, demographers, and epidemiologists, Buettner discovered five areas of the world where people live the longest and are the healthiest.

He called them the Blue Zones:

1. Ikaria, a Greek island
2. Okinawa, a Japanese island
3. The Barbagia region of Sardinia in Italy
4. Loma Linda, a small city near Los Angeles, California
5. The Nicoya peninsula in Costa Rica

Interestingly, the people in these five groups had common characteristics. For example, they were active throughout the day, had a sense of purpose, practiced stress-reducing rituals, ate mostly plants, stopped eating when their stomachs were 80% full, ate their smallest meal in the early evening, and had strong social ties with family and friends.

We'll talk about all these habits throughout this book, but here was a surprising discovery: the large majority of the world's healthiest and longest-lived people belong to a faith-based community—just like Nicole. Of the 263 centenarians that were interviewed in the original Blue Zones, 258, or 98 percent, of them belonged to a faith-based community.[23]

Buettner called "the simple act of worship," a "subtly powerful habit" that seems to improve the likelihood of a longer and healthier life whether you are Muslim, Christian, Jewish, Buddhist, or Hindu.[24]

While the causal relationships weren't clear, Buettner observed that spirituality as practiced in a community is associated with improvements in both our mental health and physical health, the two major components of vitality:

Spirituality's benefits to mental health were lower rates of:

1. depression
2. stress
3. suicide

Spirituality's benefits to physical health were:

1. less cardiovascular disease
2. stronger immune systems[25]

I noticed that "stronger immune systems" was on the list. That meant community-enhanced spirituality seemed to play a role in fighting off disease. This would give spirituality a significant role in treating illness, and, therefore, contributing to longevity. Dr. Harold Koenig came to the same conclusion.[26] Dr. Koenig, a psychiatrist on the faculty of Duke University and Editor-in-Chief of the *International Journal of Psychiatry in Medicine*, wrote, after years of research, that there is a link between a strong immune system and a strong faith.[27]

When I was a pastor, I noticed another benefit of community-enhanced spirituality: happy relationships. Healthy spirituality seemed to enhance marriages, families, and friendships.

The health benefits of happy relationships have been emphasized by many social scientists. It's particularly evident in the work of Dr. Nadine Burke Harris, a pioneering pediatrician and first Surgeon General of California. Dr. Harris is known for her groundbreaking work on understanding the impact of adverse childhood experiences (ACEs) and toxic stress on long-term health.

She said, "Nurturing relationships…literally change our biology. When we have safe, stable, and nurturing relationships in our lives it improves our neurologic functioning. It improves our hormonal regulation. It improves our immune functioning. And these social supports are a critical part of healing."[28] In other words, compassion, a characteristic of healthy spirituality, is a therapy that rewires our brain's circuitry. Healthy spirituality leads to healthy relationships. And healthy relationships lead to many physiological and psychological advantages (which we'll explore in the next chapter).

When I began implementing some of the spiritual practices listed below, I too experienced what the science seemed to predict—more zest for life, greater meaning in my life, less stress, more peace in relationships, and more peace even when alone. I felt stronger and less needy—a little more like Nicole and her friends.

4. TIPS TO BOOST HEALTHY SPIRITUALITY

Over the years, I developed tools to help people boost healthy spirituality. You may be a person from any or no faith background. When it comes to benefiting from spirituality, it doesn't matter. All you need is to be a seeker of health and happiness and you're on the spirituality spectrum. Here are suggestions to experiment with, all of which aim to help you leverage the link between spirituality and vitality.

Locate Yourself on the Spirituality Spectrum

Look at the Spirituality Spectrum and explore the accompanying practices within each concentric circle. They can provide insight into your current position or offer guidance for future directions.

Longing for Something More

Recognize within yourself the longing for something better. Longing may be the invitation to a spiritual life. Dr. Miller suggests that even our times of doubts, struggles, and depression can serve as portals to the awakened life. Some types of depression might even be a natural craving for spirituality.[29]

Quiet Connection

Setting aside a time for quiet meditation before your day begins is like "sharpening the axe" for the work ahead, strengthening you for the day's interactions and challenges. When every other voice is hushed, the quietness of our mind makes more distinct the voice of wisdom. Reading something inspiring, then thinking about its application to life, can help in personal growth.

Clarify Values

Clarifying the values or principles you will live by can protect you against being led astray by whimsical feelings. Values could include authenticity, integrity, creativity, compassion, community, or personal development. In your personal time, search for the word "values" online and pick out the ones you want to live by. Let your conscience be your guide. Enlighten your conscience through wisdom reading. Then look for ways to live out your values.

Connect with Fellow Journeyers

Balance the moments of meditation with moments of connection. Meet up with people who have similar goals—people who want to experience something more meaningful in their daily lives. It could mean attending a weekend retreat, joining a weekly small group, or getting together with fellow journeyers in a home or online. Interaction with like-minded people can kindle a compassion within us, motivating us to act on noble intentions. Research has repeatedly shown that positive connections bring body-mind benefits. Greater community leads to greater immunity.

Connect with Nature

Walk among the trees, on the beach, on the mountain, by a river, in a meadow, or in a desert. These are ways people connect with nature. For some, it increases awareness of the presence of a higher power. For others, it's therapeutic. For some, it's both.

Working in a garden and watching seeds turn into plants is another way people connect with nature. Research from the U.K. suggests that a type of friendly bacteria found in soil may affect the brain in a similar way to antidepressants.[30] For some, walking the dog, playing with their cat, or listening to the birds sing is a spiritual experience.

Follow Your Conscience

Follow your conscience, that inner guidance that gives you a sense of right and wrong. While ignoring ego and desire for self-indulgence, balance self-compassion with compassion for others.

When making a decision, pretend you are advising a stranger. That substitution removes the emotional entanglement or resolves the "conflict of interest" in decision-making. Apply the advice to yourself. Some recognize this internal moral guide as direction from above. An uneasy feeling in the stomach, a tightness in the chest, or a flushing in the face before acting or reacting are signs to stop and consider the long-term consequences of the action. This spiritual practice leads to personal growth.

Continually sharpen your conscience by increasing your wisdom.

Use Your Talents

As we discovered in the last chapter, knowing and using your talents is a vital part of claiming your destiny. It unlocks hidden strength. My journey of discovery was a spiritual experience for me, partly because I was discovering my authentic self. Some, like Hollywood producer Devon Franklin, see using their talents as using an ability given by a higher power.

Putting talents to use not only leads to finding purpose, it adds a deeper spiritual dimension to life. Many people find that serving humanity through their talents fights depression and makes them feel more alive.

Read Inspiring Books

Books about the lives of noble people who are moved by a "higher purpose" can be inspiring and motivating—especially books about people who have similar talents as ours. Examples of biographies of noble and/or inspiring people include Dietrich Bonhoeffer, Brooksley Born, George Washington Carver, Marie Curie, Terry Fox, Gandhi, Martin Luther King Jr., Florence Nightingale, Abraham Lincoln, Nelson Mandela, George Müller, Treana Peake, Wilhelmina Rudolph, Mother Teresa, John Wesley, and William Wilberforce, among others.

There are thousands more. None of them are or were perfect. But they do or did something with their lives that makes us want to be a better person. The desire to be a better person is, for some, a spiritual calling.

Most spiritual traditions have their own books. Many of them contain principles of health and vitality. Sometimes, the words in an inspiring book are the exact words we need to hear.

For example:

> Find an inspiring book with a list of wisdom sayings.
> Keep reading until a proverb catches your attention.
> Don't read any further.
> Read it again several times.
> Memorize it.

Ask yourself, "How does this insight guide me?"

Stay silent for 30 seconds.

Dwell on that thought until it becomes your own.

Make it the motto for your day.

Read it again, asking how you will apply this insight in your day or week.

Look for opportunities to put the words into action.

At the end of the day, reflect on how the guidance enhanced your day.

Continue reading from that spot the next day.

Whenever I do this, I feel stronger and more alive. Reading inspirational material is one way in which spirituality guides us into a life of adventure. There's nothing like an exciting adventure to ignite personal growth.

Spiritual texts sometimes make claims that can even be tested in the laboratory of daily experience. Some spiritual texts boost our sense of purpose or give us something to aspire to. Other times, they kindle a desire to be a person of integrity or motivate us to explore a new avenue of self-development.

Discussions with Wise People

Before making an important decision, seek the thoughts of wise, humble people who want the best for you. Check their advice against other sources you trust.

Join a weekly small group that uses the spiritual principles of health and happiness as a foundation. You can use this book as you develop your spiritual center. It is in these discussions you may receive support, inspiration, or guidance.

Meditation/Mindfulness

For some, meditation means emptying the mind. For me, meditation means filling the mind. For example, by meditating on a daily proverb, which fills my mind with sage advice, I have found guidance for well-being and success.

Those passages can become part of the inner voice that speaks to our heart of hearts. Living in harmony with our inner voice (closely related to our conscience) gives peace and reduces stress. The resulting reduction in cortisol, a stress hormone, even contributes to disease prevention.

Read at Mealtime

Each morning at breakfast, our family—June, Michael, and I—took 5-15 minutes to read one paragraph from an inspiring book. Each person around the table asked a question to the others about what we read.

It didn't matter how many breakfasts it took to get through the book. What mattered was that we were talking to each other about the principles of life, values, ethics, gratitude, love, friendship, health, and a higher purpose. It contributed to a daily family discussion. It connected our family and brought us closer together. Sometimes we laughed. Sometimes we argued good-naturedly. It was a wonderful way to be a family and to deepen our connection with each other.

Color-Coding

Buy a package of colored pencils and color-code your inspiring book by underlining words in specific colors according to a theme. For example, underline with yellow all verses that give practical wisdom. Use green for all the words that deal with health, blue for happiness, red for success, pink for relationships, etc. Go back and read everything underlined in one color. By doing this, you can make your book a colorful handbook for positive living.

Guided Journaling

Guided journaling" works for a lot of people, too. This type of journaling starts with a wisdom quote you read rather than relying on your own initial thoughts. Writing it out in your own words helps to process and clarify the wisdom. The power of words, thoughts, and concepts sink in more when we write them down. Write out what the quote means to you and how it can make your life better.

Inspiring Music

Listen to, play, or sing inspiring music. I often do it while I walk or run by myself. Studies show that relatable words, when connected to music, reduce stress, and can help us express our emotions in a positive way.

Prayer

For some who believe in a higher power, prayer can be very strengthening. It's like talking to a friend. Some write out their prayer as they journal. Some pray as they read their most inspiring book.

Art and Writing

As with the expression of all talents, creativity in art and writing can provide a "flow" experience. We introduced "flow" in the last chapter. Creativity confers healing aspects to our existence. Some call their creative efforts a spiritual experience in that they do it as an act of gratitude to their higher power, or they feel a higher power working through them.

Health

Care for your physical health. What is good for the body is good for the mind. When the brain is unclogged from the fat, sugar, salt, and white flour that come from refined foods, the mind can discern more clearly the voice of wisdom. And the body is energized to act in response to the inspired mind.

Grit

Angela Duckworth popularized the concept of grit in her 2016 book: Grit: The Power of Passion and Perseverance.[31] The combination of passion and perseverance comes to everyone who has found their higher purpose and uses their superpower to accomplish it. They do whatever it takes to get the job done—and to get it done well.

Pursuing a passion born of a noble purpose can be a spiritual and vitalizing experience for many people. It gives clarity on when to say "yes" and when to say "no." It also can put them on a pathway that connects them to people who can help them on the next step of their journey.

Others' Needs

We can't take care of all the needs in the world, but by tending to the needs of those who have come into our circle of influence, we become an uplifter of humanity. By being alert for opportunities to build up others, we build up ourselves. But be careful not to burn yourself out by neglecting your health in a never-ending effort to help others.

Serendipity

Remember that chance meeting with an old friend you didn't want to run into but you knew you needed to? Or that time your sister called exactly when you needed a friend to lean on. That's serendipity. Some call it "providence" or "God winks." Some say it's the universe having your back. Not every coincidence is from a higher power, but some may be.

Throughout the day, be on the lookout for the kind of coincidences that set you up to serve others. If it doesn't interfere with a higher commitment, it could be a cue to change your plans. These seemingly insignificant circumstances that may take us out of our comfort zone often prepare us for something important in the future.

SUMMARY

To summarize, healthy spirituality—no matter how you practice it—contributes to vitality. It reduces stress and risk of diseases and increases creativity, connectedness, and a sense of purpose, making us feel strong. In the end, healthy spirituality turns out to be a surprising but essential ingredient to optimal bodymind vitality.

Complete the checklist below to gauge your level of healthy spirituality.

The next ingredient answers how social connections influence vitality levels in very unexpected and wonderful ways.

CHECKLIST FOR
"UNLEASH HEALTHY SPIRITUALITY"

	To what degree am I practicing healthy spirituality? On a scale of 0-10, answer these questions, based on the last seven days. The cumulative sum of all nine end-of-chapter checklists will result in a total out of 100.	
1	I was consciously aware that I was part of something greater than myself.	
2	I prioritized compassion and integrity over wealth and popularity.	
3	I followed my conscience but modified it as I received greater wisdom.	
4	I made decisions based on spiritual principles.	
5	I read something inspiring each day.	
6	I connected with others for spiritual purposes.	
7	I practiced meditation, prayer, or a spiritual activity each day.	
8	I spent time in nature each day.	
9	I practiced gratitude each day.	
10	I practiced forgiveness (when needed) for myself and others.	
	Total out of 100	
	Divide by 10 for average out of 10	

CHAPTER 4

LOVIFY YOUR LIFE

WHY LOVE MATTERS TO YOUR SUCCESS

Love is deeply biological… [It] has a profound effect on our mental and physical state.

C. Sue Carter and Stephen W. Porges,
Research Scientists

HOW TO BE A HERO WITHOUT TRYING

The animal leaped from the shadows into the dim light of the streetlamp, crouched, back up, tail straight, fangs gleaming slobber, growling low. The ugliest, meanest dog I had ever seen, three feet in front of me, readied to attack. Adrenaline surged in my body. My heart beat faster, rushing more blood to my muscles, preparing me for the well-studied response to perceived danger: "fight or flight."[32]

My nighttime jog through the forested country roads and sleepy homes of Rosedale Avenue, Lacombe, Alberta, Canada, instantly turned into a sprint for life. I sidestepped the dog and ran as fast as my legs could carry me. The chase was on. My would-be attacker, panting hard, paws pounding behind me, was not letting up. He wanted me for a midnight snack.

I reached the bottom of the hill, breathing heavy, and swung left onto University Drive. I had a half mile to go, uphill to my dormitory home at

Burman University. The panting dog, snapping at my heels, made the turn as well.

Lungs burning, legs screaming, I despaired, "How am I going to run another half mile at top speed uphill?" But no sooner had I thought that than a surge of adrenaline carried me, like the wind, soaring up University Avenue. When I reached the top, I peered back. The dog sat in the shadows at the bottom of the hill.

I was in the habit of jogging in the evening from the university library to the highway and back—about two miles. Out of shape at first, it took me 21 minutes, then 19 minutes, then 17. But this night, I made it in 15 minutes flat.

As hard as I tried, I could never run that fast again. I needed the dog.

Flash forward three years when I stumbled across another disgruntled dog—this time, in the early morning hours with my wife, June, by my side. We had just married six months before, graduated from Burman University, and moved to the small harbor town of Botwood, Newfoundland, Canada. We were in the habit of jogging together each morning at dawn before she headed off to teach elementary school.

This morning, loud barking pierced the morning stillness. It came from my distant left. Scanning the horizon for a possible threat, I saw it was a German shepherd three backyards away, running toward us. The yards were divided by white picket fences. There was no way the dog could jump that high, especially three times.

Then he shocked us.

He vaulted his fence like an Olympian. Now only two backyards away, and snarling, the dog sped toward the second fence. He cleared it with ease and accelerated toward us. Only one fence, three feet to June's left, protected us from the dog. She was in his direct path.

Adrenaline surged in my body preparing me for "fight or flight." This time it was time to "fight." I stepped in front of my wife to protect her.

The German shepherd and I locked eyes in mid-motion. My muscles tensed as I prepared to rip him apart with my bare hands. There would be blood, both his and mine. But there was no way that dog was going to touch my wife.

Suddenly, the dog thrust both paws in front of him and slid on the grass, coming to a screeching halt. There he sat, motionless, on the other side of the fence, staring, breathing hard as my wife and I jogged by.

WHAT MADE THE DIFFERENCE?

When I tell this story to audiences, I ask the question, "What made the difference? Why did I run in fear from one dog, yet stand up fearlessly against the other?"

The answers are always the same.

"Your wife!" someone calls out.

"Love!" someone else calls out.

Both are right.

Both dogs represented a threat—a source of stress that activates the emergency system in the body.[33]

In both situations, I didn't have time to think. When alone, faced with danger, I instantly defaulted to fear and ran. However, when I was with my wife, I instantly defaulted to love and stood ready to fight. I didn't ask myself, "Should I risk getting bitten by a dog to protect my wife?" Or "Should I take this opportunity to impress my wife, or prove my love to her?" No. I just acted.

I was a hero without trying.

In the context of love, courage rules. That's the power of love.

Matthew McConaughey wrote in his autobiography, Greenlights, "Cool doesn't try. Cool just is." Same with love. Love doesn't try. Love just does. No conscious effort needed. It is like going to the store to buy a package of love, and courage is thrown in for free. Love releases chemicals in the body that powerfully contribute to a life of optimal vitality.

Love flips on the power switch.

LOVE AND "LOVIFY"

"Love," as we are using it in this book, is "positive connection to others." It encompasses everything from "romantic relationships," to "a sense of belonging to a community," to "friendship." Love's main characteristic is that it is other-focused. That's its power.

When I officiated at weddings, I strived to inspire the bride and groom to put love in action throughout their relationship. I'd ask the couple to hear their own name every time I read the word "love" in the following words:

Love is patient,
love is kind.
It does not envy,
it does not boast,
it is not proud.

It does not dishonor others,
it is not self-seeking,
it is not easily angered,
it keeps no record of wrongs.
Love does not delight in evil but rejoices with the truth…
[Love] always perseveres.[34]

It's not just about giving love, though. The bride and groom needed to actively receive it as well. As a matter of fact, they needed to know how to attract love in the first place. Both giving and receiving are necessary for a life of vitality. In other words, we need to "lovify" our lives.

"Lovify" means to fill your life with love by:

1. strengthening your capacity to love others.
2. enhancing your ability to attract and receive love from others.

THE BEST PREDICTOR OF HAPPINESS AND HEALTH

Love does more than give you courage. Harvard University conducted two studies that highlighted more surprising by-products of the lovified life. The first study, "Harvard Study of Adult Development," is one of the world's most comprehensive longitudinal studies on health, happiness, and longevity. It began in 1938 at Harvard College and tracked the lives of its second-year students, including the future U.S. president, John F. Kennedy, along with teen boys from Boston's disadvantaged families.

The list below shows attributes researchers scrutinized to determine the top predictor of health, happiness, and longevity:

1. fame
2. fortune

3. social class
4. cholesterol levels
5. IQ levels
6. personality
7. genes

After reviewing tens of thousands of pages of data, they found that none of these things predicted health, happiness, and longevity. The top predictor was a surprise: close relationships.[35]

Amazingly, the quality of our relationships has a very powerful influence on our physical health. The study found that "the people who were the most satisfied in their relationships at age 50 were the healthiest at age 80."[36] Not only does love strengthen you to fight off attacking dogs, it keeps you healthy throughout life.

People in healthy relationships could even have physical pain and still be happy. But poor relationships increased the likelihood that physical pain will magnify emotional pain. Sadly, the health and brain function of lonely people declines earlier in life than those who are not lonely. "Good relationships don't just protect our bodies," said Robert Waldinger, director of the study, in a TED talk. "They protect our brains."[37]

The research also found: "Loneliness kills. It's as powerful as smoking or alcoholism."[38]

This research could not be plainer. If we want optimal vitality, we must lovify our lives. Our bodymind depends on it.

There's more.

THE BEST PREDICTOR OF SUCCESS

Another Harvard study about the effect of positive social connections was led by the head teaching fellow for positive psychology and New York Times best-selling author of The Happiness Advantage, Shawn Achor. He went on a mission at Harvard to uncover which individual attributes predicted happiness and success in the stressful, anxiety-ridden university environment.[39]

In his study of 1,600 students, he looked at the family income, SAT scores, high school GPAs, number of friends on Facebook, degree of extroversion, etc. None of these factors correlated with happiness, success, or thriving as a student.

He was about to give up hope of finding a predictive indicator of student success. It seemed there was no trait that directly correlated with thriving at Harvard. All of them were held by people who thrived, and people who didn't. Then he stumbled upon what he called a "massive exception": social connection.[40]

Social connection (not to be defined by the number of friends on Facebook), he said, was the "greatest predictor of thriving both personally and academically at Harvard."[41] Social connection had more power than fame, money, or medication. That finding is huge.

Achor reported that social connection was "the strongest predictor of emotional well-being, optimism, the greatest buffer against depression, and it also predicted how much stress one felt in the face of exams and competition."[42]

More than that, he found that social connection became "one of the greatest predictors of long-term performance in their careers."[43]

In other words, if you want to be successful, lovify your life.

By the end of his study, Achor had discovered that social connection predicted a total of seven advantages, all related to personal growth. They are:

1. personal thriving
2. academic thriving
3. emotional well-being
4. optimism
5. a buffer to depression
6. a reducer of stress
7. positive long-term career performance

Achor's work wasn't the only research to show the power of social connection. In a study published in The American Journal of Psychiatry, researchers from the Massachusetts General Hospital identified "social connection as the strongest protective factor for depression."[44]

Since "depression is a leading cause of disability worldwide," as reported by the World Health Organization, "and is a major contributor to the overall global burden of disease," [45] gently integrating social connection into treatment of depression may prove helpful in treating depression.

We must be careful not to conclude that social connection is a cure for depression. But we do see reason for hope suggesting it could benefit many people. For some, it can even be life-changing.

If love expels fear (like the fear of an attacking dog), then lack of love allows anxiety, a form of fear, to creep in. That effect may be what happened to the Harvard students who did not, or could not, make room in their schedule for social connection. They did not thrive. Social isolation correlated with more stress. With no feeling of belonging, life's challenges can be more overwhelming.

Dr. Bessel van der Kolk confirms the effect of social connection on stress reduction in his New York Times bestseller, When the Body Keeps the Score: Brain, Mind and Body in the Healing of Trauma. Dr. van der Kolk is the founder and medical director of the Trauma Center in Brookline, Massachusetts, and a professor of psychiatry at Boston University School of Medicine. He wrote, "Social support is the most powerful protection against becoming overwhelmed by stress and trauma. . . . No doctor can write a prescription for friendship and love."[46] It is a prescription written by nature's laws of cause and effect.

LOVE'S STRESS-BUSTING POWER

Not only does connection help with depression, success, thriving, optimism, etc., it can also help us when we have to take on a stressful project. For example: giving a speech. Research suggests public speaking is ranked among the top fears—right behind fear of snakes, according to one Gallup poll.[47]

At the beginning of my second year as a student at Burman University, I was asked by the university president, Malcolm Graham, to give a speech at a gathering of approximately 500 students, staff, and guests at the next Friday evening's assembly hall. The president wanted us to give a 10-minute talk sharing a summer experience that gave us a breakthrough in personal growth.

"Sure," I said, "I'd be happy to."

The second after I blurted out those words, my body shivered and my stomach turned upside down. All I could do was think about how I would embarrass myself in front of my professors and fellow students.

While eating with a friend in the cafeteria, I opened up about how nervous I was.

My friend raised his eyebrows and asked, "Did you learn any lessons over the summer?"

I took a bite of my lasagna. "Yes."

"Do you think others could benefit from those lessons?"

I stared at him. "Sure."

He leaned in. "Stop thinking about yourself and focus on how it will help them."

That reframe gave me what I needed.

That Friday evening, when President Graham introduced me, my stomach twisted. I took a deep breath and thought about someone in the audience who really needed to hear my story. After the first few words were forced out, I lost my nervousness, finished the speech, and was soon thanked by the president for a job well done.

Without my social connections and other-consciousness, I would not have been able to do it. The support I received empowered me. In turn, I gave support to others. When I tapped into my compassion for others, I became less self-conscious and felt more alive.

Dr. Bonnie Betts of the Mayo Clinic Health System also found that positive relationships can boost happiness levels and reduce stress levels. Consistent with the findings above, her research uncovered these bodymind benefits of positive relationships:

1. improved confidence
2. more ability to cope with traumatic life events
3. reduced risk of depression

4. lower blood pressure
5. a healthier body mass index (BMI)[48]

RAGS TO RELATIONSHIPS

All other things being equal, the one with quality relationships will outdo the one without them. I witnessed it firsthand with a homeless man, Bill. I often saw him slumped on the large cement stair entrance to the library of Andrews University, Berrien Springs, Michigan. He wore old baggy brown clothes. He lifted his eyes when a student passed by and dropped his head when they didn't return eye contact. He reeked of loneliness.

I was one of the many students who had passed him without eye contact. One afternoon, though, I saw him hobbling away, dejected, from the stairway. He hunched over as he walked.

"Hi," I said with a smile. "How are you?"

Immediately, his eyebrows lifted, and he smiled faintly as he joined me for a walk. I was on my way to the bookstore but decided to keep walking with him around the campus. After small talk, he told me about his lost dreams.

It turned out he wasn't homeless after all. He lived alone in an old messy house and was not motivated to clean it. He was plagued by depression, had high blood pressure, and worried about being overweight. He revealed a lot of personal tragedies to me that afternoon. Mostly, he just needed a friend.

I invited him to a weekly get-together of a small group the next Saturday morning. When he arrived, I introduced him to my friends who welcomed him. He took to joining us every Saturday. Within a few months, he was smiling and laughing. It was heartwarming to watch him make new friends.

A few years later my wife and I came back and visited the group. To my surprise, Bill jumped out from the crowd to greet me. I barely recognized him. He was thinner, stronger, and more vibrant. He walked tall. It was obvious his lovified life brought him many of the benefits mentioned above. What a difference it makes to belong to a loving community!

Love doesn't happen on its own, though. We have to do something to attract it. Bill recognized his need for connection and took the only action he could think of. By sitting on the library steps waiting for a passerby to say hi, he initiated a chain reaction that brought love into his life.

These emotional rags-to-riches stories play out whenever there is love.

Following are "Lovify Your Life" principles that have worked in my life and career as well as for others. If you'd like to try an experiment, choose at least one of the following to act on this week and see what happens.

PRINCIPLES TO LOVIFY YOUR LIFE

Happy social connections are essential for a life of optimal vitality. They make you feel strong. When it comes to your social environment, identify the three categories of people who feed your soul and consider balancing your social life between these three types of relationships:

Three categories of people who feed your soul:

1. People in your life who occupy the role of big brother/big sister, caring senior, or loving and wise mentor. It could be a family member but doesn't have to be.
2. People in your life who occupy the role of buddy, partner, or peer. Someone with whom you can laugh.

3. People in your life you mentor such as children, or someone who has not walked the distance you have walked in a certain discipline or area of life or work. See yourself as a model for the ones you love. Let them see you doing what you wish they would do.

TIPS ON HOW TO PUT MORE LOVE IN YOUR LIFE

Strategic Listening

My friend Jim Gaull said listening feels so much like love that people can't tell the difference. Particularly powerful is the practice of asking questions and just listening. This especially works in the context of conflict. Take Priscilla, for example.

Priscilla came with her sister to my office looking for some advice regarding a tumultuous relationship with her teenage daughter. She talked a long time, sharing with me how much she loved her daughter. She would tell her daughter she loved her all the time and tell her how heartbroken she was over their constant arguing and power struggles, but none of that seemed to make their relationship better.

I asked Priscilla whether she was willing to try an experiment.

"Anything." She scooted closer to the edge of her seat to hear what I was about to say.

"Stop telling her you love her, especially since you've done that many times already. It hasn't fixed anything so far. Instead, show her that you respect her. Then she'll feel how much you love her."

Her brow crinkled. "How do I do that?"

"By strategic listening," I said. "That's when you ask your daughter what the issues are from her perspective. Then you promise her you will listen without interruption no matter what she says. You'll be tempted to defend yourself or give your opinion. But resist. Don't interrupt her to defend yourself no matter what. Just listen. And when she is finished, ask her this question: 'Is there anything else?' Then listen more.

"She might falsely accuse you. She might hurt you with harsh words and even make you cry. Let your tears show. But listen. Your daughter might go on for hours. But listen."

"This is going to be hard." She shifted in her seat. "But I'll do anything to save my relationship with her."

She left my office with a strategy to lovify her life and that of her daughter's.

Two weeks later Priscilla called me.

"I told my daughter I was willing to listen without interrupting. At first, she didn't believe me. But when she spoke for 20 minutes and I just listened and said, 'Is there anything else?' she really started in on me, telling me how unfair I was. I really wanted to tell her where she was wrong. But I listened and said, 'Is there anything else?'"

"That must have been hard," I said.

"It was. But I kept on saying, 'Is there anything else?' It took six hours for her to say all she wanted to say. She said things that were hurtful. I cried. But I kept on listening without interrupting. And as I did, I began to feel her pain. I just wanted to hold her."

"Wow."

"In the end—what a moment. It was so beautiful. We hugged and cried together. It has changed our relationship forever."

Her daughter experienced love through her mother's gift of listening.

Years later, I learned that mother and daughter are still enjoying a wonderful relationship.

True listening and being open to feedback can be hard. But it is a powerful way to lovify your life and ensure you are making another step toward optimal vitality. It works.

Bids for Connection

Another subtle but powerful form of social connection is often overlooked in the office, school, family, and social circle. It is called "turning toward." This insight comes from the groundbreaking research of John and Julie Gottman. They give the example of a couple sitting at the breakfast table.

The wife looks out the window and says, "Oh, look, honey. Our garden is growing." The Gottmans call that innocent attempt to direct her husband's attention a "bid for connection."

When the wife makes a bid for connection, the husband can respond in one of three ways. He can "turn against" by saying, "Can't you see I'm busy?" Or he can "turn away" by ignoring her and turning the page of his newspaper. Or he can "turn toward" by looking out the window and saying, "Well, look at that. It's growing quite nicely. I wonder if that means we're going to get lots of tomatoes this year."[49]

Here's why the response is important: 86% of the "turning toward" couples were happy in their marriage six years later. But 33% of those who didn't "turn toward" were unhappily married or divorced six years later.

For many, just a few seconds of attention determines their long-term relationship success. It's that powerful.

Here are more examples of bids for connection:

1. "Look, Mom. No hands."
2. "Wow. Look at that."
3. "What a day I had."
4. "I can't believe my boss."
5. "Just thought I'd email this to you."
6. Sometimes it could be as simple as a sigh.

Lovify your life by searching for opportunities to use turn-toward bids for connection in daily conversations.

Here are some quick tips on how you might find more positive connections:

Join a Club

Find a way to strengthen social connections by joining a group that meets regularly, like a book club, a running club, or the Rotary Club. Something that gives you opportunities to consistently connect with others. It doesn't need to be that formal. Just pick something you like doing and do it with others. Serendipity will take over from there, and you will easily learn if the club resonates with you.

Empower Yourself by Forgiving Others

Forgiveness can be very hard. But when we let go of past hurts, we often find freedom and strength to start "living" again. Forgiveness doesn't need to start with trying to change our emotions. It can start with an act of will. Make a determined decision to let go of thoughts of revenge that can take over and get in the way of loving relationships. Often positive emotions of peace will follow an act of forgiveness.

For many, forgiveness has the added benefit of increased self-confidence because they no longer cling to victimhood. Forgiving somebody can even strengthen the immune system and lower blood pressure. Many people have experienced that true forgiveness is more freeing for themselves than for the offender.

Volunteer

Go online and type in "volunteer organizations in [your city]" and choose the organization that most taps into your talents. Call them and ask how to join. Doors will open to new friendships and sense of purpose.

Self-Care

Lovify your life by caring for yourself. This is not being selfish. It is being strategic. Wise parents know that taking the time to keep themselves healthy in mind and body is the best long-term strategy for their children's well-being. Set boundaries by learning to say no to some things so you can say yes to the best things.

Soft Answer

An ancient proverb says, "A gentle answer turns away wrath."[50]

I had a chance to test the validity of that principle when I was the editor of the college newspaper at Burman University. I allowed something to be printed that, although true, showed a student in a bad light.

He was angry and confronted me, towering over my table, as I was eating with my friends in the dining hall. His voice was loud and accusatory. Three hundred students suddenly stopped talking and turned their heads to hear the argument between him and me.

I was tempted to defend myself by attacking him with the truth I knew about him. But I remembered this principle and decided to give a soft answer. "I'm sorry," I said.

He turned his accusations into explanations. I listened as he explained his point of view. With every sentence he spoke he became less and less angry. Within two minutes his anger dissipated, and his voice calmed down. People in the dining hall resumed their lunch and conversation.

He and I are friends to this day.

I also learned there are truths that don't need to be made public.

The Power of Kind Words

Catch someone doing something nice and express gratitude for it. Look for positive characteristics in everyone you meet and tell them about it. Use words to build up people. They will more likely build you up, too.

Love Embraces Another's Power to Choose

Love does not coerce or manipulate. Love allows choice—even the wrong choice. In marriage when one partner compels the other to yield to their wishes, love is lost. The same principle shows up at work, school, politics, and religion. When choice is removed by someone with more power, it can feel like oppression to those with less power. Cortisol levels rise. The resulting stress can trigger adaptive responses such as anger or rebellion. Or it may be fear and submission. But in both cases, the social fabric is damaged.

By allowing freedom of choice in a relationship, we allow love and, therefore, health to flourish.

The Golden Rule

When we don't know how to interact with people, a helpful guide is to treat people as we'd like them to treat us. This ancient piece of wisdom is the famous "golden rule." But before applying it, consider their temperament.

An introvert, for example, doesn't always want to be treated like an extrovert. Respect and empathy are the main principles behind the golden rule.

Eliminate Toxic Relationships

Sometimes, toxic people need our help. But an ongoing toxic relationship can be a threat to our bodymind vitality. It doesn't take long before we feel drained of energy and self-worth.

Again, practice self-care. Balance your life with nourishing people. Look for people who know you and like you just the way you are. Perhaps you can find them in your contact list on your smartphone. Call them to rekindle or strengthen the relationship.

Apply one of these ideas and see where it leads. Then try the others as you have opportunity. In this way, you will find that the law of love is the law of life.

Complete the checklist below to see how much you've lovified your life this week.

Now, let's delve deeper into how to make real-life transformation happen.

CHECKLIST FOR

"LOVIFY YOUR LIFE"

	To what degree am I lovifying my life? On a scale of 0-10, answer these questions, based on the last seven days. The cumulative sum of all nine end-of-chapter checklists will result in a total out of 100.	
1	I maintained a healthy balance of give-and-take in my relationship interactions.	
2	I am a part of a community of people who share my core values.	
3	I expressed gratitude to people.	
4	I knew when to say no and how to set boundaries that people respect.	
5	I respected others even though I may have disagreed with them.	
6	I served the people who most need my strengths.	
7	I've been maintaining loving relationships without giving up my authentic self.	
8	I showed humility and confidence when I was with people.	
9	I didn't force or manipulate people to get my way.	
10	I actively listened before I spoke, interrupted, judged, or gave unsolicited advice.	
	Total out of 100	
	Divide by 10 for average out of 10	

LAUNCH YOUR PLAN—PHASE 1

RESTRUCTURING THE HABITS OF THE MIND

If habits made me who I was, then new habits will remake me into whom I choose to become.

Ernest J. Brake

I stepped out of the shower, wiped the vapor from the mirror, and peered at the shape of my body—a cross between a barrel and a marshmallow. I grimaced as I looked at my sagging muscles, sloped shoulders, rounded midsection. My body testified to poor self-care. Every roll of fat was there because I put it there. I didn't mean to…it just happened.

Actually, no. It didn't just happen. The shape of my body was not something that formed as if I was a passive bystander. I was an active participant.

How did I get to this point? Well, I can tell you, it wasn't overnight. It took me years to sculpt my body into a barrel.

It was the last 100 bags of potato chips I ate, the last 500 cookies, the last 50 pieces of cake, the last 50 orders of french fries, the last 50 scoops of ice cream, and the last 50 pizzas. They all sculpted the "me" in the mirror. With every bite of processed food, with every surrender to cravings, I built my body, one fat molecule at a time. In the end, those thousand little pleasures conspired against me.

My habits made me the "me" I didn't want to be.

It wasn't only the food I ate. It was about where I put my time and energy. It was everything I repeatedly did and didn't do that produced the man I was that day.

I recalled a certain dark city street from a few years before. The promise I made to myself on that night came back to me.

"You can do better than this," I said to the man in the mirror.

I stood straight, pulled my shoulders back, tightened my abs, and imagined what I could be—stronger and fitter physically, mentally, and professionally, too. If habits made me who I was, then new habits will remake me into whom I choose to become.

That intention meant a change in my lifestyle—immediately. To get started, I read a book on health and fitness. Then I read one on nutrition. I took notes about what I could do and made changes.

It worked. But not for long.

So, I broadened my reading to include books on the mind-body relationship, self-discipline, self-improvement, success, lifestyle medicine, happiness, and productivity. I pored over ancient books that have endured through the centuries and modern books with the latest research. I discovered many of the authors gave presentations on YouTube and podcasts. I watched and listened.

But the man in the mirror didn't change.

The books didn't work. The lectures didn't work. The videos didn't work. I had a lot more knowledge, but I was still the same. Disappointing.

But not surprising.

It turns out, knowledge doesn't work unless you apply it. I hadn't yet committed—really committed with all my being—to turning the knowledge into action. I mostly dreamed about it.

What can a person do when their dreams crash against the wall of reality?

THE SECRET TO FULFILLING A DREAM

For years, I'd known that to achieve success individuals must have a burning desire for change. And a clear goal—that picture in their head of their photo finish. For me, that photo finish was symbolized by a man standing on top of a mountain pumping his right fist into the air.

But as I discovered in front of the mirror, desires and goals are not enough. Far from it.

The international best seller and thought leader, James Clear, put desires and goals into a new perspective with this revolutionary insight: "We don't rise to the level of our goals. We fall to the level of our systems."[51]

That was my problem. I had no "system." I had desires, visions, dreams, and goals. But I had no system to turn them into reality.

A system is a set of habits driving us toward a goal. It could be called a strategy, a program, or an action plan. Whatever we call it, committing to it is what we mean by "Launch Your Plan." It means actually doing something. If we want to be something different, we have to do something different.[52] Applied to optimal vitality, it's about initiating lifestyle changes—ones that maximize our personal development and strengthen our bodymind.

In calling it a "system," we may be tempted to think it's impersonal. But activating new habits is very personal. And it's the only strategy for turning a mediocre life into an extraordinary life.

Confucius said 2,500 years ago, "All [humans] are equal, it is their habits that separate them." A system of habits separates the winners from the majority. Life champions do what the majority won't. To position ourselves for success, therefore, we can't rely on advice from the average person. We need to look to those who have accomplished what we want and learn how they did it.

When I studied the people who were at the top of their field, the power of habit was a feature in almost every success story. It showed up in sports, entertainment, education, relationships, parenting, leadership, healthcare, and business.

For example, in The Billion Dollar Secret, Rafael Badziag, award-winning author and entrepreneur, writes about traveling the world to interview 21 self-made billionaires. He had one main question for them: "What is the secret of your success?" The answers could be summarized in one word: "habits."

More specifically:

1. They rise early in the morning.
2. They exercise regularly.
3. They read regularly and widely.
4. They take time for daily contemplation.
5. They commit to morning and/or evening routines.
6. They are disciplined.
7. They take calculated risks.[53]

We don't need to be billionaires, and not all their habits need to be ours. But we, too, can become life champions by creating a system of daily actions. In time, the new actions turn into habits and routines that advance us toward our goals.

Studies have shown that a habit takes between 18 and 253 days to form, and an average of 66 days depending on the actions and situation.[54] But when good habits do form, something wonderful happens. The new habits create "the new you,"[55] that champion standing at the top of the mountain. Or in front of the mirror.

I had that vision. I knew I needed a new set of habits. Yet, standing in front of the mirror that morning, I had to acknowledge another problem: I was an unstructured person. Incorporating lifestyle changes into my day conjured up pictures of restrictive rules, rigid routines, and exhausting drudgery. I could only take the grind for so long before losing motivation and giving up.

The only kind of system that would work would be one with built-in motivators. Every part of it would have to tap into something deep within me. First, it would have to tap into my superpower and spark that sense of higher purpose, making it fun to keep pushing. Second, the plan would have to build on my personal values and identity, making it deeply spiritual. Third, the plan would have to leverage the strength of social connection.

Fortunately, these three sources of motive power are the very principles we discussed in the three preceding chapters. They are the first three principles of FULL POWER:

1. Find your superpower (Chapter 2)
2. Unleash healthy spirituality (Chapter 3)
3. Lovify your life (Chapter 4)

Without these activating principles, I couldn't successfully launch a plan because I'd be missing the motive power to keep going when the things got tough. Like gasoline in a rusted-out gas tank, motivation leaks. Any plan or system for optimal vitality would have to take that leakage into account. The first three principles of FULL POWER fill up the motivation tank for the fourth principle, Launch Your Plan.

Ignoring these principles is, perhaps, why many weight-loss programs fail. Jumping into a weight-loss program without the necessary psychosocial and spiritual preparation undermines potential for success.

That's why launching your plan requires two phases:

> Phase 1: Restructure the habits of the mind through the principles of FULL.

> Phase 2: Restructure the habits of the body through the principles of POWER.

If you want to lose excess weight or conquer any other personal growth challenge, start by identifying your higher purpose. Identify your higher purpose by finding your superpower. Then unleash the power of healthy positive spirituality and lovify your life.

When you determine to score high on these FULL principles in PART 1, you are then prepared for the POWER principles in PART 2. That's where we get physical and physiological. As you advance to PART 2, note the new habits you want to adopt. We address harmful habits in a very specific way in Chapters 7 and 8.

In PART 3, we'll put it all together—Phases 1 and 2—in a complete FULL POWER plan for optimal bodymind vitality.

Congratulations. You've laid the foundation. Complete the checklist below to assess your score in launching and living out your plan. Remember the checklists are just benchmarks against which to compare your future score. You'll have a chance to improve your score when you implement your plan.

But, right now, we need to build on the mental foundation we've laid in PART 1. Adventure and discovery await us in PART 2.

CHECKLIST FOR
"LAUNCH YOUR PLAN"

	To what degree am I launching or living my plan? On a scale of 0-10, answer these questions, based on the last seven days. The cumulative sum of all nine end-of-chapter checklists will result in a total out of 100.	
1	My habits aligned with a purpose that inspired me.	
2	I tracked my progress in maintaining healthy habits.	
3	I have been intentionally living out a plan for my personal growth and health (vitality plan).	
4	I read, watched, or listened to material that supported my vitality plan.	
5	My environment (physical and relational) supported my vitality plan.	
6	My habits were strong enough to help me overcome self-sabotaging behaviors.	
7	I put knowledge into action.	
8	My habits enriched my mental health.	
9	My habits enhanced my physical health.	
10	I practiced morning and evening routines that supported my vitality plan.	
	Total out of 100	
	Divide by 10 for average out of 10	
	Double it for score out of 20	

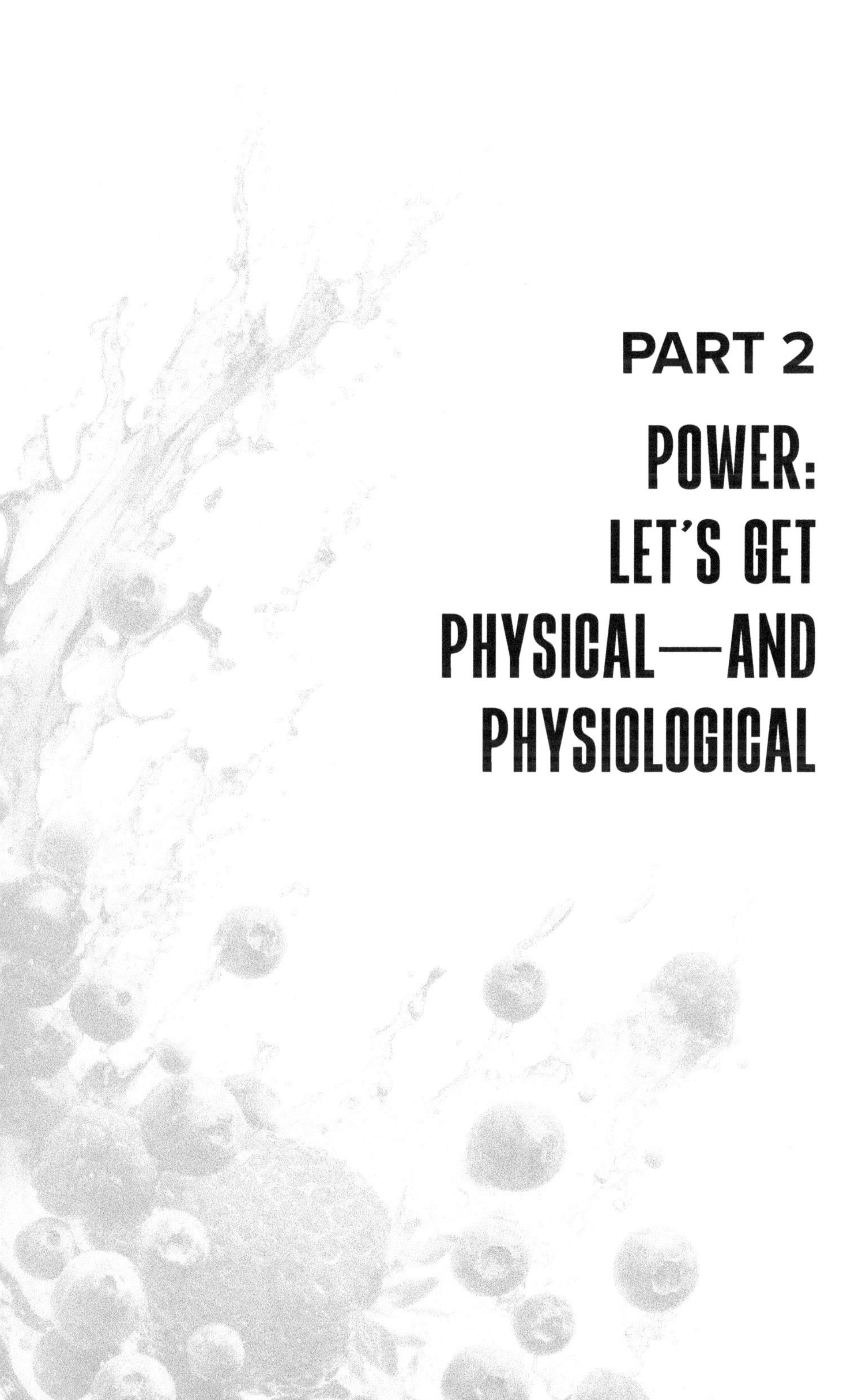

PART 2

POWER: LET'S GET PHYSICAL—AND PHYSIOLOGICAL

CHAPTER 6

PRIORITIZE HIGH-OCTANE FUEL

*Nutrition, when done right, can create more health
than all the pills and procedures combined.*

Dr. T. Colin Campbell

At 65 years of age, Frances received devastating news. Poor circulation prevented her heart from getting enough oxygen, resulting in angina pain, a dreaded squeezing pressure in the chest. Physical activity became excruciating as Frances's muscles strained to work in an oxygen-deprived environment. After several bypass surgeries, there was nothing more the doctors could do. Frances had end-stage heart disease. She was sent home in a wheelchair to die.

But Frances heard about a program on the other side of the country that gave her hope. Even though she was knocking at death's door, she was determined to live to see her grandchildren grow up. With the support of her family, she travelled from Miami, Florida, to Santa Barbara, California, to a live-in health center called the Pritikin Longevity Center. They specialized in reversing terminal heart disease through a menu plan that offered high-quality food along with a daily exercise routine and health education.

For the purposes of this book, we will use the term "high-octane fuel" as a metaphor for high-quality food. In the oil industry, octane, a hydrocarbon molecule $C8H18$, is added to gasoline to stabilize the fuel for high-performance, high-efficiency, and freedom from "knock." The higher the octane rating, the better the performance. It is identified at the gas pump as "premium."

At the center, Frances learned to think of her body as a high-precision machine requiring "fill-ups" on premium fuel to "run at full power." While food does not actually contain octane, the concept of food as fuel is very real. High-quality food is like high-octane fuel. The higher its rating, the better your performance.

The lowest rating comes from empty calories—calories emptied of nutrition, vitamins, and minerals, and calories filled with tasty but toxic substances. Such inferior fuel comes in the form of refined foods, usually high in sugar, salt, fat, white flour, and/or chemicals, often called "treats." In the body, these food-like substances are the equivalent of "dirty" sludge running through the system where "clean" fuel should be.

Frances's habit of feeding her cells sludge instead of fuel eventually took its toll. After many years, her cells reached a breaking point, and her body began to shut down at the cellular level.

Fuel is delivered to our 37 trillion cells[56] through our circulatory system. Think of tiny delivery trucks and tiny garbage trucks traveling through your blood highways and byways making deliveries and pickups, delivering fuel and removing waste. Top-quality food means a top-notch delivery and removal system. Operating at such a high level makes stronger cells. Stronger cells lead to more vitality. When Frances ate better quality food, her cells received "high-octane fuel" and provided the strength to heal her body.

For Frances, high-octane fuel was made of a large variety of:

1. fruits
2. vegetables
3. whole grains

4. legumes
5. nuts
6. seeds

That combination of food is the nutrition component of nature's golden formula. They are foods that can be picked off a tree or grown in the ground—unrefined and unprocessed. Herbs and spices can be added for taste and, in some cases, additional healing.[57]

This premium fuel includes macronutrients and micronutrients.

Macronutrients are:

1. **Complex Carbohydrates** – large molecules made of carbon, hydrogen, and oxygen that provide the body's primary source of sustained energy, often called "starch." Complex carbs stand in contrast to simple carbs, which are small molecules often called "sugars." Simple carbs harm the body and are often what people mean when they say "carbs."
2. **Proteins** – amino acids that form the builders and repairers of body tissue.
3. **Healthy Fats** – source of stored energy and component of cell membrane.

The micronutrients are:

1. **Vitamins**: organic compounds essential for healthy growth and required in small quantities in the diet because the body cannot make them. Examples: vitamins A, B1, B2, B3, B5, B6, B7, B9, B12, C, D, E, and K.
2. **Minerals:** inorganic elements present in soil and water, which are absorbed by the plants we eat. Examples: calcium, chloride, iron, magnesium, potassium, sodium.

3. **Trace elements:** inorganic elements needed in smaller amounts. Examples: iodine and copper, zinc, etc.

4. **Phytochemicals:** chemicals from plants. Examples: flavonoids[58] and carotenoids.[59]

An essential part of natural nutrition is the emphasis on a wide variety of nutrients. For maximum health, variety is critical. The nutrients found in an apple, for example, are different than those found in a carrot.

But what is missing in the carrot is supplied by whole grains. What is missing in whole grains is supplied by beans. What is missing in beans is supplied by nuts. Nature's formula ensures a strong balance between structure-building proteins, energizing complex carbs, and healthy fats.

Frances's new high-octane fueling plan also provided four other advantages.

They were:

1. anti-inflammatory
2. fiber-rich
3. microbiome-friendly
4. sustainable for a lifetime

Frances didn't need meat to get iron. She absorbed all she needed from beans and greens (leafy green vegetables), nuts and seeds, along with lots of vitamin C (oranges, kiwi, mango) to maximize absorption.[60] It was the same with the protein, healthy fats, and micronutrients—all came from plant-powered whole foods.

After three weeks on the program—unknowingly following many of the principles of FULL POWER—Frances was walking 10 miles a day. She left her wheelchair, marched out of that health center, and lived another 31 years![61]

Before, with no hope of living beyond a few months, she now was able to enjoy 31 more Christmas gatherings, the weddings of loved ones, and other family events. She watched her grandchildren grow up and shared her love, her joy, and her wisdom with the next generation. Such is the precious value of lifestyle medicine.

BLOWN AWAY BY PATIENT OUTCOMES

The late Dr. Hans Diehl, an epidemiologist (an expert who studies diseases in the population), was the research and education director of the Pritikin Health Center during Frances's stay there. Part of his job was to record the "before and after" medical data of each client. He was blown away with patient outcomes—including those of Frances.

In an interview with popular health show host, Chef AJ, Dr. Diehl recalled how Frances was wheeled into the health center and how she walked out three weeks later. He said, "Pritikin could demonstrate within 26 days [that] many patients with angina pain were no longer taking medications for their angina pain."[62]

Any program that removes the need for pills in 26 days is a powerful program. Especially when pain is involved.

Dr. Diehl also reported on high blood pressure. He said, "Eighty three percent of the patients on medication for high blood pressure were off the medication after four weeks and their blood pressures were normal."[63]

Dr. Diehl went on to list other benefits of plant-powered nutrition. "They showed in these residential centers [that] within four weeks 40% of the people on insulin were off insulin. And Type 2 diabetes was gone."

One of the concerns of diabetics is blood sugar spikes. Fortunately, the complex carbs in the plant-based menu reduce their frequency and intensity.

A menu filled with vegetables, fruits, whole grains, legumes, and nuts provides a slower and more sustained release of energy throughout the systems of the body, helping to keep blood sugar levels stable while giving feelings of fullness. Lentils, for example, being high in complex carbs, "slow the rate at which sugar is absorbed in the system."[64] Good news for diabetics.

Approximately one-third of the U.S. population (133 million people) has either diabetes or prediabetes.[65] Imagine the reduction in suffering, medical expenses, and deaths if the diabetics and prediabetics could find a way to fill up on plant-powered fuel! Many would find, to their great relief, that Type 2 diabetes is reversible.

When it comes to reversing angina pain, high blood pressure, and Type 2 diabetes, in many cases, the sole "medication" required is high-octane fuel. It was high-octane fuel that gave Frances the support she needed to live out her life's purpose, to do it with less pain, with less disease, and to reach well into her 90s.

WHY FRANCES WAS ABLE TO RECOVER QUICKLY

Very few understand the benefits of plant-powered eating habits more than Dr. Michael Greger. He made it his life's purpose to research every scientific journal article on nutrition to find out what constitutes the best fuel for the human body.

He wrote the New York Times bestseller How Not to Die and followed it up with How Not to Diet, each of them containing almost 5,000 scientific references and checked by nine fact-checkers. Rarely are the facts in a nutrition book verified with such thoroughness. You can find more on nutrition research on his website, nutritionfacts.org. During the writing of this book, he has published a third book, How Not to Age.

His research explained why Frances recovered so quickly. The conclusion of his research is unequivocal: The food you eat is one of the biggest contributors to long-term health. A poor diet is one of the biggest thieves of vitality and has brought years of anguish and suffering to millions of unaware people—before laying them in an early grave. Each of those reasons is why the FULL POWER Plan focuses on eating whole-food, plant-based products.

Dr. Greger not only showed that switching to high-octane fuel makes huge contributions in recovering health, reducing suffering, losing excess weight, and saving lives, he saw it first-hand. He was the 10-year-old grandson of Frances in the story above!

Inspired by the near-miraculous recovery of his grandmother, Dr. Greger entered the field that saved her life. He introduced his book, How Not to Die, with these words: "It all started with my grandmother." And then he continued to show, through many scientific studies, the power of prevention through plant-powered eating—prevention of the many chronic diseases killing people today—diseases such as heart diseases, lung diseases, brain diseases, digestive diseases, cancers, infections, diabetes, high blood pressure, breast cancer, prostate cancer, liver diseases, gallbladder disease, and kidney disease.

In many cases, the research has shown that plant-powered eating produced results better than pills and without the side-effects. Many patients also were able to avoid pending surgery.

To some, Frances's story and these studies sound too fantastic to be true. I suggest putting it to the test. See if these results can be replicated in your own life, or in the life of someone you care about. Then you would be able to answer this question for yourself: Can high-octane fuel consistently predict better health?

Although not always as dramatic as Frances's story, the answer for most willing to take the challenge is a resounding "yes."

SPREADING THE LIFESAVING MESSAGE

After seeing Frances's near-miraculous results and those of the other patients, Dr. Diehl founded the Lifestyle Medicine Institute and created the Coronary Health Improvement Project (CHIP). CHIP was built on the same principles as those of the Pritikin Longevity Center. Its aim was to make these lifesaving interventions available to communities across North America and the world through the leadership and participation of passionate volunteers. CHIP went on to help approximately 100,000 people experience the major health benefits of lifestyle medicine.[66]

In the early 2000s, when I was a pastor in British Columbia, I was inspired by the success stories that came out of the CHIP programs organized by Dr. Sid Kettner in Creston, British Columbia. Dr. Kettner partnered with Dr. Diehl to impact hundreds of people in eastern British Columbia. They saved lives and reduced suffering through the 16 evening programs highlighting the lifesaving benefits of lifestyle medicine.

My teams of volunteers wanted to make the same impact on our communities in Mission and Maple Ridge, near Vancouver. We had a vision of helping people gain back control of their health.

We became convinced that the CHIP program aligned well with the healing power of lifestyle medicine. I called Betty Steinke, an experienced OR nurse, who had organized many CHIP programs in nearby Langley, a suburb of Vancouver. While assisting surgeons in procedures like inserting stents, Betty saw the results of the Standard American Diet (SAD) firsthand—yellowish fatty deposits, known as cholesterol, clogging the blood vessels, which lead to heart disease.

Many times, Betty saw the surgeon's tweezers pulling out the strings of this fatty substance from an artery. It was the devastating effect of clogged arteries that brought most patients into the operating room. Betty longed to have been able to talk to the sedated patient on the operating table: "If only I could have talked to you a year ago, I might have been able to help you avoid this operation by giving you more choices. Then maybe you wouldn't have to be lying here today trying to save your life."

Betty became determined to give people a better, less intrusive alternative. With her mentorship and the leadership of dedicated church volunteers led by Dr. Hilda Rainda, our Mission team set out to make a difference in the city of Mission, and later our Maple Ridge team did the same in Maple Ridge.

HOW A LIFESTYLE-INTERVENTION PROGRAM WORKS

For each CHIP program, we organized two blood-draw clinics—one before and one after the four-week CHIP program.

We took 10 measurements:

1. total cholesterol - type of lipid (fat) in the blood and a marker of cardiovascular health
2. high-density lipoprotein (HDL) cholesterol - "good" cholesterol
3. low-density lipoprotein (LDL) cholesterol - "bad" cholesterol
4. total LDL to HDL ratio - one marker of heart disease risk
5. triglycerides - fat in the blood, indicator of cardiovascular disease
6. fasting plasma glucose (blood sugar) - risk factor for diabetes
7. blood pressure - indicator of cardiovascular health
8. resting heart rate – indicator of heart health
9. weight – indicator of general health
10. body mass index (BMI) – body-fat composition for non-athlete adults

Measuring the change in these biometric risk factors over a 30-day period allowed us to evaluate the effects of the program. The blood work also made the results submissible for scientific study. It's important to note that focusing on any one of these biomarkers may, in some cases, be misleading. It's only when they are taken together that they provide a useful assessment of health.

Other biomarkers that could prove helpful in evaluating overall health:

1. Hemoglobin – a protein that transports oxygen in blood
2. C-Reactive protein – a marker for inflammation
3. Cortisol – a hormone marker for stress that correlates to many diseases
4. A1C – a measure of average blood-glucose levels over a two- to three-month period, commonly used to diagnose and monitor diabetes

For four evenings a week for four weeks, in a hospital lecture room or community hall, we invited the participants to watch Dr. Diehl's health presentations on video. We interspersed the videos with live discussions on nutrition and lifestyle, vegetarian cooking demonstrations, and tasty taste tests.

We encouraged our participants to eat two or three meals daily of a large variety of fresh fruit, vegetables, whole grains, seeds, and nuts, and drink only water between meals. This way they could eat as much as they wanted even though they would be consuming fewer calories. We also encouraged them to walk every day and recorded their mileage on a chart. We even hosted friendly competitions between groups to see which group walked the farthest. It was a fun and charged social atmosphere.

The improvements were spectacular.

After the four weeks, the average weight loss for our class of 25 participants was seven pounds. One male participant lost 15 pounds in the month.

There were marked decreases in blood sugar, cholesterol levels, triglycerides, blood pressures, and resting heart rates.

At the end of each of our programs we held a graduation celebration. In the ceremony, we handed out prizes and lab results. People cried with tears of happiness realizing, for the first time, there was hope they could be healthy and strong without pills or procedures. They loved their newfound energy and were revived with a new sense of control over their future. Some even felt they had new identities.

Our results were similar to those later reported in many scientific peer-reviewed journals. For example, the American Journal of Lifestyle Medicine reported:

> On average, males with the highest levels of total cholesterol at program entry (i.e., 240-279 mg/dL) experienced a 22% reduction in 30 days. Comparatively, females with the highest levels of total cholesterol experienced a mean decrease of 11%. Noteworthy, in the same year that these data were published, a systematic review of the effectiveness of dietary interventions for lowering total cholesterol in free-living subjects, published in the *British Medical Journal*, concluded that improvements of only 3% to 6% could be expected.[67]

The CHIP program worked. Since improvements in the biometric risk factors correlate with a decreased risk of heart disease, many kinds of cancer, diabetes, lung disease, depression, and more, we knew we were making a positive difference.

We found that the degree to which health programs aligned with the principles of FULL POWER was the degree to which that program was successful.

HEALTH CHAMPIONS

One man in his 60s came up to me after doing the program and said, "I feel shiny and new!"

His wife said with tears in her eyes, "Thank you for giving me my husband back."

Words like those stay with you a long time.

The most dramatic story starred a man in his early 60s who took our Maple Ridge CHIP program. Fred was a mean, disruptive, arrogant, angry grump. In our first session, he angrily reported he couldn't walk across the kitchen without wheezing. The doctors, after doing all they could, including three heart bypass surgeries, gave him one year to live. He was on 23 pills a day. We were his last chance—although you wouldn't know it by how many times he interrupted our presentations with accusatory questions.

Despite his belligerence, the team treated him with compassion. We knew that poor health conditions often put sufferers on edge.

After the first week on a plant-based diet, Fred noticed it was easier to walk across the kitchen. After two weeks, he rode his bike around the neighborhood. By the end of the four weeks, he was riding his bike from Maple Ridge to Mission and back—30 miles (48 kms)! He proudly announced to the group at graduation that he was off most of his pills.

But what we noticed most was that his personality changed. He became happy, respectful, and kind. He had strength in his body, a new purpose, and he started making plans for the future. His personality had changed so much that his family and friends wondered what magic was happening at our health program. When we conducted the program a year later, four of them attended.

Dr. Larry Shipowick found similar results. He has organized lifestyle health programs, including CHIP, in Kelowna, British Columbia, for over 20 years. When he was a young dentist, Dr. Shipowick had severe allergies. He said, "I was coughing and hacking so much I needed medications to be able to work and go to sleep." Upon the advice of a doctor in Seattle he switched to a plant-based diet, "and within two weeks," he said, "the coughing and hacking were gone."

He was so inspired by what a plant-based diet did for him, he had to help others.

After measuring for the medical markers outlined above, Dr. Shipowick said in a phone interview, "the average drop in cholesterol for participants in his programs was 20 points – milligrams per deciliter (mg/dL)." He added: "We have had cholesterol decreases of over 40% in one month." In many cases, these participants, under their doctor's care, could eliminate the need for cholesterol medication, such as statins.

One of his participants "lost 17 pounds in the first month and continued to lose 40 pounds within the year." The biggest change he made was to eat plant-based whole foods. Another man in the program lost 100 pounds in a year.

One of Dr. Shipowick's participants, a lady in her 50s, had been told by a medical doctor that her failing eyesight couldn't be fixed and, in fact, in the next few months she would go blind. Also, she could barely walk. She hobbled into the Kelowna Lifestyle Centre with a walker. Within 30 days, she was walking 2 kms a day with no walker with her eyesight restored.

Restored eyesight is an unusual response to switching to a plant-based diet. Dr. Shipowick theorized that fat particles plugged up the small arterioles (tiny arteries) at the back of her eyes. When she ate plant-based, she eliminated those fat particles. With her health restored, she and her husband bought a motor home and toured the country, fulfilling a lost dream.

CHIP AND FULL POWER

Unfortunately, CHIP[68] no longer exists as a public service program. However, the health principles upon which it was based are encapsulated in the FULL POWER Plan. While FULL POWER places more emphasis on the psychological and emotional contributors of vitality, both programs are based on lifestyle medicine and include "before and after" assessments to measure their impact on health.

DID IT STICK?

The big question comes: Did the participants of the CHIP program return to their high-calorie diet? Dr. Greger's analysis of aggregated research of various CHIP programs found that participants continued to consume 400 fewer calories a day 18 months after the program.

Dr. Greger suggested that the CHIP program's success could be attributed, in part, to the participants' freedom in determining their own food intake—no requirements to count calories or carbs—making the program more sustainable than other weight-loss programs. Participants reported that the social support and outdoor exercise were also contributing factors.

DOCUMENTARIES ADVOCATING A PLANT-BASED EATING PATTERN

Documentaries have a way of stimulating us to reevaluate our viewpoints by providing insights into unfamiliar realms and challenging our preconceptions. At the same time, many of them seem to have their biases, and often ignore confounding variables when advocating for their causes or conclusions. The same holds true of documentaries recommending food choices. This is why the FULL POWER Plan advocates a whole "formula" over a "silver bullet" approach to achieving bodymind vitality. For example, it's important to get our Vitamin C. But Vitamin C is not a "silver bullet" for health. There are many contributing factors, and we don't want to miss out on any of them.

With this in mind, here are some documentaries that advocate a plant-based eating pattern. Each has their own, and sometimes controversial, perspective. But each gives "food for thought" regarding lifestyle change:

1. *Fat, Sick, and Nearly Dead*, 1 and 2[69]
2. *Hungry for Change: Your Health Is in Your Hands*[70]
3. *FOOD, Inc.*[71]
4. *Forks Over Knives*[72]
5. *Meat Me Halfway*[73]
6. *PlantPure Nation*[74]
7. *The Game Changers*[75]
8. *Vegucated*[76]
9. *What the Health*[77]
10. *You Are What You Eat: A Twin Experiment*[78]

BEYOND THE PHYSICAL

No matter what program you use, the benefits of filling up with high-octane fuel extend beyond the physical. Lorrie Erho, a personal growth coach in the Vancouver area, organized a whole-food plant-based (WFPB) health program, complete with food demonstrations. Dean, a mechanic from Vancouver, showed up at one of her programs. He was 30 pounds overweight and had so much pain in his knees and feet he contemplated giving up his job. But what worried him most was having to live with "brain fog."

After eating a high-octane fuel diet consistently for three months, the pain in his knees and feet disappeared. His brain fog lifted, and within six months, he lost the 30 pounds. It wasn't just the physical benefits he enjoyed. It was the mental as well. In an interview he exclaimed that he would never go back to his old life and suggested there would be fewer hospitals if more people went on a plant-based diet.

Of course, there are always individual differences. What works for most people may not work for others. When it comes to addressing health challenges, contributions from the environment, stress, various health conditions, and genes come into play. But no matter the accommodation we need to make, we give ourselves the best chance when we eat unrefined high-octane fuel.

If healthy eating is new to you, the best thing may be to experiment based upon a knowledge of your personality. For example, if you know yourself to have an "all or nothing" kind of personality, you might do better to go all in.[79] Like Susan Peirce Thompson wrote in her book, Bright Line Eating, "Be prepared to change your life, not just your body size. Anything short of total change is a waste of time.[80]

Still, if you tend to adapt slowly to new things, resources abound to try healthy eating slowly, including free trials for plant-based meals delivered directly to you.

EXAMPLES OF HOW TO FUEL UP WITH HIGH-OCTANE FUEL

For some, it might be best to make one food change at a time to make sure that they don't have an allergic reaction to an ingredient. After you have found what foods work for you, eat a large variety from the incomplete "Examples of High-Octane Fuel" below. There are hundreds of ways to plan it out.

One way is to center your breakfast around these four high-octane foods:

1. fruits
2. whole grains
3. nuts
4. seeds

If you are in a hurry and want all four in one quick meal, try a banana hotdog, which I created to save time as I rushed to the office each morning. It couldn't be any simpler: Spread Nut & Seed Butter (in British Columbia, we get it from Costco) on multigrain bread (Silver Hills Bread is the best), then wrap it around a banana like a hotdog and eat it with one hand.

Center your dinner around:

1. vegetables
2. grains
3. legumes

A fast way to remember it is to say "beans, greens, and grains." But keep in mind that we need more vegetables than just greens. Otherwise, there are no rules. Personal preference and culture may come into play. Just focus on eating a large variety.

Two meals per day may work best, especially for sedentary workers. If you need a third meal, again choose a small amount from the lists below:

EXAMPLES OF HIGH-OCTANE FUEL

Fruits:

Apples, apricots, avocados, bananas, blackberries, blueberries, cranberries, cherries, coconuts, dates, durian, figs, grapes, guava, jackfruit, kiwi, kumquat, lemons, limes, pears, mangos, oranges, papaya, prunes, plums, pomegranates, peaches, pears, persimmons, pineapple, raspberries, strawberries, watermelon

Vegetables:

Artichokes, arugula, asparagus, beets, broccoli, brussels sprouts, cabbage, calabash, carrots, cauliflower, celery, chayote, chili peppers, corn, cucumber, edamame, eggplants, fennel, garlic, ginger, jicama, kale, leeks, lettuce, mushrooms, okra, onion, peas, potatoes, pumpkin, radish, squash, rutabaga, sweet potatoes, parsnip, shallots, spinach, tomatoes, turnip, watercress, yams, zucchini

Whole Grains:

Amaranth, barley, black rice, brown rice, buckwheat, bulgur, chia seeds, farro, flaxseed, freekeh, hemp seeds, kamut, kaniwa, millet, oatmeal, popcorn, pumpkin seeds, quinoa, Red River cereal, rye, sesame seeds, sorghum, spelt, sunflower seeds, teff, triticale, wild rice, whole rice, whole wheat

Nuts:

Almonds, Brazil nuts, cashews, chestnuts, hazelnuts, macadamias, peanuts, pecans, pistachio, walnuts

Legumes (Beans):

Adzuki beans, big broad beans, black beans, black-eyed peas, chili beans, chickpeas (garbanzo), green beans, green split peas, kidney beans, lentils, lima beans, mung dal, pinto beans, red calypso beans, Romano beans, scarlet runner beans, soy beans

THE IRON-MAN WALK

My wife and I attended a lifestyle-change center that served a plant-powered diet and ate solely from the list above. It is called Silver Hills Guest House, an hour east of Vernon, British Columbia.

When we arrived, we were exhausted and depleted from stress and 80-hour workweeks. In his health presentation on the first day, director Phil Brewer had the audacity to announce that after 21 days on a plant-powered diet, we would be able to complete the Iron-Man walk, an 18-mile hike (29 kilometers) through the mountains.

June and I didn't believe him. But in 21 days, after eating a balance of complex carbohydrates, plant-based proteins, and healthy fats, we proudly crossed the finish line with the other participants. Along with the daily walks in the fresh mountain air, it was the gourmet high-octane fuel that powered us for the full 18 miles. We, as non-athletes, had never accomplished anything close to this feat before.

GOURMET HIGH-OCTANE FUEL

In those 21 days we fueled up on the most delicious gourmet meals imaginable. We ate fruit cobblers, granola, crepes, coconut millet, muesli, multigrain bread with raspberry jam, rice pudding, banana muffins, oat cakes, Italian bread sticks, salads with healthy dressings, walnut rice burgers, baked squash, veggie chili, super soups (minestrone, black bean, corn chowder, cream of asparagus, etc.), sauces, spreads, cooked greens with delicious toppings, zucchini casserole, flavored rice and beans, pear cream, cashew cheese, jack cheese, and healthy desserts galore like apple strudel, mango pudding, banana cream pie, carob delights, tofu cheesecake, to name a few. You can get many of these recipes from their cookbook, Silver Hills Spa Cuisine by Cecile Gordon and Eileen Brewer, on Amazon.

When we returned home, our friends said they could hardly recognize us because we looked so young and energetic. We glowed with health.

This was our version of the Frances Greger story.

"WHERE DO YOU GET YOUR PROTEIN FROM?"

When faced with the evidence of the benefits of a plant-powered diet, people ask, "Where do you get your protein from? Don't you need protein from meat to build muscle?" This question has long been settled by science. Observations from the animal kingdom can teach us much.

Ask the great apes where they get their protein from. Ask the African elephant, the strongest animal on land, where he gets his strength. Ask the galloping stallion or the charging buffalo. Their energy and strength come from plants.

It is no different with human beings. We get our best protein from plants. When we eat animals, we get our protein secondhand. Not only are plants the best source of protein, they also have the added benefit of providing complex carbohydrates and fiber. Meat is deficient in these necessary nutrients.

HIGH-OCTANE FUEL CHAMPIONED BY PERFORMERS

One of the greatest tennis champions of all time, Serena Williams, filled up on plant-powered fuel to conquer her opponents. Kendrick Ferris, record-breaking Olympic weightlifter, fueled his muscles with plant protein to beat out the Olympic competition. Tom Brady, an NFL superstar into his 40s, credits his predominantly plant-based diet for his record-breaking performances on the field year after year.

These, and many other athletes, have found that plant-fueled muscles gave them more endurance, resilience, and stronger bodies, plus faster recovery time after a hard workout than when they ate meat.

It works for entertainers too. Multi-genre singer/songwriter, pianist, composer, and actress, Gina Williams, told me in an interview, "I was impressed to give up meat and, as far as I was concerned, 'all things tasty.' I fought against the idea and finally gave it a shot. Here we are years later, and I have more energy than I ever had. Embracing a plant-based diet and eliminating processed sugar, especially during concert week, is a large contributor to the longevity of my career. In the business of entertainment, it's important to have the mental clarity that this job demands almost 24/7." I meet Ms. Williams from time to time at various events in Vancouver. I can testify, she is always energetic.

BEING HEALTHY, NOT NORMAL

The problem with starting a plant-powered eating pattern after a constant diet of refined food is the taste. Veggies don't taste like french fries and a lot of us don't like vegetables. One strategy some athletes and others use to overcome the distaste for vegetables is to drink them. Here's what I do. Once or twice a week, I put handfuls of spinach or kale in a high-powered blender such as a Vitamix with frozen banana chunks and diced pineapples, water, and sometimes flaxseed. You can throw in other vegetables, too. The sweetness of the banana and pineapple make eating the vegetables much more palatable. In our house, we call it a "greens drink." A lady at one of our seminars said, "This is the best trick I use to get my husband to 'eat' his vegetables."

If you want more motivation, read or listen to Dr. T. Colin Campbell. He is renowned for his ground-breaking book, The China Study. It reveals one of the most comprehensive and well-researched studies on nutrition and health ever conducted in the world. Dr. Campbell dedicated over 60 years to researching the diet-disease link, notably cancer. His cutting-edge book, Whole: Rethinking the Science of Nutrition, is also a must-read for everyone who wants to know the science behind the best way to eat. [81]

Dr. Campbell, in a TEDx talk at Cornell University, made a profound statement: "Nutrition, when done right, can create more health than all the pills and procedures combined."[82]

Dr. Campbell's nutrition advice makes sense. But doing nutrition "right" was a big challenge for me. I had to reprogram myself on how to eat high-octane fuel. I learned to replace the sugary breakfast cereals with fruits, grains, and nuts. I learned to put rice milk in mashed potatoes or pour cooked lentils on a baked potato instead of sour cream. I learned to spread avocado or "better butter" (recipe follows in the box below) on Silver Hills multigrain bread.[83] I learned to eat vegetable and zucchini stew, and to eat beans, nuts, and grains to replace my steak.

Fruits and nuts we can eat raw. Many vegetables, grains, and legumes need to be cooked to maximize nutrient absorption. Not all vegetables are alike, though. So, include raw vegetables in your daily menus.

Some of your friends or relatives might say, "I like to eat real meals" or "You are missing out on a juicy steak, cheeseburger, or a soft drink." Or they might turn up their nose and say that vegetarian food tastes strange or has no taste.

The truth is eating healthy is different than the norm. But the norm is not designed for optimal health. Following the norm, in many ways, is toxic. The only way to rise above the toxic norm is to be different. Be willing to do what the majority are not doing.

RECIPES

Tastes in food and cultures are so varied, so I will refrain from listing the top 10 natural cooking cookbooks. Instead, use the health principles in these chapters as a guideline in your online or bookstore searches for healthy recipes. See the "Menu for Life" in the appendix for general guidelines.

When searching online, don't limit your searches to "plant-based," "vegetarian," or "vegan" food recipes. Include searches for recipes using these words: unprocessed, unrefined, natural, whole food, simple, WFPB, natural lifestyle.

In our household, we have been helped by recipes from:

1. T. Colin Campbell and his team in the *China Study* and *Forks Over Knives* material.
2. Michael Greger in the *How Not to Die* cookbook.
3. Material from Caldwell and Rip Esselstyn.
4. www.Straightupfood.com, which follows the John McDougall program and gives gluten-free recipes with no added sugar, salt, or oil.
5. 21daykickstart.com, which is from the Physicians Committee for Responsible Medicine (PCRM) headed by Neil Barnard for those who want a structured program to go vegan.

For most of us, it is within our power to make ourselves significantly stronger and healthier by fueling up on high-octane fuel. Assess your effectiveness in achieving this goal by completing the checklist below.

However, some of the biggest challenges—and rewards—come from what we don't eat. Turn to the next chapter to understand what's behind the struggle to omit the tasty toxins we know are killing us.

Recipe: Better Butter

1 tbsp Agar-Agar gelatin

¼ cup cold water

1 cup boiling water

¼ cup cashews

1 cup cooked cornmeal (1/4 cup cornmeal to 1 cup water)

1 tsp salt

2 tsp lemon juice or to taste

In blender soak Agar-Agar gelatin in cold water for a few minutes. Pour boiling water over gelatin and whisk (slowly at first as tends to splash due to heat) to dissolve. Add and blend cashews until very smooth. Add remaining ingredients and blend thoroughly until smooth as cream. Cool and refrigerate.

CHECKLIST FOR

"PRIORITIZE HIGH-OCTANE FUEL"

	To what degree am I prioritizing high-octane fuel? On a scale of 0-10, answer these questions, based on the last seven days. The cumulative sum of all nine end-of-chapter checklists will result in a total out of 100.	
1	I followed an eating plan consisting entirely of whole-food plant-based (WFPB) options.	
2	I ate four or five fruits, including berries every day (unless I was fasting).	
3	I ate four or five vegetables, including cruciferous vegetables and greens every day (unless I was fasting).	
4	I ate a few nuts, including almonds every day (unless I was fasting).	
5	I ate a few seeds every day - like pumpkin seeds, sunflower seeds, flaxseeds (unless I was fasting).	
6	I ate whole grains every day (unless I was fasting).	
7	I ate legumes every day (unless I was fasting). (For those with sensitive stomachs just starting on a whole-food plant-based eating plan, even one bean counts.)	
8	I had between one and four bowel movements each day.	
9	I ate two or three meals daily.	
10	I ate nothing between meals.	
	Total out 100	
	Divide by 10 for average out of 10	

CHAPTER 7

OMIT WHAT IS HARMFUL—PART 1:

THE SITUATION

I'm getting tired of intelligent choices. I want french fries!
June Brake

One evening my friend, Evert, and I were relaxing at his kitchen table after playing guitar together. He took a drag from his cigarette, glanced at it, then he looked at me, and said, "I've never loved or hated something so much in my life as this cigarette."

He loved smoking, but he hated that it was killing him.

Inside many of us rages a similar battle. We are stuck in a dilemma that makes us choose between short-term pleasure and long-term health, between what we want now and what we want most.[84]

This dilemma is especially true for tasty, processed food.

When it comes to the harmful effects of certain foods, a few people are fortunate. All they need is the knowledge about its effects, and they give it up right away, no problem. But for many, it's not so easy. To give up something that brings so much pleasure is almost impossible. This chapter is for that second group. It includes me.

As hard as I tried, I found that what I wanted to eat (fresh fruit, vegetables, legumes, nuts, and whole grains), I didn't eat—at least not consistently. And what I wish I didn't eat (potato chips, french fries, pizza, ice cream, chocolate bars, white bread, rich desserts, and many other processed foods), I ate with pleasure. I would have had no problem cutting down on potato chips if they tasted like Brussels sprouts. And I would jump on the "Eat your vegetables" bandwagon if vegetables tasted like chocolate.

But for many of us, food doesn't work that way. In my teens, using only taste as a guideline, I enjoyed unhealthy high-fat foods with no apparent side effects…emphasis on "apparent." Who doesn't love a burger, fries, a coke, and a soft ice cream cone? I am pretty sure my friends and I single-handedly saved the fast-food industry from bankruptcy. (You're welcome, McDonalds!)

But I was like the poor fish that saw the worm and not the hook. As I grew older, I paid for every tasty morsel by packing on the pounds, losing my physique as well as my energy and clarity of mind. This worried me—when I thought about it.

Evert and I are not alone. Some studies show two-thirds of the population fight this battle every day to a greater or lesser degree.[85] Most of us long to be fit, healthy, self-disciplined, confident, happy, and successful human beings. In other words, we want a life of optimal vitality. But temptation can overpower us like a great adversary, whether through tasty toxins (my demons) or cigarettes (Evert's demons).

It turns out, omitting what is harmful is just fine…until you're hungry.

It's one thing to satisfy that hunger with a cheeseburger and a soft drink every now and then. But it's quite another when we desire something so much, we continually eat it even though we know it hurts us.

That's when a healthy hunger becomes an unhealthy craving.

A daily habit of eating highly refined food initiates and fosters diseases in our bodies that are very costly—costly not only to our well-being, but to our bank accounts. First, we drain our bank accounts to hand over our money to the junk-food industry. Then, after we get sick from years of processed food, we drain our bank accounts to give our money to the pharmaceutical industry to treat our suffering from the effects of the food. The pharmaceutical industry must be very appreciative of the junk-food industry. Big Pharma makes big profits from our pain.

I'm glad pharmaceuticals are there when we need them. But what if we didn't always need them? What if we could prevent some of the illnesses that cause the pain in the first place?

It's not the responsibility of the junk-food giants to curb our cravings. That's on us. But there's a problem. And it's bigger than we thought.

The surprising revelation is this: Continuous self-sabotaging behavior may be part of, or a precursor to, addiction. To illustrate what I mean, let me share a very personal story.

One social Saturday night when I was in my 40s, I was indulging in potato chips, ice cream, and sugary snacks. Even though I knew it wasn't good for me, I kept on eating.

The next morning, I was ripped awake with fierce pain in my stomach. Last night's food didn't digest well throughout the night. On top of that, I had gained four pounds in 24 hours, most likely from salt and water retention. As I writhed in pain, disgusted with myself, I vowed, "Never again. Never again."

Those words. There was something about those words "never again" that triggered a childhood memory—one that gave me an insight into what I feared might be my true condition.

When I was 10 years old, my parents took my three siblings and me on our annual summer vacation to visit my two sets of grandparents in Halifax, Nova Scotia. Our grandparents lived only three miles apart. It was like visiting Magical Kingdom, with two sweet grandmothers who gave us lots of hugs and food. We played games on the big double-seat lawn swing and turned the wooden boat into a little swimming pool. These happy times formed in my young mind an association of food with happiness, fun, comfort, and connectedness.

One night, I was fast asleep in Grandma's guest bedroom on the main level. I was abruptly awakened by my granddad hollering obscenities from the living room. He was yelling at my dear grandmother. As I shook in fear, with blankets pulled up to my wide-open eyes, I listened in the darkness, stunned that my gentle granddad was so verbally violent.

The next morning, my parents rushed the four of us children to the basement suite for our breakfast. It felt strange and disorienting to be eating down in the basement. After I gulped down my breakfast, I asked to go back upstairs.

My parents sternly told me, "No."

They were hiding something.

"But I want to see Grandma."

They kept dismissing me.

Suddenly, two of my younger siblings became fussy, calling for my parents' attention. I snatched the opportunity to sneak upstairs.

The main floor was eerily silent and dark. Passing through the kitchen, I slowly tiptoed toward the living room. But I stopped frozen at the entrance and gasped in horror. Before my eyes, my grandfather, like a dead body, was sprawled out on the floor on his back, bare belly bloated. His head awkwardly crooked up against the couch, mouth gaped open, drool and vomit stained his chin, neck, and shirt. In his hand, limp at his side, was an empty rum bottle.

The shock of seeing my dear grandfather taken down and stripped of his dignity by the power of alcohol has never left me.

Two days later, cleaned up, he sat in his La-Z-Boy chair with a large smile for his grandchildren. We talked with him for a while before he stopped us and said in a firm, determined voice, "I'll never drink again. Never again. Never again."

A month later, my mother told me he was drunk again.

Over and over, the pattern repeated until he eventually died from alcoholism. My grandfather was one of the approximately 280 million people worldwide who suffer from alcohol-use disorders, and became one of almost three million who died that year from addiction to alcohol.[86]

Years later, the day after my junk-food binge, I made the same promise, full of fierce determination: "Never again. Never again."

And just like my granddad, a month later I binged again. As he succumbed to the call of the bottle, I gave into the taste of processed food. Over and over again. Though we suffered from different habits, they led us down a similar path to self-destruction.

It seemed to be more than taste, though, that caused my granddad and me to make a habit out of destructive pleasures. Why did we repeatedly indulge them knowing full well of their long-term damage, especially when we swore "never again?"

AM I AN ADDICT?

Did an addictive personality run in my genes? My anatomy and physiology professor, Dr. Cyril Dean, contradicted that notion. He used to say, "Genes load the gun; lifestyle pulls the trigger." Many scientific studies have since borne that out. We may be predisposed by genes, but we are not predestined.

Despite that fact, I wondered whether processed food was a "substance" I "used"—like the alcoholic used alcohol, or the smoker used nicotine, or the cocaine addict used cocaine. While the substance was different, there were behavior patterns that, at least to some degree, are similar. For many, the habit of enjoying and welcoming harmful substances into our bodies has become commonplace. It seems quite normal. But is the "normal" life really an "addicted" life? Or maybe "addiction" was too strong a word for it. I had to know.

Interestingly, Dr. Gabor Maté expressed a similar concern in his book, The Myth of Normal: "Much of what passes for normal in our society is neither healthy nor normal."[87] If so, it's not the culture I needed to go to for answers. "Our culture's skewed idea of normality is the biggest single impediment to fostering a healthy world."[88] I didn't want to be normal. I wanted to be healthy.

My guiding question was, how can we be released from the destructive power of our cravings?

The answer began with understanding the nature of addiction and what kinds of things are addictive.

I needed a definition of addiction, though, before I could go on. So, I turned to the Diagnostic and Statistical Manual of Mental Disorders – 5 (DSM-5), published in 2013. It's one of the most authoritative resources for mental health clinicians. Its term for addiction is "substance use disorder."

The DSM-5 describes the "essential feature of a substance use disorder" as "a cluster of cognitive, behavioral, and physiological symptoms indicating that the individual continues using the substance despite significant substance-related problems."[89]

The definition focuses on behaviors we continue despite the problems the substance causes in our life. To one degree or another, that fit Evert, my grandfather, and me.

The DSM-5 goes on to describe the types of behaviors I would have to exhibit for me to be diagnosed as an addict. That diagnosis would be "based on a pathological [harmful] pattern of behaviors related to use of the substance."

These four major "groupings" of addictive behaviors further divide into 11 criteria or symptoms. Here is a partial sampling:

1. **Lack of self-control** – symptoms such as unsuccessful efforts to cut down or stop using, sometimes due to uncontrollable cravings.
2. **Social problems** – symptoms such as neglecting major[90] role obligations or relationships at work, school, or home.
3. **Risky use** – symptoms such as using the substance despite the problems it causes.
4. **Physical dependence** – symptoms such as tolerance and withdrawal. Tolerance is needing more of the substance to achieve the desired effect or a "markedly reduced effect when the usual dose is consumed." Withdrawal is signaled by a psychological and/or physiological discomfort when the reward is not reached.[91]

Checking myself against these criteria, I lacked self-control and I practiced a "risky use" of food. But, as far as I knew, I did not have the "social problems" or "physical dependence." So, I self-classified my issue as a problem, not a disorder or an addiction. Glad I checked.

It further alleviated my concern to read in the DSM-5 that addictions occur on a scale from mild to severe, based on the number of symptoms. Remember, there are 11 possible symptoms spread throughout the four groupings of behaviors.

"As a general estimate of severity, a mild substance use disorder is suggested by the presence of two to three symptoms [out of the 11], moderate by four to five symptoms, and severe by six or more symptoms."

Since I only had two of the symptoms, I was "mild."

But if I was being honest with myself, this rating wasn't comforting. My personal guidelines for food choices—mainly, a craving for unhealthy fats, sugars, and processed food—were still enough to threaten my health.

For clarity, I checked the DSM-5 to see if food was on the list of addictions. In the section on Substance-Related and Addictive Disorders,[92] nine classes of drugs to which someone may have a "substance-related disorder" (such as alcohol, caffeine, cannabis, hallucinogens, inhalants, opioids, sedatives, stimulants like cocaine, and tobacco) are listed. But food as a category was not on the list.

The DSM-5 did, however, list a 10th category. They called it "Other (Unknown)." Perhaps they were leaving room for peer-reviewed evidence to sufficiently accumulate before claiming certain foods could be addictive. Maybe food addiction doesn't fit their description of a substance-related or a substance use disorder. The DSM-5 was clearly talking about the continued use of drugs, not food, being the cause of the "substance-related problems."

But what about food? Was there something else in the DSM-5 that addressed eating?

Yes. There is another section in the DSM-5 entitled "Feeding and Eating Disorders." It provides diagnostic criteria for such disorders as "pica, rumination disorder, avoidant/restrictive food intake disorder, anorexia nervosa, bulimia nervosa, and binge-eating disorder."[93]

It compared the symptoms of those with "eating-related disorders" to the symptoms of those with "substance use disorders." In other words, it compared my symptoms to my grandfather's symptoms. The two groups do have overlapping symptoms, such as "craving and patterns of compulsive use" and may even "reflect the involvement of the same neural systems." But what was not fully understood was how both common and unique factors of each disorder developed.[94]

In other words, according to the DSM-5, I and the millions like me are not food addicts. That's because addictions are associated with drugs, not food, even though both produce the same neural pattern in the brain. Furthermore, there was not enough research connecting eating-related disorders to addiction for the DSM-5 to be conclusive.

But I wanted more understanding. To further clarify whether food addiction is a "thing," I went beyond the DSM-5 and checked online with the "12 Steps" people—those associated with Alcoholics Anonymous—to see if there was such a group as Food Addictions Anonymous. Sure enough, there is.

Here is what they said:

People who are addicted to food:

1. have an obsession - constantly thinking about what, when, and how they eat.
2. chronically overeat at mealtimes by a large margin.
3. try to control eating and can't.
4. fall into a pattern of binging and purging.

5. use unhealthy practices to lose weight such as laxatives and vomiting.
6. associate eating with other pleasurable activities such as watching TV.
7. eat when they are bored or feeling bad.
8. eat when they are full.
9. hide their eating much like alcoholics or drug addicts do.
10. associate food with either reward or punishment.[95]

First, according to Food Addictions Anonymous, food addiction is real. Second, many of us may have some but not all these symptoms.

Since the DSM-5 was published, other scientists have weighed in with research of their own. And their insights are invaluable. Dr. Anna Lembke, for example, warns that people may still be vulnerable to "compulsive over-consumption, even when not meeting clinical criteria for addiction."[96]

A leader in food-addiction research is Dr. Susan Peirce Thompson. She taught a college class on the psychology of eating and body image before launching the Bright Line Eating (for weight loss) movement. Peirce Thompson, a neuroscientist and weight-loss expert, diverges slightly from the DSM-5.

She wrote: "Science had finally proven what anyone who has ever been in a 12-Step program for food already knows: Food addiction is real. As real as cocaine addiction. As real as heroin addiction. There is no physiological difference."[97]

No physiological difference? That was a shocker.

AN ADDICTION STRONGER THAN COCAINE

Peirce Thompson referenced a 2007 research study[98] that compared cocaine-addicted rats' preference for sugar over cocaine. Yes, you read that right. The rats wanted sugar more than cocaine. Scary. Especially since I love chocolate bars and sugary desserts.

Peirce Thompson points out that generally every addictive substance had to be extracted from its natural environment and concentrated into a powder, whether it's heroin, cocaine, or sugar. Ever noticed how many people are addicted to broccoli? Or have you ever found a Spinach Eaters Anonymous group? Me neither. Turns out, you can't get hooked on sugar when you eat it in its natural setting—like in a fruit, vegetable, legume, whole grain, or nut.

Dr. Gabor Maté shares a similar concern over sugar. He is one of the world's top addictions experts, has worked with drug addicts on Vancouver's downtown east side, and has written weighty top-selling books on addictions and the mind-body connection.

He wrote: "Junk foods and sugar are also chemically addictive because of their effect on the brain's intrinsic 'narcotics,' the endorphins. Sugar, for example, provides a quick fix of endorphins and also temporarily raises levels of the mood chemical serotonin."[99]

Hmmm…I imagined that if sugar were personified as a character in a movie, he would be the villain. He'd greet us with a sweet smile, hook us with deliciously deceptive food, and watch us slowly kill ourselves.

Sugar is not the only culprit, however.

THE FAT EFFECT ON THE BRAIN

Most of us know there is a difference between healthy fat and unhealthy fat. But let's be specific. Healthy fat is the fat naturally occurring in a whole food, like in a nut, seed, olive, or avocado. Unhealthy fat is extracted from its natural environment, whether animal or vegetable, and concentrated into oils and added to foods and cooking.

Dr. Michael Greger wrote in How Not to Diet, "Fat appears to have a similar effect on the brain as sugar. Feed people yogurt packed with butterfat, and within thirty minutes, they exhibit similar brain activity changes to those who had just drunk straight sugar water."[100]

Dr. Greger cited another study done on food addiction in 2018, five years after the DSM-5 was published. It involved over "100,000 women from the Harvard Nurses' Health Study." The study found, "greasy foods—hamburgers, french fries, and pizza—were the types of fare most linked to food addictions."[101]

Add white flour and lots of salt to the sugar and fat, and you have the four killer ingredients for a million deadly recipes—tasty but toxic. All these combos are harmful. Many are addictive. It is a cruel irony that the foods we love most are the foods that hurt us most.

BUT THERE IS HOPE

If you are struggling with unwanted cravings, understanding and addressing the underlying causes of addictive eating can clarify your path forward. Dr. Gabor Maté provides profound insights in this area.

His simple definition of addiction is "any repeated behavior, substance-related or not, in which a person feels compelled to persist, regardless of its negative impact on his life and the life of others."[102]

Maté's definition is broad enough to include refined food. But to be a food addict, we would have to:

1. eat harmful foods repeatedly, or
2. overeat food repeatedly, and
3. feel a compulsion to persist, knowing it will hurt us, and
4. feel a compulsion to persist, knowing it will hurt others

Food consumption may hurt us in two possible ways:

1. the eating of refined food, and
2. the overeating of any food, even healthy food

Overeating, though, is mostly associated with refined foods because of their addictive design. Addictive foods are designed by people—usually with a profit motive. Non-addictive foods are designed by nature. Nature's formula forms the solid foundation for the healthy "Whole Foods Plant-Based" (WFPB) movement that is gaining widespread popularity.

HOW TO TELL IF YOUR EATING HABITS ARE HURTING YOU

Here are eight general guidelines on how to tell if your eating habits are harmful:

1. Pain in the gastrointestinal tract or digestive organs may be a sign that you've put your body in danger due to eating. Try to discern the source of the hurt. Is it overeating processed or sweet foods? Eating too much? Etc. If you experience stomach pain when eating new, healthy foods such as vegetables and beans, it's advisable to introduce the foods slowly so the body can get used to them—even if it's one bean at a time.

2. Schedule a blood test, checking to see if the results are within healthy ranges for blood pressure, triglycerides, cholesterol, lipids, blood sugar, etc. In the U.S., especially, it's cheaper to get bloodwork done now than medical treatment for a disease later.

3. Schedule a yearly medical checkup. Don't ask the doctor, "Am I normal?" Ask, rather, "Am I healthy?"

4. Looking for something quick and easy? Try the pinch test. If you can pinch more than an inch of fat at your waist just above the hip, you have fat you don't need and are overworking your heart and other parts of your system to keep it alive. The local gym or a personal trainer will have a more detailed pinch test procedure.

5. Check your body mass index (BMI), which is our height to weight ratio. According to the National Institutes of Health, "The higher your BMI, the higher your risk for certain diseases such as heart disease, high blood pressure, type 2 diabetes, gallstones, breathing problems, and certain cancers."[103] Various online tests are available. With exceptions, a BMI of 18.5-24.9 is considered healthy. A BMI of 25 or over indicates overweight. A BMI of 30 and above indicates obesity.[104] BMI is not gender-specific, but its accuracy is limited to non-athletic adults because it will incorrectly assume that the extra muscle on a lean athlete is fat and render a false-high BMI score.

6. Measure your waist to determine health risks related to overweight and obesity. Health risk escalates with a waist size exceeding 35 inches for women or 40 inches for men. To obtain an accurate waist measurement, stand upright, positioning the measuring tape above the hipbones, and measure after exhaling.[105]

7. Look at your waist-to-hip ratio because not all excess weight carries the same health risk. For a more complete picture of your health risk, compare your waist measurement to your hip measurement. The waist-to-hip ratio provides a more useful assessment than BMI, weight, or waist measurement alone because excess fat around the waist indicates visceral fat in and around the internal organs, which is associated with a higher risk for heart disease, cancer, stroke, and Type 2 diabetes.[106]

The waist should be smaller than the hips. Compare the circumference around the smallest part of your waist to that of the largest part of your hips. The World Health Organization (WHO) defines abdominal obesity as a waist-to-hip ratio of 0.90 or more. For women, it's a ratio of 0.85 or more.

8. If we are eating mostly foods designed by manufacturers, we are hurting ourselves even if we don't feel it. Manufactured food doesn't fuel our body with the life-enhancing nutrients that plant-based whole food does.

"JUST THIS ONCE"

For Wendy, the first sign on her pathway to addictive eating was when she said to herself, "Just this once." Then there was another "just this once." The next time, she said, "I know I shouldn't but…" Then she said, "This is good. I deserve this." Then, "This is good. I want more of this." Then, "I need this." Then, she just stopped talking to herself altogether and let her tastebuds enjoy the party. And the next party, and the next party, and on and on.

Little exceptions became a lifestyle.

Each time Wendy gave into her craving it became harder for her to resist the next time. This low impulse control – or weak self-regulation – is part of the addiction process as explained by DSM-5 and Food Addictions Anonymous earlier in this chapter.

These compulsions are rooted in the circuits of our brain from childhood and are "triggered whenever [we are] stressed, fatigued, unhappy, or bored."[107] When we are stressed, the rational part of our brain—the "impulse controller"—is weakened. When that happens, we lose the power to "regulate" ourselves. And it shows up as less self-control. That, in turn, drives us to pleasure-seeking but self-destructive behaviors.

But Wendy is not to be blamed for having a damaged impulse controller. Blame the "faulty incentive-reward circuits" in her brain.[108] Faulty "brain wiring" is one of the underlying contributing factors for addiction.

DOPAMINE IS THE DRIVER

"Brain wiring" is a metaphor for pathways of connected nerve cells in the brain. Those pathways transmit messages in the form of electrical signals. Between each nerve cell, a neuron, is a tiny gap called a synapse. It is in the gap between neurons that problems—and solutions—occur.

To "jump the gap," the electrical signal must turn into a chemical that can "swim" across to the receptors at the end of the next neuron. That's the only way to transmit the message on down the line. Those chemicals that swim across the gap are called neurotransmitters.

Dopamine, sometimes called the pleasure hormone, is the neurotransmitter that creates and transmits the message of "want" and "anticipation." It's the "motivation" molecule that helps us concentrate and feel good. Think of an aroma that triggers a craving for a homemade cookie. Or the ad photo that triggers a craving for chocolate ice cream. Or the finish line that spurs you on to win the race. That's dopamine kicking in. It says, "I want it now, and I am willing to do what it takes to get it." It's desire, motivation, and ambition. That's a good thing because dopamine "increases mood, confidence, courage and tolerance to pain."[109]

But dysfunction of the dopamine pathway can turn a healthy "want" into an unhealthy uncontrollable "craving." It leads to addictive behaviors—wanting more and more without constraint. Any pursuit, activity, or substance that makes us want and anticipate a reward "will activate the same brain systems as drug addictions."[110]

Here's the kicker: The dopamine pathway is impaired when there are too few dopamine receptors to receive the dopamine coming from the other side of the gap. Studies have found that a shortage of dopamine receptors correlates with a brain that is more welcoming of external substances—anything that has a chance of increasing dopamine supply.[111] Tragically, this condition exposes a person to a host of vulnerabilities. A picture comes to mind of a desperate, needy soul ready to embrace anything or anyone as a friend regardless of the potential dangers they may pose.

This brings us back to Wendy. Addictive eaters, like addictive drug users, have a shortage of dopamine receptors, which results in a reduced sense of satisfaction. They attempt to compensate for that feeling of not being satisfied by taking more drugs or eating more food. Wendy had a low dopamine receptor count in her brain, and it made her vulnerable to addiction.[112]

The correlation relates to obesity too. In one study, Maté noted, "the more obese the subjects were, the fewer dopamine receptors they had."[113] The association between obesity and dopamine receptors helps us to understand people who have issues with overeating.

Obesity-related medical costs have risen to over $260 billion in the U.S. alone.[114] With approximately 42% of the U.S. population classified as obese,[115] and approximately 74% classified as overweight,[116] obesity has become a national crisis requiring immediate interventions.

Did a low dopamine receptor count predispose Wendy to overeat junk food so compulsively? Or did eating junk food cause the low dopamine receptors?

If we could understand the cause, we would be in a better position to identify a solution.

Maté said it can go both ways. But "all addictions start in the mother's womb." As an embryo, the brain is in its most critical and sensitive stage of development. "Brain development in the uterus and during childhood is the single most important biological factor in determining whether or not a person will be predisposed to…addictive behaviors of any sort.[117]

When babies don't develop a positive emotional connection with a primary caregiver, dopamine receptors don't multiply as fast in the developing brain. Therefore, the baby's environment—pre- and postnatal—plays a major role in its susceptibility to addiction of any kind as an adult.

American talk show host and producer Oprah Winfrey had her share of adverse childhood experiences and has shared many times her struggle with food. She partnered with neuroscientist Dr. Bruce D. Perry, an expert on the long-term effects of trauma in children, to write a profoundly insightful book called What Happened to You.

Winfrey wrote these insightful words: "What I've learned from talking to so many victims of traumatic events, abuse, or neglect is that after absorbing these painful experiences, the child begins to ache. A deep longing to feel needed, validated and valued begins to take hold." If not addressed, a "frustrating pattern of self-sabotage, violence, promiscuity, or addiction" follows.[118]

In other words, addictions begin in the early stages of life when a natural emotional need goes unmet. Here's the big takeaway: Addiction is not the problem. It's the person's attempt to solve the problem.[119] The problem is disconnection.

Disconnection may be caused by a host of factors stemming from an emotionally distant primary caregiver. Such disconnection could have been in the form of abuse, neglect, stressful environment, or a feeling of unsafety.

The resulting non-optimal brain development is why low self-control (a weakened willpower) is part of addiction. Because "on the neurobiological level, all addictions…bypass the impulse-control part of the brain."[120] No wonder Wendy couldn't control her eating. Her faulty dopamine pathways omitted the self-control part of her brain. Not only did she have an abundance of stimulating and convenient junk food at her fingertips, but she was also set up from early childhood to be predisposed to eating too much of it.

Which brings us to another contributing factor for addiction: the processed-food industry, which preys on the faulty incentive-reward circuits in the brain.[121] Sugar/salt/fat/white flour combos are purposely designed to hijack our natural drives and appetites and turn them against us.[122] For the sole purpose of making their products more addictive, food manufacturing companies and fast-food restaurant chains hire scientists to hook us.[123]

Add to that the fact that junk food is easy to grab and go. It requires little or no prep time. In our fast-paced modern lifestyle, the ease of snatching something can be extremely appealing. But it contributes to a culture of addiction.

Prioritizing Maté's definition of addiction over the DSM-5's definition gave me more insight into my behaviors and helped me to identify strategies to overcome self-sabotaging behaviors, such as binge junk-food eating, and truly omit what is harmful.

TALKING TO MY ALCOHOLIC GRANDDAD

So, what can we say to the addict? Or those with addictive-like behaviors? What can we say to the alcoholic or overeater? We can start by saying, "It's not your fault." That doesn't mean we should abdicate responsibility for our own personal growth and healing. But it does give us a place to start.

If I had a chance to sit with the younger version of my grandfather, I might say something like this:

Granddad, I know you want to stop drinking. You saw how it hurt us. And I know you don't want to hurt us because you say, "Never again."

Your addiction is not the problem. At least, it's not the root of the problem. It's your attempt to solve the problem. The problem is a sense of dissatisfaction. It began with an insufficient number of dopamine receptors in your brain. With fewer dopamine receptors, less dopamine gets through to the next segment of your neural pathways. You feel this as dissatisfaction, and it creates a want for more dopamine just to reach the same level of life satisfaction that other people have.

To address this dissatisfaction, this emptiness, you turned to alcohol, just as other people go to drugs, gambling, stimulating food, pornography, shopping, or risky behavior. It's to fill a void—a void not of your making.

You want the same amount of dopamine as anyone else. That's natural. But because you were stuck with fewer dopamine receptors to do all the work, they are overloaded. It's like 10 workers on the loading dock who are forced to do the work of 12 because two of them were let go. The same work needs to get done. But the workers have to work harder to do it. And it wears them out.

Your dopamine receptors are overworked—overstimulated—trying to do the work of more. This overwork has the long-term effect of weakening them. They are less able to convert dopamine into an electrical signal to pass down the neuron. That means you must stimulate them even more to get the same effect. That's called tolerance—the body's increasing need for more of the substance to receive the same amount of pleasure—and then you need even more of the substance to feel normal. So, your addiction grew.

Those who have the healthy number of receptors don't need to overstimulate with alcohol or junk food, etc., because there are enough receptors to receive the dopamine and easily pass it on down to the other end of the neuron allowing it to travel its brain circuit.

But for you, one reason you may have fewer dopamine receptors is that you experienced emotional disconnectedness in your early childhood. Mom told me you had an alcoholic father. It's very likely your mother was a stressed-out mother trying her best. Then she died when you were nine years old, and you were forced to live in an orphanage. All that must have been traumatic. You had emotional needs that went unmet. This drove you to compensate for those unmet needs the only way your child brain knew how. You eventually found coping mechanisms that became maladaptive as you grew up. That's not your fault.

The answer is that you need new dopamine receptors. New healthy neural pathways form as you develop new healthy habits. The old neural pathways will still always be there, but more analogous to a dried-up riverbed. Let the old pathways dry up and start new ones. How? Come with me to the next chapter of your life and I'll show you some things I've learned.

Maybe my grandfather, with loving support and the principles of FULL POWER, would have walked a different path. There are so many more like my granddad who are searching for that different path. The principles in this book can be a guide.

All around the world, individuals struggle with self-sabotaging behaviors due to diminished dopamine receptors stemming from childhood trauma. Sadly, this state of being affects their vitality levels and social interactions, which in turn affects the quality of their relationships. And, as we learned in Chapter 4, the quality of our relationships impacts our physical health. Sadly, like falling dominos, dysfunction in one component of life brings down other components of life in a vicious downward cycle.

When some of these traumatized children grow up to be powerful people, it makes one wonder about the role of their psychopathologies in shaping some of the tragic episodes of history. Exploring childhood trauma could unveil the underlying causes of crime, corruption, and conflict, and by extension, become a crucial target for research in our efforts to prevent global challenges in the future.

Understanding the root cause of addiction and addictive-like behaviors shows us where to start the healing process. It gives hope. But what does this start look like in a practical sense? How can we understand our self-sabotaging behaviors in such a way as to stop them and cultivate positive habits for lasting change?

In the next chapter, we'll learn how the FULL POWER principles play a crucial role in guiding this process.

OMIT WHAT IS HARMFUL—PART 2:

THE SOLUTION

You do not rise to the level of your goals. You fall to the level of your systems.

James Clear

When I lived on Canada's east coast, I loved vacationing on Prince Edward Island in the summertime. The sunshine, sandy beaches, family togetherness, and down-home eastern hospitality was like Paradise. In 1997, engineers built Confederation Bridge, an eight-mile (13-kilometer) bridge to the island.

To me, that bridge is a metaphor for our "path to Paradise." It represents the transition period between the old life and the new life. We long to get to the other side so we can start living that life of optimal vitality.

But there's a problem.

THE SABOTEUR

Like the enemy in the old war movies, a villain awaits beneath the bridge. With dynamite in hand, he is poised to sabotage our path to Paradise.

But the irony is this: The enemy is a force within ourselves. Susan Peirce Thompson, author of Bright Line Eating, aptly calls this enemy "the saboteur."[124] The saboteur is the inner force that drains our willpower, tempting us to give in to tasty toxins or clickbait even though we know it sabotages the bridge to our long-term goals. The saboteur is the dark voice that convinces us to give up on our long-term goals to settle for instant gratification. It's the mindset that makes us settle for information without application and sedates us with a dream without a plan.

It represents those inner cravings that hijack our best intentions and cause us to betray our future selves.[125] The resulting emptiness leads to a lifestyle that saps our life forces, driving us to an early grave from addiction, heart disease, cancer, stoke, diabetes, depression, Alzheimer's disease, etc.[126] Ultimately, it's our self-sabotaging behavior that destroys the bridge to our own happiness. In this way, we are our own worst enemy.

We need strength to fight the saboteur. Our happiness, health, and success depend on it.

Where does such strength come from?

It starts with a growth mindset inspired by the FULL principles from PART 1 (Chapters 2-5), from finding our superpower and knowing our higher purpose, unleashing positive spirituality, nurturing and being nurtured by loving relationships, and then turning that knowledge into habits. There's more, as we will see, but that's where it starts.

Therefore, we don't have to see ourselves as weaklings fighting a cruel enemy. We can see ourselves as superheroes with the potential to save the world, but only held back by one challenge.

Kryptonite.

Let me explain. When I was a small boy, I imagined possessing the powers of Superman. He was strong, fast, and confident. He didn't need a bridge. He could fly. But even Superman had his kryptonite. When he was exposed to kryptonite, he grew weak, clumsy, and unreliable—vulnerable to his enemies. But even in this weakened state, he knew he wasn't a weakling. He knew, deep down, he was strong and destined for a purpose. His inner strength sustained him through the kryptonite exposure until he eventually triumphed.

Even when weakened by our own personal kryptonite we know that we, too, can triumph. We know it because deep down inside, we can tap into sources of strength—the power of knowing that we have abilities to achieve our higher purpose, the power of healthy spirituality, the power of loving connections, and the power of habit.

Internalizing the FULL principles comprises the first steps to success. They are what transforms the weakling with no hope into a superhero with a conquerable challenge. Yes, the superhero has a challenge. But he also has hope. And that makes all the difference.

At this point, you might be saying, "Yes, I'm going to conquer my kryptonite. I'm going to resist the junk-food cravings and all other temptations. I'm going to flex my willpower muscles and stop my self-sabotaging behaviors. I'm going to cross the bridge to the new me."

Great. I love your enthusiasm. Let's set ourselves up for success. Here's our next step: understanding the role of willpower and habit.

UNDERSTANDING WILLPOWER AND HABIT

Mary, an office worker, is trying hard to live a healthy life. She begins her day with gusto. After a quick shower, she works with her husband to put breakfast on the table for their two children. For her own breakfast, she skips the doughnut and sugary cereal because she's decided to live a healthy lifestyle. So, Mary tops her hot, seven-grain cereal with sliced banana, berries, almonds, a handful of pumpkin seeds, and a teaspoon of flax meal.

She responds wisely to her youngest child's complaints about her older sister. Meanwhile, she helps them prepare their lunches—spreading hummus on multigrain bread topped with tomato, cucumber, and green romaine lettuce. They add carrot curls on the side and grapes for dessert. With a few loving words to her husband, she guides the children to the car and drives them to school on her way to the office.

As Mary enters the office, she resists the chocolates in the jar on the counter on her way to her desk. She has meetings throughout the morning—both formal and informal. For lunch with her coworkers, she eats her homemade vegetable bean soup with Silver Hills Sprouted Power Squirrelly bread (nutritious high-fiber whole-grain bread made with digestible sprouted wheat, sesame, and sunflower seeds) with no butter…all the while peering longingly at her coworker's doughnut. She thinks of her children and hopes they can resist the tasty toxins they face in the school cafeteria.

She resists the candy jar on the coworker's desk as she returns to her office. In the afternoon she makes calls, answers email, and has one last decision-making conversation with a coworker before heading home to have dinner with her family.

At home, exhausted and achy from the long day, Mary wants to unwind. She opens the refrigerator, sees lettuce, tomatoes, and carrots, then glances to the counter where the lonely doughnut calls her name.

Hmmm…Make a salad? Or grab the doughnut?

All she wants is to grab something comforting to eat and take a quick nap.

"One doughnut won't hurt," she says to herself. "I'll make a salad tonight when I have more energy." She grabs the doughnut and though it's a bit dry, she savors the soft chocolate coating.

What just happened?

Mary's willpower dried up. She couldn't resist yet another temptation. So, she gave in. She didn't have the strength to fight the saboteur, so she sabotaged her bridge.

I know I'm being a little dramatic over a doughnut. But why did she give in, especially when she went through a successful day of making healthy choices and resisting temptations?

A well-known study on ego depletion suggests that resisting temptations can drain our willpower, making it harder to resist later temptations.[127]

Mary's willpower is like a gas tank that is full at the beginning of the day. Let's say it holds 100 units of willpower. Willpower is weakened by common everyday experiences, including self-regulation, fatigue, stress, resisting temptation, decision-making, and thinking hard. Every time Mary resisted a temptation or made a decision, she drew upon her willpower, which depleted her willpower tank by the end of the day. It was as if Mary was exposed to her kryptonite, and she weakened.

We all have our temptations. For Mary, it's doughnuts. Think of that doughnut she resisted at breakfast as using up 10 units of willpower. Those chocolates she resisted in the office: 20 units. Now she's down to 70 units of willpower. Those decisions she made at the meetings, on the phone, and on her email added up to 40 units. That butter she resisted putting on her healthy bread for lunch: 10 units of willpower. (She loves butter.) That doughnut she watched her coworker eat but she didn't: 10 units. That last decision she made with her coworker: 10 units. By the end of the end of day, her willpower tank was running on empty.

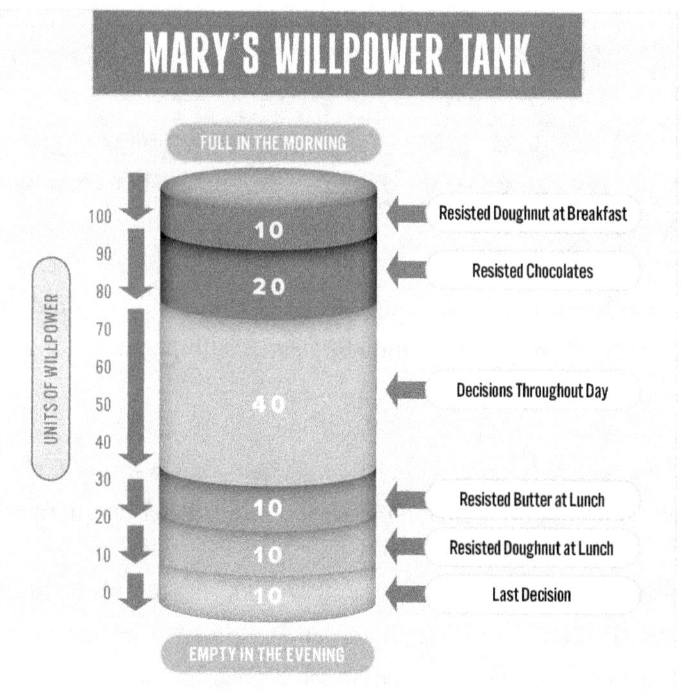

THE SECRET TO WILLPOWER

Many people like Mary experience willpower depletion every day. If you are like Mary and want sustainable self-control, here's the secret:

Don't depend on willpower. Depend on habits.

More specifically, depend on a system of habits that align with your purpose and goals.

We introduced this concept in Chapter 5 when we quoted James Clear: "You do not rise to the level of your goals. You fall to the level of your systems." In other words, our habits—our systems—influence our inner strength and our chances for success.

To understand how willpower and habits work, let's look at Mary's brain—two parts of the brain in particular: the basal ganglia and the prefrontal cortex.

The basal ganglia form a group of structures in the middle of the brain associated with emotions, patterns, and memories—all things necessary to form a habit. The basal ganglia automate repeated actions, reducing the need for conscious effort. Thanks to the basal ganglia, there is little need for conscious effort. In other words, after an action becomes a habit, it's easy. But Mary wasn't quite there yet.

The prefrontal cortex, on the other hand, is where Mary's willpower resides.[128] It's where conscious decisions are made, emotions are regulated, and impulses are controlled. Because of this mental effort, the prefrontal cortex uses up significantly more energy than the basal ganglia. And it can get tired, depleting the willpower tank. Whenever we use the basal ganglia instead of the prefrontal cortex we save energy, and life becomes much easier.

So, if Mary wants to establish a new behavior—for example, eating beans and greens each day, or doing 20 pushups each day, or replacing doughnuts with salads—she is going to drain her willpower each time she performs the behavior until it becomes a habit. As already noted, studies have shown it takes between 18 and 253 days, and an average of 66 days depending on the actions and situation, for a habit to be formed.[129] To oversimplify, when Mary's habit is finally formed, that's the point at which her behavior switches from the prefrontal cortex to the basal ganglia. Her behavior shifts into autopilot.

So, people who look like they have strong willpower may actually be those who have simply developed strong habits. This automaticity makes their success appear effortless. They've reached the stage where maintaining their daily routines no longer requires self-discipline. Now, they can use their surplus willpower for higher levels of productivity.

Eliminating the need for willpower is what makes a system of habits so powerful. What would make the system even more powerful is identifying your particular set of habits that bring you optimal vitality, including those habits that slay the saboteur. For new habit ideas, check out the chapter checklists and suggestions throughout this book.

But what can Mary do during the average of 66 days while waiting for her new, healthy eating behavior to turn into a habit? Is she condemned to run an agonizing endurance race until the habit kicks in?

Yes and no. Yes, genuine effort and self-control will be essential until the habit forms. But "self-control is a short-term strategy, not a long-term one."[130] Mary will have to use her prefrontal cortex to make conscious decisions every day to establish or discontinue certain behaviors. So, yes, she will be running on willpower during a transition period. But it is enhanced willpower because she is buoyed up by the FULL POWER principles.

Here's how it played out for me with my chocolate addiction.

OUR CHOCOLATE CHALLENGE

Years ago, I came across an alarming article detailing how sugar damages blood vessels, which is the main reason diabetics go blind or require foot amputations. It was shocking that something so sweet could lead to something so bitter. After I shared the article with my wife, we talked about our diet. She challenged me with, "I bet you can't go without chocolate for a year."

I loved my chocolate. It was my favorite sugar substance. But that article was sobering. It sparked the motivation to quit chocolate. Plus, I had gained weight and needed to lose a few pounds. That was an added motivation. However, I couldn't do it alone. I looked at my beautiful wife and said, "Only if you join me."

The competition was on. Unless sugar was in its original form, like in an apple, we went off all sugar, including chocolate. It was hard. The cravings were intense. For the first two weeks, it felt like I was losing a friend. I'm pretty sure I went through all the stages of grief. No matter what I ate, it didn't satisfy like chocolate. We were drawing heavily from our willpower tank.

Fortunately, we buoyed up each other to resist the urges. We reminded ourselves often about why we were doing this. That mutual support system was very necessary.

I didn't know it at the time, but I was experiencing the benefits of the third principle of FULL POWER: "Lovify Your Life." It helped to get me through the transition period—to cross the bridge. If you have to cross a bridge, there's nothing sweeter than crossing it hand-in-hand with the one you love.

Loving connection was only part of our motivation strategy. Our plan also included reading health books every day and attending health seminars when we could.

After a month, something happened. I stopped thinking about sugar. I stopped seeing chocolate everywhere. It was like it didn't exist. The struggle to resist vanished.

If you saw me coming out of the grocery store and asked me, "Were there any chocolate bars at the store?" I would have said, "I don't know. I didn't notice any."

They were probably in front of me at the checkout stand or on the periphery of my vision. But I wasn't triggered by the sight of a chocolate bar because I didn't see them, and I didn't look. There's an old saying, "Out of sight, out of mind." But it works in reverse too: "Out of mind, out of sight."

My willpower tank stopped draining, and I was now running on power of habit. No effort needed. Together, June and I made it over to the other side.

A bonus was I lost that weight I needed to lose, and I went for several years without chocolate.

Double bonus, the brain fog that I didn't know I had cleared up, which made it easier to solve problems in my work, resolve conflicts, prepare presentations, and speak in public.

Kryptonite begone!

On a walk one morning, June and I discussed our transition to toxin-free living. We admitted that we felt deprived at first. Giving up tasty foods felt restrictive, as if we were losing our freedom. Then, as we analyzed what we really wanted in the long term, it all became very clear. Our thinking shifted to this:

We face a choice between leveraging the laws of nature or facing the consequences of disregarding the laws of nature. Adhering to nature's laws of cause and effect may indeed feel restrictive at first. But ultimately, it leads to freedom and strength. In contrast, enjoying tasty toxins offers momentary pleasures, and it feels like freedom. But eventually, it results in debilitating restrictions due to chronic illness.

We knew we couldn't change nature's laws of cause and effect. So, we accepted the short-term restrictions for the sake of the long-term freedom and vitality.

Since then, we've gleaned more practical tips on how to form good habits. Here are some strategies that may be useful:

HOW TO FORM A HABIT

An effective way to form a habit is to attach the new behavior to a current habit.

For example:

1. As soon as we rise in the morning, that's the cue to drink one or two cups of water.
2. Every time we see the elevator, that's the cue to take the stairs.
3. After we brush our teeth, that's the cue to stretch. Or we could even do some stretching while brushing our teeth (e.g., tree pose, or runners lunge, or rotating your ankles).
4. When breakfast is finished, that's the cue to go for a walk.
5. After we brush our teeth in the evening, that's the cue to write in our journal.
6. Every time we walk through a particular door, that's the cue to tighten our abs and straighten our shoulders.
7. Every time we receive a call on our cell phone, that's the cue to walk around our office or house. (Hint: this doesn't work if you receive that call while driving.)

What new habits could you attach to your current routines? For more ideas, fill in the blanks:

1. Every time I rise from sleep, I will _________.

2. Every time I come home from work, I will __________.

3. Every time I take off my shoes, I will __________.

4. Every time I get dressed, I will __________.

5. Every time I see the __________, I will __________.

6. Every time I hear the __________, I will __________.

7. Every time I sit at the table to eat, I will __________.

8. Whenever I open my computer, I will __________.

9. Every time I go for my morning walk, I will__________.

10. Every time I brush my teeth, I will __________.

11. After my breakfast, I will __________.

By attaching a new behavior to an existing daily habit, the two behaviors become intertwined. The new behavior becomes part of the daily routine.[131]

We've seen a glimpse of how the brain works when it comes to turning new behaviors into habits. But are there some practical tips for stopping harmful habits, especially if we have strong cravings or addictions?

Yes. Let's explore other weapons in our arsenal that help to fight off cravings and temptations. These weapons are activities that give us dopamine in a natural way—something I wish I could have discussed with my granddad. I call the list "How to Conquer Your Kryptonite."

HOW TO CONQUER YOUR KRYPTONITE

1. "What's My Purpose for This Phase of My Life?"

In Chapter 2, we saw the power that springs from a sense of purpose. We saw how a sense of purpose clarifies priorities and goals. Now, we call upon the power of purpose to conquer self-sabotaging behaviors, harmful habits—our kryptonite.

The secret to resisting harmful habits is to aggressively focus on healthy ones. When the mind is fixed on an absorbing purpose, temptation finds little foothold. Distractions disappear. It's easier to pass by the junk-food place when we are on our way to something else. It's easier to resist the chocolates when we are concentrating on a deadline.

Champions do not have time to agonize over resisting the negative when they are wonderfully absorbed by the positive.

As a bonus, focusing our superpower on a purposeful activity increases our dopamine production the natural way.

Decide on this: "What positive thing will consume my attention?" See Chapter 2, "Find Your Superpower," for tips.

Or chose something exciting to focus on that jumps out at you from this list:

    a. health goals
    b. career goals
    c. talent-development goals
    d. relationship goals
    e. spiritual goals
    f. character goals
    g. creativity goals
    h. humanity goals
    i. financial goals

Avoiding the negative begins with focusing on the positive. Omitting what is harmful starts with focusing on the helpful. Therefore, set goals. Anticipate reaching them because you're going to have a plan.

2. *"What Is My Kryptonite?"*

Now that we've established a goal, what self-sabotaging behaviors are getting in the way of reaching it? Is it alcohol, drugs, or cigarettes? Sugar, milk chocolate, candy, soft drinks, doughnuts, cookies, cakes, or ice cream? White flour, salt, or fats? Potato chips, french fries, pasta, bread, cheeseburgers, hotdogs, or pizza?

Our personal kryptonite may go beyond food or substances. It may be certain behaviors such as binge-watching TV, internet gaming, gambling, pornography, and shopping. All of these can be addictive and sabotage the bridge to our preferred future.

When it comes to consuming harmful substances like the ones listed above, it's helpful to train our minds to think, "None of these substances are real food. They are manufactured tastebud titillaters, artificially designed to stimulate the pleasure centers of my brain. They are not there to nourish the cells of my body. They are there to entertain my tastebuds. And my goal is to nourish the cells of my body so I can be strong."

A primary purpose of manufactured "food" is to get our money into the pockets of the fast-food manufacturers. Increasing their shareholders' wealth is their legal obligation. And they are motivated.

I don't expect the junk-food giants to back down anytime soon. So, it's up to us to protect ourselves from their predatory practices. Fast-food scientists and marketers know our brains better than we do and deploy marketing strategies to exploit our weaknesses. They lure us in by saturating our environment with slick invitations to tasty toxins at every turn. That's their strategy.

What's ours? Start by asking: "What am I doing, or not doing, that hinders me from accomplishing my purposes and goals?"

3. The 30-Day Tastebud Reset

Try an experiment. Abstain from manufactured food for a month. "A month is usually the minimum amount of time it takes to reset the brain's reward pathway."[132] Eat only whole food, plant-based meals using foods that come from a garden, field, tree, or bush such as vegetables, fruits, beans, grains, legumes, and nuts. Cravings will decrease over that time.

Tastebuds take approximately two weeks to regenerate. As we age it takes longer.[133] Depriving our tastebuds of sugar and other manufactured stimuli for at least two weeks will give the new tastebuds a chance to appreciate the subtle tastes found in natural foods. Dr. Anna Lembke, the author of *Dopamine Nation*, noted in many of her patients that when they made the effort to abstain from drugs for one month, they experienced a newfound sense of freedom they had never felt before.[134]

Withdrawal can be hard, especially for those with high susceptibility to addiction or other conditions. See your doctor for any concerns.

4. Arrange Your Environment to Reduce Temptations

Arrange your environment—your cues—to support goals, not impulses. A cue is something that triggers a certain behavior. It could come from something we see, hear, feel, taste, touch, smell, or read.

The cues around us could be the foods on the kitchen counter or the feeds or ads on our screens. It could be a fellow worker eating candy, the billboards with smiling people eating refined foods, the stores we pass by with the aromas of sugar-rich coffee.

Be proactive by strategizing how you will avoid, bypass, or omit everything that doesn't support your purposes and goals. It means enriching your surroundings wherever possible to make them supportive of your new identity. Being proactive means tossing out anything within your control that forces you to use your willpower to resist.

"Make the cues of your good habits obvious and the cues of your bad habits invisible."[135] It means turning your environment into a Blue Zone as much as possible. The original Blue Zones had few negative cues. They were environments where healthy cues were everywhere. So, healthy choices were easy to make—no willpower necessary.

Examples of reducing temptations:

1. Minimize the triggers at home by throwing out the processed foods (foods with added sugar, salt, oil, and white flour) and stocking the refrigerator and cupboard with healthy foods like fruits, nuts, seeds, grains, vegetables, and legumes.
2. Minimize the triggers in the car by removing the junk food and coffee smell.
3. Minimize the triggers in the workplace.
4. Subscribe to a newsletter that gives you positive reinforcement of your good intentions.
5. Avoid driving by the favorite fast-food restaurant where irresistible aromas beckon us to drive in.

Changing your environment to support your long-term goals takes time and effort. But it's well worth it. Setting a date to implement a new habit may be helpful. For example, my wife and I scheduled the first day of the month to start our new healthy habits. In PART 3, you have a chance to implement a 28-day FULL POWER Action Plan.

5. Lovify Your Life

As we learned from the last chapter, it is often the feeling of disconnection in our early years that leads to the underdevelopment of dopamine circuits in the brain. This deficiency makes us vulnerable to addictions and addictive-like behaviors as adults. Simply put, "disconnection is a major driver of addiction."[136]

Reconnection, therefore, is a major driver of healing. It's part of personal growth. Knowing how to maintain healthy, loving relationships is vital for establishing new, healthy brain pathways. Love empowers the tempted to withstand trial and temptation (see Chapter 4 on how to lovify your life).

Weight loss expert Susan Peirce Thompson relied on this strategy as she struggled with obesity and addictions for years and finally conquered her demons. She wrote, "Social support has been the single most effective tool for keeping me on track."[137] Find friends who understand you and will support you during your makeover period.

6. Keep Consistent Mealtimes

Our bodies thrive on regularity whether it be bedtimes or mealtimes. We can achieve optimal vitality more rapidly by maintaining a consistent eating schedule, even on weekends. A 2017 study on meal frequency and meal timing found that "eating breakfast and lunch 5-6 hours apart and making the overnight fast last 18-19 hours may be a useful practical strategy [for preventing long-term weight gain]." It also found that snacking, defined as eating more than three meals per day, was linked to a relative increase in BMI.[138]

Sticking to regular mealtimes of two or three whole-food plant-based (WFPB) meals per day also stabilizes blood sugar. This fact is important because fluctuations in blood sugar levels can affect mood, cognitive function, and self-regulation. When blood sugar levels drop significantly, it can lead to feelings of irritability, fatigue, and difficulty concentrating, which may increase cravings and addictive behaviors.

7. Leverage Spirituality

"The spiritually engaged brain is a healthier brain," wrote psychologist Dr. Lisa Miller, who also says we are wired for spirituality.[139] Many people in 12-step recovery programs such as Alcoholics Anonymous or Overeaters Anonymous say they find strength to resist temptations through various spiritual practices.

Practicing gratitude and meditating to calm the mind are natural dopamine releasers and keep your mind from seeking harmful food and other damaging behavior. In one study, researchers used brain-scan imaging to confirm that meditation naturally increases dopamine release by 65%.[140]

See Chapter 3 for tips on how to increase spiritual strength.

8. Measure What Matters: Markers of Progress

One evening a few years ago, I came home from the office excited to take my wife shopping for pedometers. We were determined to use vacation time to regain our fitness by exercising outdoors. With this new tool in our hands, we committed to each other to walk 10,000 steps a day. And to keep us accountable, we could now easily measure our daily steps.

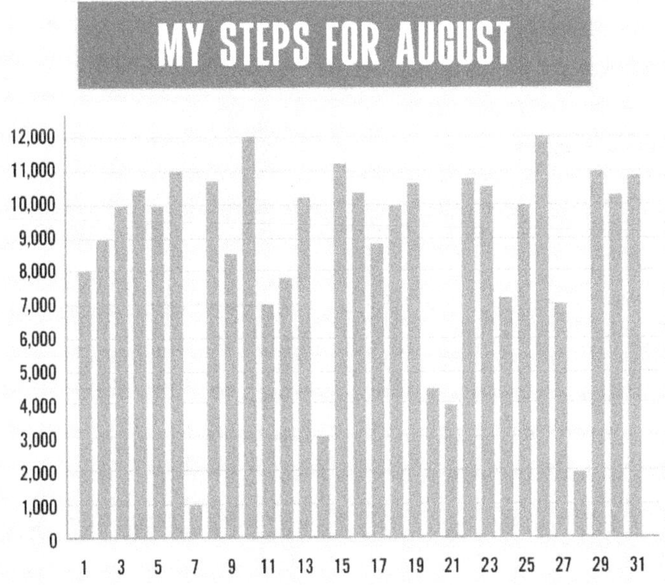

Measuring my steps motivated me to want to take more steps. Recording my progress on a chart gave me a dopamine hit each time I met my goal. Check out my chart to see how I did.

To conquer your kryptonite, find a way to measure your new habit. See the checklist at the end of this chapter for the best habits to measure. For a plan to follow, check out options in PART 3.

9. *What to Do When a Craving Hits*

Another strategy for resisting temptation is to create "trigger protocols." This entails preplanning your response to a craving before the craving hits you.

For example, before Martin goes to a party or dinner, he resolves what he will do when a temptation appears before him. He establishes his trigger protocol or routine clearly in his mind so that when he is offered that drink, fatty appetizer, or sweet dessert he knows exactly how to respond.

Normally, the unhealthy routine goes like this:

Trigger > Craving > Acting on the craving > Guilt.

Now, it goes like this:

Trigger > Craving > Protocol against the craving > Success.

Notice how the craving now triggers a pre-established action—a protocol—instead of succumbing to temptation. The trick is to execute the plan immediately on cue, without stopping to think about it. We arm ourselves so we don't harm ourselves. The protocol might involve a getaway plan, a stroll outside, a drink of water, a call to a friend, engaging in a hobby, offering service to others, or playing a game. Reward yourself (not with a chocolate bar ☺) when you stick to your designated protocol.

Dr. Maté suggests recognizing the craving as a belief that something is urgent when it isn't. If it were real hunger, a handful of nuts or an apple would satisfy. But if the craving is for french fries and a cheeseburger, or ice cream and a soft drink, something else is at play. The appetite centers of the brain tend to be separate from the hunger centers of the brain.[141]

When observing the craving, ask, what need is this craving filling? The goal, then, would be to identify an alternate way to address that need. For example, some food cravings can be associated with chronic stress.[142] If stress is the cause, find alternate ways to relieve the stress.

Another common cause of food cravings is boredom. A helpful protocol may be to start working on a creative activity, push toward a goal, play music, or call a friend. These are natural dopamine boosters.

Here are some other questions we can ask:

1. Is this craving about wanting comfort?
2. Is this craving about wanting to alleviate emotional pain?
3. Is this craving about wanting to eat to fill an emptiness?

Then ask, what can I do instead to take care of this need?

Another possible response to a food trigger is to choose healthy foods that increase dopamine: almonds, apples, avocados, bananas, beets, green leafy vegetables, green tea, lima beans, oatmeal, oranges, peas, sesame and pumpkin seeds, tomatoes, turmeric, watermelon, and wheat germ.[143]

When we get off track, no need to beat ourselves up. Instead, say, "Hmmm, I just got off track. What can I learn about myself so I do better next time?"

MORE THAN OUR BODIES

Omitting what is harmful is a principle that can work for our minds as well as our bodies. Paying attention to what we let into our mind through reading, seeing, or hearing can alert us to what builds us up. Or it may cause us to ask, "Is this a productive use of my time?" Shawn Achor in his book, *Big Potential*, referred to research from Dartmouth and Ohio State that discovered when readers are engrossed with the main character of a book, they take on their main characteristics.

"For example," he said, "if you read a book about someone with a strong social conscience, your likelihood of doing something socially conscientious rises."[144] We can use this effect to our advantage by choosing to read about or watch characters that are who we'd like to be.

Then Achor added:

> I now find myself not wanting to enter fictional worlds that glorify the negative, because I find that they have real-world ramifications

on my mood and self-image. Instead, I gravitate toward things that make me feel stronger, smarter, and better, not angry, disillusioned, and reactive.[145]

Just as our bodies are made up of food assimilated, our minds are made up of thoughts assimilated.

Throughout these last two chapters we've highlighted the principle of distinguishing between short-term pleasures and long-term outcomes, mainly when it comes to our eating choices. But this potent and potentially life-saving principle can be used in many other areas of life.

Imagine a society whose leaders used this approach by asking the following question when considering potential actions: Will choosing this action produce only short-term advantages or will it produce positive long-term outcomes?

Or imagine asking this guiding question in areas such as finances, politics, business, economics, parenting, gardening, farming, environment, law, medicine, leadership, sports, education, or spirituality. The answer might very well lead our world into long-term health in other areas too.

So far, in PART 2, we've looked at what to put into our bodymind and what to leave out. As we end this chapter, assess your level of omitting what is harmful by completing the checklist below.

Now it's time to look at the one thing that gives our bodies and brains the most efficiency. That's next.

CHECKLIST FOR
"OMIT WHAT IS HARMFUL"

	To what degree am I omitting what is harmful? On a scale of 0-10, answer these questions, based on the last seven days. The cumulative sum of all nine end-of-chapter checklists will result in a total out of 100.	
1	I avoided refined food (foods with processed sugar, oil, or white flour in the ingredients).	
2	I limited my daily sodium intake to ¼ teaspoon per day.	
3	I stopped eating before my stomach felt full.	
4	I avoided alcohol, smoking, and illicit drugs.	
5	I avoided meat consumption.	
6	I avoided dairy consumption.	
7	I resisted distractions (things that take me off a healthy track).	
8	I adhered to a preplanned strategy to stay on course whenever I had a craving for something harmful.	
9	I avoided the non-productive use of screen time.	
10	I considered the long-term effect of my actions and decisions.	
	Total out of 100	
	Divide by 10 for average out of 10	

CHAPTER 9

WATER UP

*No other molecule comes even close to the unique
life-supporting, healing properties of water.*

Ernest J. Brake

Gladys winced as she tried to close her hand into a fist. She hoped that maybe, just maybe, this time would be different. But, sadly, like every morning for the past year, pain shot back. As hard as she tried, she couldn't close her fingers into a ball. Using scissors was very uncomfortable. Knitting was painful. She loved cooking in the kitchen, but gripping the handle of a pot was difficult.

She was an active 60-year-old living near Peggy's Cove, Nova Scotia, and reported that her pain came from arthritis. At work she was sometimes required to make harnesses for aircraft by twisting wire into place. She loved her work and her colleagues, but the wire twisting was agony—one she couldn't endure much longer. She hated the thought that she might have to give up her job.

Gladys, my dad's second wife, showed us one evening how hard it was to close her hand. She explained that was the reason she asked us to carry a pot of boiled potatoes to the sink, and a big dish to the oven, and eventually to carry the food platters to the table. Ordinarily, she did all the meal prep on her own with gusto. But her requests for help brought to light how serious her issue was becoming. We all knew, with no one saying anything, she must really be hurting.

"Gladys, do you drink much water?" I asked her.

I had been teaching health seminars based on Loma Linda University health research and at Hans Diehl's CHIP program. They emphasize how proper hydration is necessary for good general health, and that dehydration can cause symptoms associated with arthritis.

"Not really." She folded her hands on her lap. "I'm not used to drinking water."

"I read about some studies showing that drinking water first thing in the morning and throughout the day can reduce certain types of arthritic pain," I responded. "Maybe drinking water would help with your pain."

She raised her eyebrows, looking at the back of her hands still on her lap. "That almost sounds too good to be true. Imagine if getting out of pain could be that easy?"

Flash forward three years. We were back visiting and gathered around the dinner table with my brothers, sister, aunts, and uncles for a big feast of mashed potatoes, roasted beans, garden vegetable dishes, broiled salmon, homemade bread and jams, and an excited Gladys.

After we all had gathered at the table, she raised her hands. "Look." She put her hand into a fist and squeezed. "My hands work!"

The room gasped.

She beamed. "I didn't think I'd ever be able to do this again." She raised her hands in fists again with a huge smile. "A miracle."

Someone gasped, "How?"

"Water."

"Water?" my uncle mumbled. "What does water have to do with it?"

"Well, after Ernie said my hand pain might be because of dehydration, I started to drink two glasses every morning as soon as I woke. Plus, more water throughout the day."

"That's it?" my Aunt Kathleen asked.

"Water. That's it. Within five days, I could squeeze my hands into fists, which I couldn't do before—pain free. It's like I got my life back."

That was 20 years ago. Gladys is now in her 80s and still lives without that pain.

Unfortunately, it may not be so simple for everyone. Arthritic pain has stolen joy from too many people. "During 2019–2021, about 1 in 5 US adults (21.2%) or about 53.2 million people had doctor-diagnosed arthritis."[146] Arthritis is more common in women (20.9%) compared with men (16.3%)[147]—likely due to genetics, hormones, and relative joint laxity.[148]

Arthritic pain isn't the only symptom of dehydration. Far from it. And pain relief isn't the only benefit of water.

In this chapter you will discover that water is one of nature's best medicines. Those who live with optimal vitality understand both the threat of dehydration and the advantages of hydration.

First let's look at the difficulties that can come from dehydration.

DEHYDRATION – SYMPTOMS AND CAUSES

"Hydro" comes from a Greek word meaning "water." If we're hydrated, it means we're watered up. If we're dehydrated, it means there is not enough water in our body to run everything efficiently. Every bodily system, every organ, and every cell needs water, especially our brain.

Sir Edmund Hillary knew this well. He, and his climbing partner, Tenzing Norgay, were the first men to conquer Mount Everest. During their expedition in 1953, they remained vigilant about the risk of dehydration that often occurs at high altitudes.[149]

He wrote, "We were both very conscious of the great dangers of dehydration and were determined to stock our bodies up with an ample supply of water."[150] So they took extra snow-melting equipment and had the endurance to make it to the top.

Dehydration stresses the body and can quickly become a serious life-threatening issue if it is not addressed right away, especially for young children and older adults.[151] Some health professionals have attributed Hillary's extra mountain-conquering endurance to the fact that he took water drinking seriously.

Dehydration happens when the amount of fluid entering the cells is not enough to replace the amount of fluid leaving our bodies through urine, perspiration, breath, and from the bowels.

THE CRITICAL IMPORTANCE OF CIRCULATION

Our blood, a water-based solution, transports oxygen and fuel to every cell. That is, if there is enough water. Think of the circulatory system as a river system—billions of connected rivers transporting and delivering energy packages (oxygen and food) to stops along the way and removing their waste products (like carbon dioxide and lactic acid).

Those stops along the way are the trillions of cells in every organ, muscle, bone, joint, nerve and tissue. Our cells live or die depending on the efficiency of a delivery system that requires adequate H2O. No other molecule comes even close to the unique life-supporting, healing properties of water.

To oversimplify, when the body is dehydrated, it's like the rivers are polluted and sluggish. Even if the blood has healthy food and oxygen to deliver to the cells, without water, the delivery system slows down, and waste isn't removed efficiently. As a result, we feel tired.

The Arthritis Society says:

> Hydration is vital for flushing toxins out of your body, which fights inflammation, and well-hydrated cartilage reduces the rate of friction between bones, meaning you can move more easily.[152]

When Gladys drank more water, she gave her body the ability to flush out the toxins that kept her from being able to use her hands. Water was the best internal tissue cleanser, keeping her joints well lubricated and reducing her suffering.

There are other contributing factors to arthritis, like wear and tear, injuries, infections, diseases, and genetics. But making water our first line of defense might be all we need to manage the pain, and in some cases, alleviate it.

Arthritis is only the tip of the iceberg, though. Dr. Roger Seheult, co-founder of MedCram, the popular medical channel for doctors, reported "a strong association between low water intake and chronic diseases and premature death."[153] It's amazing how much damage we do to ourselves by not drinking enough water. But it's equally amazing how easy it is to fix—just add water.

The Harvard School of Public Health offers a list of potential symptoms of dehydration:

1. fatigue
2. confusion or short-term memory loss
3. mood changes like increased irritability or depression
4. urinary tract infections
5. kidney stones
6. gallstones
7. constipation[154]

The Cleveland Clinic adds more symptoms to the list:

1. headache, delirium: According to the Cleveland Clinic, dehydration causes tissues to shrink, including those in the brain – much like a grape shrinking as it is dried. As the brain shrinks, it pulls away from the skull, which puts pressure on nerves. That's what causes the headache.[155]
2. dizziness, weakness, light-headedness
3. dry mouth and/or a dry cough
4. high heart rate but low blood pressure
5. loss of appetite but maybe craving sugar
6. flushed (red) skin
7. swollen feet
8. muscle cramps
9. heat intolerance or chills
10. constipation
11. dark-colored urine[156]

If you experience these symptoms, the first step is to hydrate by drinking more water. Only if this fails to bring relief do you need to consider exploring other potential causes.

POP QUIZ

Choose the best answer.

What's the easiest way to tell if you are dehydrated if a doctor is not around?

a) if I am thirsty
b) if my urine is dark yellow
c) if I have lost weight recently
d) if my face is pale
e) if I am feeling full
f) if I live in the desert
g) if I just finished a marathon

Answer: Use urine color as your main guide. The darker it is, the more dehydrated you are. Matthew Solan, executive editor of Harvard Men's Health Watch, wrote, "If you drink enough water, your urine color should be pale yellow. If you're even slightly dehydrated, the color darkens."[157] Note, though, that certain foods (beets, blackberries, carrots, asparagus), supplements, and medications can change urine color temporarily.

Generally, simple thirst is a good sign we do not have enough water. But as we get older, the thirst mechanism decreases in reliability and may fail to tell us our body needs water. Therefore, short of a doctor's examination, urine color is a good home measurement.

THE REMARKABLE BENEFITS OF DRINKING WATER

The simple habit of drinking water is easily one of the best returns on investment a person could make for their bodymind vitality. It's also one of the easiest habits to start. Water plays many roles in keeping us healthy, from reducing arthritis pain to slowing down memory loss.

Research from Johns Hopkins University suggests, "The more hydrated you are, . . . the more efficiently your body works at tasks that range from thinking to burning body fat."[158] A hydrated body is an efficient body; the hydrated brain is an efficient brain.

Here are a few benefits we receive from drinking enough water:

1. **Mental sharpness**: Water enhances mental sharpness and alleviates brain fog. In a research experiment on 75 children, "kids assigned to drink 2.5 liters of water a day had significantly better scores on the cognitive flexibility test than those assigned to drink 0.5 liters."[159] It's like knowing the secret to smartness.

2. **Complexion:** Water is the real foundational beauty treatment for a clearer complexion.[160] Water brings moisture and nutrients to our organs. Many scientists say water helps flush toxins from the skin, which can reduce acne and blemishes.[161] Some research indicates water improves skin elasticity, causing it to bounce back from sagging.[162]

   Water has antiaging qualities in that it improves skin physiology.[163] Water also speeds up the healing of sunburned skin.

3. **Cancer risk**: Water reduces the risk of some cancers. For example, a Harvard study of 48,000 men concluded, "a high

fluid intake is associated with a decreased risk of bladder cancer in men."[164]

Dr. Michael Greger, commenting on this study, wrote: "The risk of bladder cancer decreased by 7% for every extra daily cup of fluid we drink. Therefore, a high intake of water—like 8 cups a day—may reduce the risk of bladder cancer by about 50%, potentially saving thousands of lives."[165]

Water also reduces the number of episodes of cystitis, inflammation of the bladder. The risk of colon cancer in women who drank more than five glasses of water was reduced by 45%. Water also affects risk of urinary stone disease; cancers of the breast, colon, and urinary tract; childhood and adolescent obesity; mitral valve prolapse; salivary gland function; and overall health in the elderly."[166]

4. **Weight loss**: According to some studies, drinking water between meals can help you lose weight. A study by researchers from the University of Illinois reported in the *Journal of Human Nutrition and Dietetics* that "the participants who drank the most plain [clean] water in their daily diet consumed fewer total calories, drank fewer sweetened beverages, and took in less total fat, saturated fat, sugar, salt, and cholesterol."[167]

All these factors contribute to weight loss. Water also gives you that full feeling between meals when you are tempted to snack on calorie-laden food. In another study, Dr. Greger noted that, "increasing water intake per se was independently and significantly associated with less weight gain over the long term."[168]

Water also staves off hunger during intermittent fasting, which can be part of a weight-management strategy.

5. **Toxins**: Adequate water increases the rate at which impurities, waste, and toxins leave the body. As such, water is a big contributor to feel-good bodymind efficiency.

6. **Preterm labor**: Water can even reduce preterm labor. Lisa, mother of eight, said, "I suffered from preterm labor with almost all my babies. Finally, a midwife told me to try drinking water. It reduced my preterm labor by 60%. I wish someone would have told me earlier."[169]

7. **Digestion:** Water helps digestion and absorption of nutrients. It's needed to make saliva, which in turn breaks down food in the mouth.

8. **Circulation:** Water improves circulation.

9. **Blood pressure:** Water normalizes blood pressure.

10. **Body temperature:** Water maintains and regulates body temperature.[170]

11. **Short-term memory:** Water improves short-term memory.[171]

12. **General brain health:** Dr. Lisa Mosconi wrote *Brain Food: The Surprising Science of Eating for Cognitive Power*. She said in an interview with Jim Kwik, "The best tip for brain health is water."[172]

13. **Nerves:** Our brain needs water to create hormones and neurotransmitters, which strengthen exhausted, irritable nerves.

14. **Pain:** Water decreases chronic pain.

15. **Fatigue:** Water fights fatigue.

16. **Body's chemicals:** Water balances our body's chemicals.[173]

The only side effect of taking in adequate water is using the bathroom more often. But think of it this way: Every time you use the bathroom, you get rid of more toxins, which is exactly what your body wants to do.

HOW MUCH WATER SHOULD WE DRINK?

Many people wonder about how much to drink. They've heard that people need to drink eight glasses of water a day. Is that true?

Yes, it is true for some, but not all. It depends on several factors such as how active we are, our weight, the weather, our diet, medications, and illnesses (such as kidney disease or heart failure). For example, a 250-pound man who doesn't eat many fruits or vegetables, living in hot Arizona, will likely need more water than a 120-pound woman who eats a lot of fruits and vegetables and who lives in chilly Alaska.

The bigger we are, the more cells we have, and therefore, the more water we need to support them. The more fruits and vegetables we eat, the less water we need to drink because we get water in the food. The hotter the weather or the more active we are, the more water we need to replace water lost through perspiration.

According to Dr. Greger, "probably the best evidence we have for a specific recommendation for how much water you should be drinking comes from the Adventist Health Study."[174] In this research, over 20,000 men and women were studied.

> Those who drank five or more glasses of water a day had about half the risk of dying from heart disease compared to those who drank two glasses or less daily. About half the cohort consisted of vegetarians, so they were also getting extra water by eating more fruits and vegetables. As in the Harvard study, this [heart] protection remained even after controlling for other factors,

such as diet and exercise, suggesting that water indeed was the cause, perhaps by lowering blood "viscosity" (that is, by improving blood flow). [175]

Yet again, water is the hero. By upping our water intake to five or more simple glasses of water a day, we could be the one who averts that heart attack. As water intake goes up, heart disease risk goes down.

To better understand how much water we need to be drinking on a daily basis, consider how much water we lose. On average we lose 10 cups of water a day. But we may gain back three or four cups from food depending on its water content. Fruits and vegetables have the most water content.

Below is a chart that gives a general breakdown on daily water losses.

Approximate Daily Water Losses for an Adult in Temperate Climate:

Perspiration	2.1 cups
Water lost from lungs by exhaling	1.7 cups
Water lost with feces	0.5 cups
Water lost in waste removal as urine	6.3 cups
Total daily water lost	**10.6 cups**

We compensate for these losses in three ways:

Water produced by oxidation of carbohydrates and fats	1.5 cups
Water contained in the food we eat	3.6 cups
Drinking water needed to balance water loss	5.5 cups
Total water gained by body	**10.6 cups**[176]

Note that at least five and a half cups are needed to take care of the essential needs. More water is needed in cases of hotter weather, exercising conditions, or sickness, especially sicknesses accompanied by diarrhea and vomiting.

CAN YOU DRINK TOO MUCH WATER?

Yes. It's possible to drink too much water. It's rare and very unlikely to happen by accident.[177] But in extreme cases, drinking excessive amounts of water can be harmful and even fatal. It can cause an imbalance of electrolytes in the body. Electrolytes are essential minerals like sodium, calcium, and potassium that regulate motor, digestive, and neurological functions.

Marathon runners, for example, who don't consume electrolytes with water while running can lower the sodium concentration of their blood. This effect is called hyponatremia. Exercising in extreme heat can also put people in danger of drinking too much water, unbalancing the electrolytes in the body.

Consult your doctor regarding your water intake when:

1. taking chemotherapy.
2. you have certain diseases, such as kidney disease, heart disease, or liver disease.

WHEN NOT TO DRINK WATER

Is there a time when we should not drink water?

Yes. At mealtimes. The more liquid we put into the stomach with meals, the more difficult it is for the food to digest. That's because the liquid must first be absorbed before solid foods are digested. Also, water diminishes the flow of the saliva at mealtime and dilutes acid in the stomach, both of which are needed to break down, or digest, the food. So, water is best taken a half hour before a meal—and, of course, as soon as we rise from sleep and between meals throughout the day.

QUALITY OF WATER

People react differently to different qualities of water. For optimal health, ensure the water you drink is clean—that is, free from microbial contamination (usually from feces). According to the World Health Organization, arsenic, fluoride, and nitrates pose chemical risks to drinking water. A growing concern is now coming from "emerging contaminants," such as pharmaceuticals, pesticides, and microplastics.[178]

If we are not sure whether our water supply is the most supportive for our health, we can get it tested and/or look into a water purifier. When using a water purifier, it's important to change filters as instructed. Otherwise, we'll have false security that our water is pure when old filters are holding the impurities and leaking them into our drinking water.

There may be reason for concern regarding drinking bottled water. First, it is not as rigorously regulated as tap water.[179] Second, a global study has shown that microplastics (plastic particles less than 5mm across) show up in 93% of bottled water.[180] While the World Health Organization says microplastics haven't been shown to be damaging to humans, more research is needed.[181]

OTHER USES OF WATER

We have seen the benefits of water inside our bodies. But there are benefits of applying water outside our bodies as well. For example, here's what happened to my friend, Cameron, who became a stress management and burnout coach after a period of burnout in his 30s.

A combination of overwork and an unbalanced lifestyle had taken its toll. To recuperate, he took his wife and two little girls on a long vacation visiting campsites along America's eastern seaboard. Then seemingly out of the blue, Cameron says, "an intense depression descended on me I would not wish on my worst enemy. For the next three weeks, I did not have a positive thought. My concentration levels were next to zero. I have never felt so hopeless or scared in my life."[182]

After three weeks on the road, he found a campsite advertising hot showers near the beach along the Outer Banks of North Carolina. He decided to stay there for the night. The next morning as he headed for the washhouse, he heard loud screams coming from inside.

As one man left, he grumbled, "That water is freezing." A hurricane had knocked out the hot water tanks a few days before.

Cameron reluctantly and cautiously went in and turned on the shower tap. The freezing water hit his body as if it had just come off a glacier. He gasped for breath and danced around trying to get out as quickly as possible. When he turned off the water, the cool air felt warm next to the icy shower. He dried off and returned to the tent to join his family for breakfast.

Surprisingly, he felt good for the first time in months—optimistic and light-hearted.

That happy feeling lasted for about two hours, then the depression returned. He decided to go for another cold shower. He did this every two hours for a total of eight showers that day. Each time he took the cold shower he felt better. He kept at it the next day. He was still tired and could not concentrate, but the heavy cloud of depression was lifting.

Cameron took two or three cold showers every day for the next month. He eventually learned that he could experience the same benefits if he merely ended a warm shower with 30-90 seconds of cold. He also discovered that the water in Florida is not as cold as in New England.

It took Cameron three years to fully recover from the burnout. But it was the cold shower that jumpstarted his recovery.

So, what happened in the shower?

Cameron stumbled upon a treatment called hydrotherapy and found a host of benefits, including a natural treatment for some depression symptoms. Cold water causes blood vessels on the surface of our skin to tighten up, thus forcing blood into our body's core as a way of conserving heat. This action increases circulation, bringing more oxygen and nutrients to our organs, including the brain.

Another feature of hydrotherapy is alternating between hot and cold, 30 seconds each, ending with cold. One lifestyle coach I know promotes the "Rule of Threes," advising three cycles of three minutes of hot shower followed by 30 seconds of cool water. The effect decreases stress hormones like cortisol and helps to bring into balance the feel-good neurotransmitter, serotonin.[183]

In addition to serotonin, a dose of beta-endorphin and noradrenaline (more feel-good chemicals) were released every time Cameron took a cold shower. That increase is consistent with a 2008 study that found a cold shower floods the temperature receptors on our skin, triggering an antidepressive effect.[184]

After hearing Cameron's story and doing some research, I now end my showers with 30 seconds of cold water. Here are some more of the benefits of ending showers with 30-90 seconds of cold water. It:

1. stimulates our immune system.[185]
2. reduces our stress response by activating our vagus nerve."[186]
   The vagus nerve is incredibly important to our overall health.
   It is "the longest nerve in the body," which "[runs] from our

brain down through our eyes, ears, vocal cords and down to all our major organs, including the heart, lungs, liver, kidneys and gut."[187] The vagus nerve helps to regulate involuntary sensory and motor functions such as heart rate, speech, mood, and urine output. It plays a crucial role in enabling the body to switch between the flight-or-fight response and the relaxed state. So, anything we can do to activate the vagus nerve optimizes vitality.

3. decreases sick days by 29%.[188]
4. decreases pain, inflammation, and swelling.[189]

Water, inside and out, goes a long way toward energizing the systems of our body and mind.

Experimenting with new water habits may show us more ways to enhance our vitality. For some ideas, complete the checklist below to gauge how you are doing on watering up.

Next, we turn to an indispensable habit that builds strength of body and mind, reduces risk of almost all diseases, helps you lose weight and build that physique you've always wanted, while at the same time building up confidence, strength of purpose, and clarity of mind.

It's in the next chapter.

CHECKLIST FOR

"WATER UP"

To what degree am I getting enough clean water?

On a scale of 0-10, answer these questions, based on the last seven days.

The cumulative sum of all nine end-of-chapter checklists will result in a total out of 100.

1	I drank enough water for my weight, activity level, and circumstances.	
2	The water I drank was clean.	
3	I drank water upon arising in the morning.	
4	I drank water up to approximately a half hour before meals.	
5	I drank water again about an hour after eating.	
6	My urine was pale yellow.	
7	Water was the only thing I drank between meals.	
8	I ended my showers with at least 30 seconds of cold.	
9	I daily counted the cups of water I drank.	
10	I distributed my water intake evenly throughout the day.	
	Total out of 100	
	Divide by 10 for average out of 10	

CHAPTER 10

EXERCISE OUTDOORS—PART 1:

THE SUPERPOWER OF EXERCISE

Let me bring clarity: Inactivity is going to kill you.
And before it does, it will make you miserable.

Ernest J. Brake

Although it was only six inches down to the pavement, my wife couldn't step off the curb. June and I were out early, walking slowly on a sunny Sunday on our way to the Halifax Common Park, Canada's oldest urban park. About a quarter the size of New York's Central Park, "the Commons," as the locals call it, boasts seven green softball diamonds, two soccer fields, blue tennis courts, a cement skate park, elaborate playgrounds, picnic areas, a swimming pool, and luscious water fountains. Our goal was to walk around its one-mile perimeter.

To get to the park, we had to cross Robie Street, the north-south artery of the Halifax peninsula. But June couldn't bear the weight of the down step to the street. She was recovering from a hernia operation, and the area was swollen and sensitive. I carefully guided her left arm over my shoulders, wrapping my right arm around her waist. I made sure not to touch near her surgical incision. She put her right hand below her abdomen where the incision was for support. Leaning into me, ever so gently, I lifted her onto the road. She grimaced as she found her footing.

That's how we started our first day of vacation—committed to her recovery. She was weak, in pain, and still under the foggy effects of medications. She was determined to regain her strength and to avoid further weakening that would come from sitting too much.

Every morning, we made the journey to the park. June was able to pick up speed as the days continued. We clocked her progress like she was an athlete in training. After a week, she felt strong enough to go twice around the park. After two weeks, she circled three times around at a much faster clip. Eventually, we jogged three times around the park. By the end of August, we were jogging five times around.

Thrilled by the progress and wanting to go further, we signed up for the Terry Fox Run, a worldwide fundraising charity run for cancer research. June, who couldn't step off a curb one month before, was now running with thousands of runners. She could not have done it unless she took that first step.

After regular daily exercise outdoors, June felt strong and recovered from surgery quickly. When she did a mental scan of her body, she found she had no aches or pains. It felt good to regain her physical fitness.

Here is what I've found from supporting people in their personal growth and health goals for over 30 years:

Recovering from inactivity is often harder than recovering from surgery—possibly because inactivity can be a habit built over years and hard to give up. It takes only days of inactivity for muscles to start to atrophy. Imagine what we do to them over years.

But convalescence, with its relatively shorter time, has the advantage of urgency and focused attention.

While chronic pain can have different causes, check to be sure inactivity isn't the culprit. When inactive for long periods of time, muscles become weak and tight, which can lead to tension and discomfort. The deficit can affect posture and alignment, which adds additional stress on joints and is accompanied by more pain. In addition, chronic inactivity can contribute to other health problems that may increase obesity, poor cardiovascular health, and poor mental health. More on that below.

Indoor activity is better than no exercise at all, especially when fresh air is allowed to flow into the indoors. But outdoor exercise is best.

Just as thirst is our body's call to drink water, chronic aches and pains may be our body's call to exercise. Increased vitality requires being responsive to our body's cries for attention. Also, being open to a friend's or doctor's observations about us, such as our posture, may be our next step toward optimal vitality.

In this chapter we will explore the uncommon insights about the incredible effects of physical activity. In the next chapter we'll discover the health secrets of outdoor activity. We will also explore how to harness this superpower for our greatest benefit.

Bad news first.

DANGERS OF INACTIVITY YOU NEVER KNEW

A sedentary lifestyle can lead to an early grave. Research shows that the damage we do to ourselves by keeping our bodies inactive is disturbing.

Let's say you have two groups of people with the same smoking, alcohol-drinking, and eating habits, and that the only difference between the groups is that one group is physically inactive, and the other group is physically active. Studies show that the inactive group will have more heart disease than the active group.[190]

Adding more clarity, the Mayo Clinic reported that those who sat for "more than eight hours a day with no physical activity" had the same risk of dying as their obese or smoking neighbors. That's a high risk. Hence, the mantra: "Sitting is the new smoking."[191] We can now put sitting—or more importantly, sitting too long—on the same list as smoking and obesity.

How long is too long? Meredith Chandler, an occupational therapist for the Ergonomics Health Association, gives some guidance: "Men who sit for five hours or more per day are at a 34% increased risk for developing heart failure as compared to men who sit only two hours or less per day."[192] As soon as I read that, I looked at the time I had been sitting. It was over two hours—into heart-risk territory. I decided, "I need to stand up." So, I stood up and continued reading.

I was glad I started moving because the next thing I read was that "prolonged sitting is associated with increased risk for at least 34 chronic diseases." That's a lot of disease I can protect myself from by just getting off the chair. Some of those diseases include cancer, obesity, cardiovascular disease, and diabetes.[193]

Regarding diabetes, Tom Rath explained in his book Eat, Move, Sleep that extended periods of sitting leads to "blood sugar and insulin levels [spiking] to dangerous levels" Yet, even "two minutes of leisurely walking every 20 minutes" proved sufficient to stabilize blood sugar levels.[194]

My conclusion: The more we sit the less we're fit.

It's not just about physical fitness. It's about mental fitness too.

IDLE BODY - IDLE MIND

Inactivity weakens the mind in two major ways:

1. It causes cognitive decline.
2. It depresses our mood.

COGNITIVE DECLINE - THE MORE YOU SIT THE MORE YOU FORGET

Sitting is one of the fastest ways to impoverish the brain. Researchers found that sitting thins the region of the brain that creates new memories. As sitting time increases, memory power decreases.[195]

In a 2018 study, researchers used MRI scans to observe the density or thinness of the MTL (the place where memories are stored) of people aged 45 to 75. The researchers found that "those who sat the longest had thinner MTL regions."[196] To prevent the decline of activity in our brain, the Mayo Clinic recommends taking a break from sitting every half hour.[197]

Sitting too much also reduces the amount of blood flowing through the blood vessels. Sluggish blood flow weakens the organs of the body, including the brain. If the blood is not flowing efficiently to and through the brain, it impairs thinking and memory.

NOT IN THE MOOD

Johns Hopkins Medicine found that inactivity "add[s] to feelings of anxiety and depression."[198] Ironically, inactivity also "leads to fatigue." Physiologically speaking, doing nothing can make us tired. Anxiety, depression, and fatigue, in turn, lead to "lower dopamine levels," which explains the lack of motivation to get up and do something.[199] So the sad downward spiral continues. In other words, too much rest can make us depressed.

Inactivity also increases the likelihood of stomach issues because the body is deprived of the natural detoxification that comes from exercise. In addition, idleness saps our muscle strength.

Walking and moving is part of our body maintenance plan. If we never move, it would be like a Ferrari sitting for five years doing nothing but being exposed to the environment. If it had any feelings, it would feel miserable with rusted-out body parts and clogged-up hoses. In time, things would fall apart, and misery would turn to hopelessness—especially if the local rats made a home under the hood, gnawing on the wires and causing more damage.

The same thing happens to our bodies. With little or no maintenance, they become hard to move and suffer damage. Instead of rats, our bodies suffer from viruses and germs gnawing at our systems. That damage can show up as stiff muscles, chronic aches and pains, tiredness, slouched shoulders, poor posture, poor balance, back pain, that "old and tired" feeling.

Maintenance is needed to get our high-precision machines working at peak performance. When it comes to physical fitness, movement is maintenance. What are the essentials to understanding fitness?

THE FOUR PILLARS OF PHYSICAL FITNESS

Many aches and pains are preventable through a proper balance of four components of physical fitness, all of which are "antiaging" activities:

1. **Cardiovascular Exercise** (a.k.a., cardio) - the kind of movement that makes our heart pump faster, increases blood flow, and makes us breathe harder. It's also called aerobic exercise because it improves oxygen consumption in the body. Examples are walking, running, swimming, cycling, and rowing.

2. **Strength Training** (a.k.a, muscle-building) - often done through lifting weights, strength training builds muscle, which is so necessary for most activities of life, and prevents injuries. An example of strengthening upper-body muscles is lifting dumbbells and doing pushups; for lower body, squats and leg presses. Pilates is an example of muscle conditioning that uses our own body weight instead of mechanical weights.

3. **Stretching** (a.k.a., stretching ☺) – gently extending muscles to improve flexibility and tone, reducing stiffness, especially needed as we age. All 640 muscles need to be stretched as part of our maintenance program.

4. **Posture** (a.k.a., "Stand up straight!") – when in proper alignment, our spine greatly reduces stress on our structure and frame, plus it keeps our muscles healthy, strong, and working correctly.

Most people feel stronger and more flexible within weeks of applying these four pillars of physical fitness results. It's what compels us to say, "I feel so much younger." See the list "16 (and Counting) Benefits of Exercise" below. Consult your doctor before beginning exercises if you have any concerns. Consider working with a trainer to make sure you perform each movement in a way that prevents injury.

THERE IS HOPE

Unlike the rusted-out car that needs to be scrapped or upgraded with new parts, our bodies have an amazing ability: they can upgrade themselves… with our help…cell by cell, muscle by muscle. Over time, most cells in our body are replaced—some within days, some within years. Exercise, together with high-octane fuel and plenty of water, will determine the vitality of those new cells. In fact, in many cases, the process works better than pills. When we exercise, our blood delivers the high-octane fuel to every system, cell, and muscle of our body more efficiently.

To appreciate the wide-ranging benefits of exercise on the entire body, consider the 11 major systems that make up our anatomy:

1. Circulatory (cardiovascular system – transports materials throughout body)
2. Digestive (breaks down food, turning it into fuel, excreting solid wastes)
3. Endocrine (produces hormones to regulate the body's functions)
4. Integumentary (covers and protects body from the outside world)
5. Lymphatic (includes the circulatory and immune system – fights invasions)
6. Muscular (works with skeletal system to allow us to move)
7. Nervous (allows us to sense and respond to stimuli)
8. Reproductive (produces babies)
9. Respiratory (part of circulatory system – takes in and distributes oxygen)
10. Skeletal (gives structure to the body)
11. Urinary (renal system – extracts waste from the blood and excretes it)

Each system requires exercise to serve us at peak capacity.

THE "UNFAIR" ADVANTAGES OF ACTIVE PEOPLE

Active people have an "unfair" health advantage over inactive people. Dr. Stephen Ilardi, a professor of clinical psychology and the author of The Depression Cure: The 6-Step Program to Beat Depression Without Drugs, explains why. "Exercise literally is medicine. It changes the brain and the body in beneficial ways that are more powerful than any pill you can take."[200]

In our pill-popping culture, the fact that there is research to support the claim that exercise—a natural remedy—is stronger than a pill is truly astounding. That fact means strolling around the neighborhood would not only improve our health but save money on medical prescriptions.

As noted earlier, there are magical places around the world where the entire culture has exercised themselves into the healthiest people in the world—the "Blue Zones."[201] In Blue Zone environments, they barely sit for more than 20 minutes before they move again. Some of us "normal" people might be tempted to think they must have ADHD. But for them, it's a lifestyle. Activity is naturally built into their environments.

For most of us, though, it's not so easy. We need to make a deliberate effort to incorporate exercise into our daily environment. Exercise wasn't built into my environment as a university student. In fact, studying late hours, barely dragging myself out of bed and rushing to class with maybe an apple in my hand, was about all the exercise I managed. But then one day, my college professor Dr. Paul Lehmann challenged me on my lifestyle.

He claimed that exercising one hour a day could help accomplish up to 14 hours of work in 10 hours. He explained that when we exercise, both the body and mind work more efficiently because more oxygen and fuel are carried to every system of the body. Fitness increases productivity.

To put the claim to the test, even though I "didn't have the time," I scheduled jogging into my day. I signed up for a PE course that included badminton and racquetball.

After a month, I noticed that studying took less effort, and I was getting more work done. My brain worked faster—just like he said it would. I almost felt guilty because I had an unfair advantage over some of my fellow students. Almost.

Years later, Dr. Wendy Suzuki, author of Healthy Brain, Happy Life, confirmed the exercise-brain connection. Suzuki is a professor of neural science and psychology in the Center for Neural Science at New York University. When she only went to the gym once or twice a week, as opposed to five or six times a week, her mood decreased, and it took more effort to write, making her work last longer. In a TED Talk, she said she became more productive, happier, and more energetic when she added exercise to her life.[202] In her book she noted that a study of 1,740 participants over the age of 65 showed a correlation between higher levels of exercise and lower incidence of dementia. Those who reported "exercising three times a week or more had a 32 percent reduced risk of developing dementia."[203]

But there is hope for the couch potato: "60 to 75 minutes of moderately intense" exercise each day could counter "the effects of too much sitting."[204]

Below is a sampling of the wonderful benefits that sedentary people are missing.

LIST OF 16 (AND COUNTING) BENEFITS OF EXERCISE

1. **Exercise Reduces Pain.**
   According to the U.S. CDC, "Regular physical activity can be an important way to reduce pain, improve function, and manage symptoms for people with arthritis and other chronic conditions."[205]

   In the last chapter, we learned that drinking water can, in certain cases, relieve joint pain. Now, add responsible exercise to that, and we compound the effects of natural pain relievers.

2. **Exercise Reduces Stress.**
    Want to bring more peace into your life? Exercise stimulates the release of endorphins—neurotransmitters in the brain that act as natural painkillers and mood elevators. Endorphins promote feelings of happiness, relaxation, and overall well-being, effectively reducing stress levels.[206]

    Physical activity also decreases the production of stress hormones such as cortisol and adrenaline. It is "probably the best anti-anxiety medication we have," says Dr. Drerup, sleep medicine psychologist.[207]

    Regular exercise also has been linked to improved sleep quality and can play a role in alleviating sleep disturbances that often accompany high levels of stress.

3. **Exercise Reduces Risk of Alzheimer's Disease.**
    Exercise reduces inflammation throughout the whole body, a major contributor to Alzheimer's disease, by triggering the immune system to produce fewer inflammatory proteins.[208] By downregulating the production of inflammatory molecules called cytokines, exercise leads to a decrease in overall inflammation, while stimulating the production of anti-inflammatory molecules, such as interleukin-10 (IL-10).

    Regular exercise can enhance insulin sensitivity, which is the body's ability to respond effectively to insulin. Insulin resistance is associated with chronic low-grade inflammation. By improving insulin sensitivity, exercise helps to regulate blood sugar levels and reduces the inflammation associated with insulin resistance.

    Exercise has also been shown to increase the production of endogenous antioxidants, which help neutralize harmful free radicals and reduce oxidative stress, known to contribute to inflammation.

4. **Exercise Makes You Feel Good.**

   Looking for a happy pill? After her research on the effect of exercise on the brain, Dr. Wendy Suzuki concluded, "Exercise is the most transformative thing you can do for your brain."[209] A single workout, for example, will "immediately raise levels of the feel-good neurotransmitters like dopamine, serotonin, and noradrenaline."[210] Exercise improves overall mood, which fights depression and anxiety. It's like taking a happy pill.

5. **Exercise Increases Your Focus.**

   Need to concentrate on your work or your teacher? Exercise boosts our ability to give attention and focus. The effect lasts two hours after the exercise is finished. An increased ability to focus also helps with willpower,[211] yet another tool to help us establish healthy habits.

6. **Exercise Speeds Up Reaction Times.**

   You are driving a car, and you see a child run out in front of you. What do you do? Immediately, you swerve and brake. Whether you do that fast enough to save his life is determined by the speed of your reaction time—that time between stimulus and response. Regular exercise speeds up the reaction time.[212] Exercise could save a life.

7. **Exercise Makes You Smarter.**

   Looking to increase your IQ? "Many experts recommend exercise as their number one piece of advice for optimal brain health."[213] The reason they make such a bold claim is because exercise forms new neurons in the brain (neurogenesis).

   Physical activity pumps more nutrients and oxygen through the blood. The improved blood flow increases neurosynaptic connections (neuroplasticity) and activity in the brain. More connections mean faster thinking—great when in a social setting or at the workplace. During that whole process, new brain cells are formed in the hippocampus, improving memory, which is needed for intelligence.[214]

8. **Exercise Gives You Better Sleep.**
Exercise helps us sleep better by reducing stress and anxiety while inducing the "sleep drive," the body's need to rest. If we exercise outdoors, the natural sunlight helps the body set the circadian rhythm—the sleep-wake cycle. With a good night's sleep, we think better, look better, and feel better (more in Chapter 12).

Research has even shown that exercise can be as effective as pre-scription sleep medication, thus saving us the expense of medication or a doctor's visit.[215]

9. **Exercise Makes You Feel Younger.**
Strengthening our muscles, especially the core muscles, gives us more physical power. The core muscles are the group of muscles that include buttocks, hip, abdomen, and trunk muscles that support the spine. A stronger core boosts independence and decreases injury risk. That's because our core is critical for nearly every move we make, from bending and reaching to twisting and standing.[216] Core strength gives that wonderful sensation of feeling younger.

10. **Exercise Helps to Shed Unwanted Fat.**
At a height of 5'1", Hulda Crooks "gorged on meat and candy," which increased her weight to 160 pounds, the "obese" category. Later, she moved to Loma Linda, California, and lived in one of the world's five "Blue Zones."

After learning about the amazing benefits of exercise and diet, she changed her eating habits and lifestyle to match those who lived there. Despite the significant impact of diet on her weight, Hulda credited exercise as the reason her weight dropped to 115 pounds.

She climbed mountains in her 50s, jogged a 12-minute mile at 80, and continued climbing mountains into her 90s. She climbed Mount Whitney's 14,505-foot peak so many times, she was called Grandma Whitney. In 1990, the U.S. Congress named "Crooks Peak" in her honor. Prioritizing exercise as a crucial part of her lifestyle, she kept obesity at bay until she died at 101 years of age.[217]

We don't have to climb mountains at 90. But we can be inspired by Hulda Crooks' example.

11. Exercise Slows Aging.
Hulda Crooks is not alone. A growing body of evidence shows that exercise can "protect brain health and function – even into old age."[218] We may not feel younger right after a wearisome workout, but after the recovery period and in time we will feel more alive.

12. Exercise Increases Longevity.
The Arthritis Foundation found that "those who exercise regularly in their 50's and 60's are 35% less likely to die over the next 8 years than their non-walking counterparts"[219] – yet another reason exercise is a major contributor to health and longevity.

13. Exercise Increases Waste-Removal Efficiency.
Since exercise improves circulation, waste removal from the body is also more efficient. Think of a stagnant stream in the woods starting to flow faster and faster. As it moves faster, the built-up bacteria are swept downstream making the water cleaner. In the same way, when exercise increases blood flow, the toxic by-products that have accumulated in the blood vessels throughout the day are swept to the liver and kidneys for later removal.

14. Exercise Boosts Your Confidence.

Exercise is known to release endorphins—the hormones of happiness and well-being. When we feel better emotionally, it can positively affect our self-esteem and confidence.

Regular exercise increases endurance, flexibility, balance, and overall physical capability. Feeling more capable and independent in performing tasks and activities can boost self-esteem and confidence.

15. Exercise Reduces Type 2 Diabetes.

Just getting off the couch and standing every half hour "removes glucose from the bloodstream." It also "decreases fat levels." This, in turn, drops our "risk for insulin resistance, a major symptom of type II diabetes."[220]

16. Exercise Saves Money.

Regular exercise minimizes expenditures on medication and hospital bills. Imagine if there were a pill that could give us all 16 benefits mentioned here. It would be the most powerful pill in the world and make the pharmaceutical company that patented it rich. But, in many cases, we don't need a pill.

Movement is medicine. And movement is free.

Here's a side benefit my friend Bill noticed. He reminded me that exercise can even save money on heating bills in cooler weather. He exercises outside in the morning, playing hockey, walking, or cycling. When he comes back into his house, his blood is coursing through his circulatory system, generating heat for hours afterward, allowing him to turn the heat down in his house. His body generated heat for free, potentially saving hundreds of dollars per year on heating bills.

POSTURE IS POWER

Physical fitness is not just about movement. It's about alignment. Those whose work is done primarily at a desk trigger structural injuries from slouching and overusing the hand and arm muscles through repetitive motions on the computer, and the damage can be debilitating.

Office lifestyle took its toll on me. It was worse because, at the time, I was overweight. My weakest area from this lifestyle was in my lower back. For years, I ignored that ache in my back and the pain in my feet until I couldn't walk.

Even though I "had no time," I visited my doctor. He referred me to a chiropractor and then to a physiotherapist. I was diagnosed with plantar fasciitis, inflammation of the band of tissue (fascia) that acts as a shock absorber connecting the heel to the toes.

"Everything is connected," the physiotherapist explained. "If you want your feet to heal, you need better posture."

Posture? I didn't believe him.

Sensing my doubt, he had me stand with feet shoulder-width apart. "Squeeze the buttocks muscles and squeeze the Kegel (pelvic floor) muscles – the ones that stop the flow of urine. Tighten your abs slightly. Put shoulders back and down and stand as if you are gently pulling the floor apart with your feet."

Immediately, I felt a release of pressure in my lower back.

"How often should I do this?" I asked. I expected him to prescribe this exercise once or twice a day for 10 seconds at a time.

"Every time you stand," he said. "Every day." He paused. "For the rest of your life."

If I wanted my freedom back, I needed a strong core that would give me proper alignment. Good posture affects the whole body, from the way it functions, to the amount of pain it is in, to the amount of oxygen intake.

It took several months with consistent focus to recover my freedom. I made sure to stand at my desk half the time and walk whenever I took a phone call. I vowed never to sit for more than 30 minutes at a time. I have continued that practice now for 10 years, resulting in my ability to walk and run for miles.

Besides freeing up airways for more oxygen, I found that good posture protects and lessens injury, especially the kind that comes from stress on the spine and joints.

A note of caution: Exercise can cause injury, especially if we have been sedentary for a long time. What is good for one body may be harmful for another. Listen to your body and seek proper instruction on the correct posture for each exercise and which exercises to do for your unique situation.

Often, to achieve better posture requires a mixture of working with professionals and trainers who know how to safely help us build and strengthen the right muscles. Instructors can also guide us in working safely with our body structure to encourage better alignment.

THE NEED FOR STRETCHING

An important factor in helping to strive for better posture is to make stretching part of our daily routine. Some of my senior friends say that when they were younger, they would jump out of bed and get to work.

Now they slip out of bed and do stretching and exercises before going any-where. Otherwise, they could hardly move because of the aches and pains.

Miranda Esmonde-White, a former ballerina, is one person who can help when our muscles and joints get stiff or "seize up." She created the stretching workout program, Essentrics, and led the long-running American PBS TV show, Classical Stretch. She a wrote a book called Aging Backwards: Reverse the Aging Process and Look 10 Years Younger in 30 Minutes a Day.

What is the secret to aging backwards according to Esmonde-White? Stretching. Our 640 skeletal muscles, 206 bones, and 360 joints are sur-rounded by a web of connective tissue. She said, "When they are all func-tioning correctly, we feel young." We enhance their functioning by gentle movement and stretching.

Esmonde-White found success in relieving the aches and pains of tens of thousands of people through this method. She has trained thousands of fitness instructors and Olympians on how to prepare their bodies for pain-free performance.

In her classes, she speaks of liberating our joints of plaque-like material that contributes to pain, by gentle stretches and a broad range of movement. The practice allows synovial fluid, a joint lubricant, to move into the joints and "relieve us of pain."[221]

She promises that if we spend the next 30 days doing healthy stretching and movement, we will start the process of aging backwards.

You can find her on YouTube at "Classical Stretch by Essentrics."

My wife and I "stretch with Miranda" almost every morning before our walk. Just yesterday, June said, "I feel more flexible after our stretches with Miranda this morning."

I did too.

By this point, you might be feeling overwhelmed with all the different types of exercises that are needed to keep a person healthy. You may be wondering how to fit it into your busy day. Start with simplifying it.

Think of the four pillars of physical fitness mentioned above:

1. Strength training
2. Cardio
3. Stretching
4. Posture

Look for opportunities to integrate them into your day.

Below are ideas of small changes you can make in your lifestyle that can make big differences. These are some of the possible habits you can be thinking about when you "Launch Your Plan."

TIPS FOR INTEGRATING EXERCISE INTO YOUR DAY

1. **Use the Stairs:** Adopt a new mindset that says, "Taking the elevator is a wasted opportunity to use the stairs."

2. **Walk:** Start your day (or end it) with a walk. You get the added benefits of fresh air and sunlight. If you walk with a partner, you are also experiencing social connection. You can also walk around the office or house while talking on the phone. I consistently clocked in 3,000-4,000 steps during an office day by walking while talking. On one exceptionally busy day on the phone, I was able to get in 9,000 steps—all before I went for my walk.

3. **Consider a Treadmill Desk:** Install a treadmill desk. Walk slowly—1 mph—while on your computer. My friend Tom installed one in his office. It helped keep him trim.

4. **Use a Desktop Riser:** What do Ernest Hemingway, Charles Dickens, Stan Lee, Winston Churchill, and Michael Dell have in common? They all stood at their desks.[222] I often stand at my desk on a soft mat with my laptop up on a desktop riser.

    After standing, practicing proper posture, it feels so good to sit again. The idea is to not stay in the same position any longer than 20 or 30 minutes. The body was made to move. Alternate between standing and sitting.

5. **Buy an Exercise Ball:** Include sitting on an exercise ball at your desk to strengthen your core with minimal effort. You have to continually make micro adjustments to keep on top of it. Again, don't think of it as something you have to sit on all day long. As above, alternate between standing and sitting.

6. **Join a Gym:** It's healthier to exercise outdoors, but some might be more motivated if they join a local gym and keep a regular schedule, especially if friends are waiting for them there. It can be fun to play racquetball with a group of friends or join a spin class and suffer together with other willing victims. It can also provide opportunities to "lovify your life" by bonding with your fellow participants. (Think of all the oxytocin you'll produce.) Gyms are also great places to meet your trainer who can tailor the right set of exercises for you and teach you how to do them properly.

7. **Play:** If it's safe for you to do, simply tumbling with your friends, kids, or grandchildren on the living room floor can increase blood flow, inducing a healthy glow. Other floor games like

Twister or table competitions like arm wrestling might be a fun option. The only rule is to move without breaking anything or getting injured.

8. **Take Short Exercise Breaks:** Every 30 minutes, stand up and do squats for two minutes, walk, drink water, say hi to a coworker, visit the washroom, do pushups, do a stretch sequence, throw in a load of clothes in the washer, or check on your children. Anything quick and active that gets the circulation going.

9. **Exercise While Sitting:** If you don't feel like standing up to counteract the damaging effects of sitting, try exercising while sitting—anything that tenses and relaxes muscle groups. You could do it while sitting at your desk, driving a car, watching a video, or flying on an airplane.

    Some examples include:

    a. squeezing your buttocks 20 times.
    b. lifting your feet two inches off the floor 20 times.
    c. squeezing your knees together 20 times.
    d. doing 20 rounds of Kegels.
    e. tightening all muscle groups in your body 20 times.
    f. tightening your abs 20 times.
    g. doing rounds of deep breathing.
    h. doing seat exercises while driving—like pushing your head against the head rest, or stretching your neck, arms, and fingers at the stop lights.

10. **Exercise Your Face Muscles:** Since your face is what most people see most of the time, why not give yourself a fit face? For example, open up your mouth as wide as you can and slowly form your mouth into a big smile. Do 20 of these smiles as part

of your morning routine. These and other face exercises will give you a non-surgical facelift. My apologies to the plastic surgery industry. There are YouTube videos that give face muscle exercise tutorials. For example, "Blush With me-Parmita" gives great pointers on how to do "face yoga."

11. **Stand Up at Every Opportunity:** Examples include when talking, reading, writing, waiting. Standing up burns twice the calories as sitting.

12. **Seek Social Support:** Walk with a friend, a workout buddy, or go to an exercise class together. That way you get the added benefit of social connection. My accountant friend Gerald and his wife, Joyce, do stretching exercises on Zoom with their physiotherapist daughter, Jerralyn, even though she lives hundreds of miles away.

We've looked at the dangers of inactivity and the benefits of healthy activity using strength-building, cardio, stretching, and proper posture. Plus, we gave a few tips on integrating exercise into your daily life.

We've learned that exercise gives us physical and mental power. But that's only part of the story. It's not just about having more power; it's about having full power. That's why we need to discover why exercising outdoors is superior to exercising indoors. We will give some fun tips on how to do it in the next chapter, which includes the checklist that applies to both chapters.

CHAPTER 11

EXERCISE OUTDOORS—PART 2:

THREE BENEFITS IN ONE

Walking is a man's best medicine.

Hippocrates

I saw no way out of a stressful situation.

In the middle of my third year of university working on a BA, like many students, I was taking a full load of courses and working a job to pay the bills. My job was the editor-in-chief of the university's newspaper, a responsibility that required me to be on the Student Association. While I enjoyed the creativity and collaboration of planning events for students, the SA drained me of time and energy.

I was such a perfectionist and had a hard time keeping on top of my studies and my always-urgent newspaper duties. Adrenaline kept me going late into the nights, many times hovering over backlit tables in windowless rooms. I often found myself falling asleep in class. I knew I had to do something about this mess I created for myself. But every time I thought about it, notions of debt and worry invaded my mind. I was anxious over whether I'd land a job once I graduated. A foreboding darkness loomed over me.

This kind of stress is not unusual for people in or out of the university setting. But for me, one afternoon, when I couldn't take it anymore, I did something "irresponsible."

I ran away.

It turned out to be the best thing I could have done. Plus, I discovered another contributor to optimal vitality.

I grabbed my hiking boots and took off. I stomped through the forest and scrambled over fallen trees. But as time went on, my stride relaxed to a stroll as I became more conscious of the warm sun spilling through the tree branches. Flowers and ferns were novel sights for my tired eyes. I watched the squirrels scurry up trees and listened to the birds singing their songs. The deeper I traveled into the canopy of trees, the more I was captured by the scents and sounds of living greenery. I inhaled the fresh air, energized with aromas of living pine, spruce, and fir.

Hours passed. Nature's serenity was working its charm. By the time I left the forest, I had forgotten why I was worried. I was fueled with motivation to face the work, studies, and challenges that laid before me. What I didn't know then, but have since learned, was something pharmaceutical companies spent decades and dollars searching for—a medicine for stress. But for many of us, stress medicine is free for the taking—compliments of Mother Nature.

That day I discovered the therapeutic power of moving in the great outdoors. What I thought was running away turned out to be a valuable coping method.

If you're feeling the pressure to get away for a while, there's a lot of science to back you up. Most of the American population is missing out on the free therapy provided by nature. According to a study sponsored by the Environmental Protection Agency, the average American spends 93% of their time indoors.[223] Unfortunately, the indoor lifestyle has a negative impact on human well-being and may even contribute to various illnesses, including respiratory diseases. Throughout the world, over two million people die of causes traceable to indoor air pollution.[224]

One of the reasons why sunlight, for example, makes us feel good is because of its ultraviolet B rays. UVB rays, when received in moderation, cause human skin to produce beta-endorphins that reduce pain. Reduced pain promotes a relaxed feeling of well-being and lowers depression.[225]

Turns out, I wasn't the only one who found the secret to serenity. Millions of people throughout millennia have enjoyed the medicine-like benefits of sunlight and fresh air. When we take regular doses of nature's medicine, it works wonders on our bodies, minds, and spirits.

The Japanese even have a name for this transformative experience. They call it a "forest bath."[226] It's simply immersing yourself in nature and letting your mind and your five senses rest on your immediate surroundings. A forest bath reduces cortisol levels (the stress hormone) and increases serotonin levels (the "feel-good" hormone).

Forest baths are catching on. Tall Tree Integrated Health in British Columbia has a certified forest therapy guide to take groups on forest therapy walks to help the participants achieve more calmness, an increased sense of well-being and positive outlook, clarity of mind, and increased vitality.[227]

In the forest, phytoncides emanate from the leaves of the trees, strengthening our immune system—the "bodyguard" of our body. They empower our bodies to combat infections and even fight against cancer. Within our immune system lives a specialized group of white blood cells known as natural killer (NK) cells. These exceptional cells have the ability to actively seek out and destroy abnormal or infected cells, including cancer cells.

Their activity is enhanced during a forest bath.[228] Studies have found that forest therapy can even be used to supplement treatment for major depressive disorder, increase working memory capacity, improve cognition, and enhance positive emotions.[229]

According to the World Health Organization, depression is the world's leading cause of disability worldwide.[230] Regular doses of Mother Nature's remedies could be one of the first lines of defense in a therapeutic strategy for treating depression.

Dr. Roger Seheult, introduced earlier, said, "There is a number of psychiatric diseases that are tied to sun and lack of sun." For example, seasonal affective disorder, SAD, "happens almost exclusively to people in the winter time who are not getting enough sun exposure."[231]

Other studies echo these findings. One analysis[232] of 10 studies found that spending time in a green environment improved mood and self-esteem. And according to the American Psychological Association, "exposure to nature" is linked to such benefits as "improved attention, lower stress, better mood and even upticks in empathy and cooperation."[233]

Imagine a world in which parents and children, teachers and students, leaders and citizens had less anxiety, less depression, lower stress, better mood, more empathy, and a greater desire to cooperate with others? We have the means to contribute to such a world.

In addition to all those pluses, the evidence also strongly suggests that experiencing nature boosts academic learning and personal development.[234] So, not only does outdoor time calm our emotions, it also stimulates our brains. It's kind of like Mother Nature helping us with our homework.

Here are other advantages of being and moving in the great outdoors.

VITAMIN D: THE SUNSHINE VITAMIN FUELING VITALITY

The sun is famous for assisting our bodies in making Vitamin D, so critical for maintaining healthy bone density and managing calcium levels. But here's a bonus: Vitamin D is also an antioxidant that strengthens our immune system.[235] Simply by being outside, we can fight off diseases and infections more easily, and heal faster.

Just taking vitamin D tablets or drops, however, isn't enough. Without exposure to the sun, taking vitamin D actually risks weakening our immune system.[236] We are better able to absorb Vitamin D and other healing properties of Mother Nature when we get outside.

Sunlight exposure has even more benefits. One scientific report said that sunlight protects us from Type 1 diabetes, multiple sclerosis (MS), several forms of cancer, including colon, breast, and prostate and non-Hodgkin lymphoma.[237]

Seeing all the research on the positive effects of sunlight and nature gave me an "aha" moment: Exercise is only part of the story. The outdoors part of "Exercise Outdoors" is significant too.

For example, when my wife was recovering from her hernia surgery and preparing to run in the Terry Fox Run, one of the reasons we believed she made such a remarkable recovery was because she exercised regularly. But now, after seeing what outdoor activity can do, we have to credit the whole package—the healing properties of sunlight, vegetation, and fresh oxygen.

Remember Frances Greger in Chapter 6? She was the 65-year-old heart patient who was given a year to live after the doctors "did all they could." Then she "plantified" her diet and exercised her body. And within three weeks, her damaged cells showed signs of recovering, and her health improved so much that she could walk 10 miles a day.[238]

But it wasn't just the diet and exercise that empowered Frances to defy the doctor's dire prediction. She also drew strength from the whole of nature's formula, which included healthy doses of sunlight and fresh air. While it would be difficult to isolate the "exercise" benefits from the "outdoors" benefits, it seems very likely that nature played a significant role in her extra 31 years of life.

WHAT ABOUT SKIN CANCER?

Shouldn't we stay away from the sun to avoid skin cancer? That depends. As one study reported in the journal Blood Purification, "Sun avoidance may carry more of a cost than benefit for overall good health."[239] Additionally, Dr. Timothy J. Arnott, medical director of Rocky Mountain Lifestyle Center, adds more punch. He said, "If you don't get sunlight, all of the cells of your body will move in the direction of cancer."[240] In other words, by trying to avoid skin cancer, many of us are doing the very thing that will trigger our cells to create cancer.

So, how do we satisfy our need for sunlight without risking exposure to skin cancer? The first counsel the scientific community gives us is to avoid sunburn at all costs. It destroys skin cells that may become cancerous years down the road.[241]

The amount of sunlight we need depends on several factors such as the pigment of our skin and what part of the world we live in. Dr. Eddie Ramirez, director of research at Weimer University in California, said, "Dark-skinned people need more sunlight whereas light-skinned people need less sunlight."[242] Note that sunlight is not the same as sunshine. Even though we may not see the sunshine on a cloudy day, we are still getting sunlight, but less so on a rainy day.

Here is what to do to take advantage of the sun's benefits yet mitigate against the risks:

1. Expose yourself to 10-30 minutes of sun a day. Stay on the lesser end of that (closer to 10-15 minutes) if you are fair-skinned, more (15-30 minutes) if darker-skinned. Some studies even suggest darker-skinned people may need 30-180 more minutes of sunlight to maintain healthy levels of Vitamin D.[243]

2. After your 10-30 minutes of healthy sun exposure, put on natural sunblock or wear a hat. Dr. Lyndi Schwartz, program director of internal medicine residency at Kettering Health, said, "Expose the majority of your skin to full sunlight, without the sunblock, for probably about 20 minutes a day, maybe you could go up to 30 maximum. Then after that, put on the [natural] sunblock." That's enough sun to get your vitamin D.[244] Most hats block out the damaging effects of ultraviolet rays but allow in the beneficial effects of infrared and near-infrared rays. Remember most hats don't protect the back of the neck.

FRESH AIR IS MEDICINE

Another healing property of spending time in nature that is rarely talked about, but extremely powerful, is fresh air.

We humans breathe in oxygen as fuel and breathe out carbon dioxide as waste. In a convenient reversal, the plant world performs the exact opposite. It absorbs our carbon dioxide and releases oxygen, the very substance we need to thrive. It's a perfect system.

So, being around forests, fields, and plants, even plants in our home, is a vitality booster. When we take deep breaths of fresh air, our heart relaxes, exerting less effort to circulate the blood around the body, which in turn, can lower our blood pressure and can help us live longer.[245]

That's not the only benefit. Breathing in greater amounts of oxygen widens the blood vessels in our lungs, "which improves cleansing and tissue repair within them."[246] During the height of the COVID pandemic, Dr. Fitzgerald, professor at the Royal Academy of Engineering at England's Cambridge University, said, "Research shows that bringing in a good supply of fresh air to dilute and disperse the [corona] virus can cut the risk of infection by 70-80%." He refuses to stay in a room that is not well-ventilated.[247] While the research is not complete, this practice may give hope to those who have suffered lung damage.

In the last chapter, we learned that exercise causes the blood to circulate better throughout the body. Breathing fresh air adds to that benefit. "As your lungs take in more fresh air, the oxygen levels in your blood go up. Higher oxygen levels mean more of it circulates to your brain, which helps you feel energized and improves your ability to concentrate and remember information."[248] Studies have shown that simply being outdoors has a way of refreshing the body and mind.

Or, at the very least, open a window.

BRING THE OUTDOORS INSIDE

The ill effects of living in close, poorly ventilated rooms are numerous. Living in homes or working in buildings with poor air circulation affects all the systems of the body. The feebleness starts with the respiratory system, which then affects the circulatory system by making the blood move sluggishly. When the body is drained of energy, we become vulnerable to higher risk levels of fevers and other acute diseases.

An article from the American Journal of Lifestyle Medicine explains why.

According to the EPA (Environmental Protection Agency), indoor levels of pollutants may be up to 100 times higher than outdoor pollutant levels and have been ranked among the top 5 environmental risks to the public. There has been a strong correlation between air quality and health.[249]

The threat of high levels of indoor pollutants alone would tell us to keep the windows open as much as possible.

To avoid toxic air in the house:

1. Open windows, unless you know the outside air is worse because of high levels of allergens or if the weather is too extreme. Also, frequently change air filters, especially the one in your air conditioner. When vacuuming, use airtight vacuum cleaners with a clean dust bag or chamber so the dust doesn't go back into the air.
2. Unless you are living in extreme temperatures, sleep with windows open. Well-ventilated bedrooms, day and night, will benefit your sleep. When you read the next chapter, you will be very motivated to do all you can to get a good night's sleep.

Now that we see the benefit of sunlight and fresh air, here are tips on how to use the outdoors as our gymnasium.

HOW TO USE THE OUTDOORS AS YOUR GYMNASIUM

Our grandparents didn't have to think about "working out" because their agrarian, labor-intensive lifestyle provided all the muscle-building protection they needed to fight off the chronic diseases we know today. They received the benefits of a workout without "working out."

Now, thanks to our labor-saving devices and indoor lifestyle, we expose ourselves to a blinding array of modern diseases. So, if you are thinking of putting the "out" back into working out, read on.

As Darryl Edwards said in a TEDx talk in Royal Tunbridge Wells, "The world is your gym."[250] Think of it as Mother Nature passing out free memberships to her outdoor gym—complete with all the lifesaving perks.

June and I take advantage of the great outdoors whenever we can and enjoy "gamifying" our walks. After we began using our pedometers, we found that one hour of walking was roughly equivalent to 6,500 steps. As we developed more fitness, we found we were taking fewer steps—only 6,200 steps—to cover the same distance, presumably because our strides were longer and more energetic. The reduction upped the challenge to find ways to add on more steps.

When we were starting out in the first couple of years of counting our steps, I noticed an unsettling pattern. By the end of the day, June always had about 20% more steps than I did. And for some fiendish reason she took great delight in this. She would put on a sweet, humble act asking me at the end of the day, with a twinkle in her eye, "How many steps did you get?"

I'd look at my pedometer, and say, "Approximately 10,200 steps. You?"

She would say, "I beat you!" She raised her arms above her head in victory. "12,342 steps."

"Congratulations," I muttered.

She smiled widely.

"How do you always beat me?" I grumbled.

She shrugged.

"I'll beat you tomorrow," I'd say. But I never do.

At least now I had a scientific basis for considering the hypothesis that a woman's life might be more active than a man's. Especially when you add her indoor steps to her outdoor steps. Or maybe I should just do the laundry more—and cooking, cleaning, vacuuming, and the other household chores that add up the steps.

Even though I always lose, measuring is motivating.

Since I started to measure my steps, I was more likely to get out more, or get up and do more things around the house. One little project might give me another 800 steps. When I added those steps, I'm sure I could feel the dopamine surging through my synapses. Plus, just once, I might surpass my wife.

June, clever as she is, found many opportunities to capitalize on my competitive nature. More than once she has poured on the sweet charm and said, "Honey, could you do this one thing for me?" And then she would add enticingly, "It would give you more steps."

Usually, it works. I love making her happy and removing an item from the "honey do" list always earns me points with her.

See? Every effort—big or small—can increase your "Lovify Your Life" score and your "Exercise Outdoors" score at the same time. Success in life is not about finding that one silver bullet. It's about finding ways to work all parts of the golden formula.

THINGS TO DO IN MOTHER NATURE'S GYM

Here are ways to take advantage of your free membership with Mother Nature's gym:

1. **Listen while you walk:** One of the most painless ways to exercise outdoors is to listen to an audiobook while walking… unless you're walking with your wife, that is. In that case, skip the audiobook ☺.

    Get free audiobooks from your local library. One day, I tallied up 21,000 steps listening to Dr. Michael Greger's book, *How Not to Die*. The book swept me away as I enjoyed fresh air, sunlight, and invigorating oxygen. Whenever I wanted to take notes, I would pause the audio and use the microphone app to dictate my thoughts.

2. **Open windows:** When you can't make it outside, bring the outside in. Open windows when possible. When the weather cooperates, I enjoy the energizing oxygen coming through open windows.

3. **Introduce walking meetings:** Turn office meetings into walking meetings, if work permits, by leaving the office and walking around the block or Zooming in from the park. I almost feel as if I am cheating…getting two things done at once.

4. **Make it fun:** Meet up with a friend at the park, listen to music, or enjoy the sounds of nature. Another option is to gamify

your exercise by charting your progress, or if it's safe to do so, counting the wildlife or wild plants you see along the way.

5. **Park farther away:** An easy opportunity that many people miss is parking at the far side of the shopping mall parking lot, allowing for a longer walk to the entrance. If you live in a busy town or city, you might even save time because you won't be fighting for the closest spot.

6. **Ride a bike:** Ride a bike for exercise or recreation. Bike to work if you can do so safely. Like most outdoor exercise, bike riding will boost your physical and mental health, immune system, muscles, lungs, heart, sleep, and brain power. It also has the added benefit of being great exercise for strengthening your knees.[251]

7. **Walk after a meal:** Leisure walking after you eat, even for 10-15 minutes, improves digestion, fights against "peptic ulcers, heartburn, irritable bowel syndrome (IBS), diverticular disease, constipation, and colorectal cancer," and improves blood sugar management.[252]

Getting outdoors for exercise, sunlight, and fresh air (three benefits in one activity) is just what Dr. Mother Nature ordered. Complete the checklist below to gauge how you are doing on exercising outdoors.

And now for the most surprising ingredient in nature's formula for body-mind vitality. If you're ready to take a lifestyle prescription that shields against cancer, dementia, and heart disease, while enhancing attractiveness, memory, creativity, happiness, and at the same time reducing food cravings, depression, and anxiety—and all achievable lying down—turn to the next chapter for the last vital principle of FULL POWER.

CHECKLIST FOR

"EXERCISE OUTDOORS"

	To what degree am I exercising outdoors? On a scale of 0-10, answer these questions, based on the last seven days. The cumulative sum of all nine end-of-chapter checklists will result in a total out of 100.	
1	I completed a strength-building routine for my core (buttocks, hip, abdomen) unless I was recovering between workout days.	
2	I completed a strength-building routine that built up my upper body unless I was recovering between workout days.	
3	I could rise from a sitting position without using my hands.	
4	I walked at least 1/2 hour a day.	
5	I rose and moved after each half hour of sitting.	
6	I stretched for 10-30 minutes each day.	
7	I performed daily exercises and stretches that enhanced my posture.	
8	I built movement into my daily routines (i.e., taking the stairs, cycling to work).	
9	I spent at least an hour outdoors, ensuring exposure to sunlight and fresh air, and applied healthy sunblock as needed.	
10	I adjusted my exercise intensity according to my fitness level.	
	Total out of 100	
	Divide by 10 for average out of 10	

CHAPTER 12

REST UP:

HARNESS THE SURPRISING POWER OF RESTORATIVE REST

The shorter your sleep, the shorter your lifespan.
Dr. Matthew Walker

Highway 19, Vancouver Island's main north-south travel route, boasted a stunning view of evergreen trees and a deep-blue sky on a spring afternoon. On this same beautiful day, however, another highway statistic was recorded. For my family, it was more than a mere statistic.

My wife, son, and I were making great time heading north past the ferry port of Nanaimo. We led a convoy of five vehicles conveying June's seventh- and eighth-graders returning from a fun class trip in the capital city of Victoria two hours south.

My eyelids grew heavy from working an exhausting week, whirlwind weekend, and a late evening the night before. Unable to stifle my yawn, I said, "Honey, I'm getting sleepy." I glanced at her relaxing in her seat. "Do you mind driving for a while?"

She also yawned. "I'm sleepy too." She shifted in her seat facing me. "How about if I sleep for 10 minutes, then we can switch?"

My eyes back on the road, I said, "Good idea."

Bad idea.

Within five minutes, sleep had overtaken me while the vehicle was going 60 mph (100km/h). The car flew off the road down a 12-foot incline that led into a green field.

I awoke bumping along the field, the noise of flying dirt grating against the undercarriage.

June awoke with a scream as we barreled toward a grove of fir trees.

I yanked the steering wheel left to ascend the embankment to maneuver our jostling car back up onto the highway.

As we crested the slide slope reaching the highway, the car tipped on its two right wheels. June, seeing the pavement inches from her window, let out another scream. The car continued its flip, crashing onto its roof, shattering glass. The driver's side took the most impact and enclosed around me like a metal shroud.

The three of us hung upside down by our seatbelts. The momentum had propelled me out the driver's window, my lower body held back by the seat belt. My upper body was out of the car being dragged down the highway like a stuffed doll.

The sound of sliding, scraping metal filled my ears. The granulated asphalt passed vividly an inch beneath my eyes as my forehead scraped along the road. I put my forearm down to lift my head, but the road instantly tore through my sleeve like giant sandpaper, driving dirt and gravel into my hand. I jerked my arm away. My head fell back on the road as the car headed straight for the concrete median barrier.

I braced for impact and the pain of broken bones. But, mercifully, we grinded to a halt.

Eerie silence hung in the air. A cold dread rippled through me. "Everyone alright? June? Michael?"

No answer.

I strained to listen, hoping for even a trace of a voice.

After what felt like an eternity, I heard my wife's voice, weakened, "Yes."

"Thank God."

"Michael? Are you alright?"

He groaned, then said in pain, "Y-y-yes."

I wanted—I needed—to jump to their aid. But I was trapped and helpless.

Later I learned June was able to unfasten her seatbelt and fall on top of the ceiling. She squeezed through her narrowed window on her stomach. Afraid the gas tank would explode, she rapidly crawled on her hands and knees over broken glass and grit around the car to save Michael and me.

She saw the metal body of the car crumpled around me and knew she wouldn't be able to help. She turned her attention to Michael, who dangled from his seat. The seatbelt had moved around his neck, cutting off part of his air supply.

"Hold on, Michael, I'm coming," June called out. "I'm going to get underneath you to push you up so you can breathe better."

She crawled through his window space, positioned herself under Michael and arched her back into his stomach. Her maneuver lifted him toward the seat and eased the pressure of the belt around his neck and chest.

Minutes later a fellow motorist rushed onto the scene and immediately unfastened Michael's seatbelt. Within seconds our boy was out of the car.

Gary and Gayle, classroom parents, and nurses rushed up. The senior nurse asked, "Can you wiggle your toes?"

"Yes." But I couldn't move my head to see them.

They took turns applying medical gauze to my bleeding forehead. I winced from the pain of their touch as the welcoming sound of sirens wailed in the distance.

Sleepiness started to take over me.

"Stay awake," one nurse ordered. "Tell us about yourself."

I started telling them about my day job when the sound of approaching sirens stopped. Heavy footsteps approached.

A man's voice near me said, "I'm going to cut your seatbelt to get you free."

"Thank you," I whispered.

Soon I heard metal creaking as they applied the "jaws of life," a hydraulic rescue tool to spread the door apart from the body of the car. Paramedics pulled me out holding my head in place to prevent further injury. I was glad for the numbness I felt as they put on a neck brace and laid me on a stretcher. They checked my vitals, then loaded the stretcher into an ambulance to take me to the hospital.

I am grateful for many things that day: the field being in the right place amid the trees, seatbelts, not crashing into the median barrier, not hitting other cars, plus gratitude to the semitruck driver who stopped the traffic behind us, the two nurses, the paramedics, the rescue crew with the powerful "jaws of life," the concerned students and their helpful parents, and Canada's emergency system. But mostly, I am grateful that my precious family survived.

June and I needed stitches, and the three of us have suffered neck problems ever after. I am thankful for the doctors, nurses, physiotherapists, massage therapists, and other medical personnel, who helped us through our recovery time.

THE DANGERS OF DROWSINESS

That's the story behind just one highway statistic. They are stories that begin with a drowsy driver and often end with injuries that bring lifelong impairment or death. Each year in the U.S., there are 328,000 more drowsy-driving crashes; 109,000 of them result in injury; 6,400 of them result in death.[253]

From our story, I draw two dramatic lessons:

1. **Accident risk increases with sleep deprivation**. Sleep deprivation can put us in very dangerous situations. My family was one of the fortunate ones. We lived. And we can cope with our injuries. But the fact remains, I ignored the warning signs—the prolonged work hours, late nights, mounting stress, heavy eyelids, and the false self-assurance that I could overcome drowsiness with sheer determination. And my family paid for my poor judgment.

Expanding the picture from drowsy driving to drowsy working, "fatigue-related errors" kill someone approximately every hour in the U.S.[254] Some of the most tragic disasters are caused by fatigue-related impairment: the Exxon Valdez oil spill that took place in Prince William Sound, Alaska, one of the worst man-made environmental disasters, and the significant accident in U.S. power plant history at Three Mile Island in Harrisburg, Pennsylvania, to name just two, each coming with their own set of devastating consequences.

2. **Our highway drama is a microcosm of life**. Accidents are a small part of a bigger picture. While our drama made the news that night, millions are living with an everyday fatigue that goes unreported. Sleep deprivation stealthily impairs our thinking, saps our physical vitality, and messes with our emotions. For many, the story of our highway accident serves as a microcosm of life. It's the story of regular Joe, going through life with tiredness and stress, ignoring the warning signs until he crashes. Or causes a crash.

Whether it's for body, mind, or spirit, my aim is to help you shield yourself from crashing.

How will you accomplish this?

By incorporating the very thing that I neglected, the final ingredient of optimal vitality: restorative rest.

Restoration, as we are using it in this book, refers to the processes by which the body repairs itself and recovers from stress, injury, illness, or fatigue. Together with the other principles of FULL POWER, restorative rest serves as a vital part of stress management, one of the six pillars of lifestyle medicine.

The word "restorative" implies something damaged is being brought back to its optimal state. Restorative sleep happens when sleep is of sufficient length and quality to provide physical, emotional, and mental rejuvenation, leaving you feeling refreshed, alert, and energized for the day.

The best chances of restoring all systems of the body, including the immune system, the circulatory system, musculoskeletal system, and the nervous system, is restorative sleep. It also helps to fight off infections and diseases. And so much more.

According to the American Sleep Apnea Association, nearly one third of U.S. adults "do not regularly get the recommended amount [7-9 hours] of uninterrupted sleep they need to protect their health."[255] Statistically, 50 to 70 million Americans suffer from sleep disorders.[256] These numbers make for a more vulnerable population, not to mention a riskier world.

After our highway accident, I was more intentional about getting my sleep to avoid another accident. Now, I have a hard and fast rule: if I'm sleepy when driving, I pull over and snooze for 10 minutes.

But until I listened to a TED talk by Dr. Matthew Walker and read his book Why We Sleep, I had no idea that sleep could be a superpower and an essential ingredient to optimal vitality. Dr. Walker, a sleep expert and professor of neuroscience and Psychology at UC Berkley, provides a list of surprising benefits of restorative sleep drawn from over 17,000 scientific reports.

I divided his list into the three areas of vitality: physical, mental, and emotional.

Physical Effects of Sleep:

1. helps us live longer
2. keeps us slim

3. protects us from cancer

4. protects us from dementia

5. wards off colds and the flu

6. lowers our risk of heart attacks and stroke

7. makes us look more attractive

Mental Effects of Sleep:

1. enhances our memory

2. makes us more creative

3. lowers food cravings

Emotional Effects of Sleep:

1. contributes to happiness

2. reduces depression and anxiety[257]

3. More than saving me from car accidents, this list gave me hope that I could be more effective in all areas of life. If restorative rest could do all that, what else could it do? Moreover, how could I ensure I reaped all its advantages?

SLEEP YOUR WAY TO WEIGHT LOSS

I noticed on Walker's list that one benefit of sleep was that it "keeps you slim." For years I struggled to keep my weight in a healthy range. But I didn't see the connection between quality sleep and healthy weight.

Until I did a little digging.

The science showed that good quality sleep makes it easier to lose excess weight. And sleep deprivation makes it easier to put on excess weight. For example, with only 5-6 hours of sleep per night, we tend to consume an additional 200-300 calories per day. For some, that amount could result in an extra pound of weight in 2-3 weeks, and an extra 20-30 pounds in a year.[258]

Explanation?

Two appetite hormones—leptin and ghrelin—explain the reason that body weight is affected by sleep. Leptin is the appetite regulator. It signals to our body, "I'm full. Stop eating." If we are trying to lose weight, we want more leptin. Ghrelin, on the other hand, stimulates hunger. It signals to the body, "I'm not full yet. I want more."

Sleep deprivation, however, flips those switches around. The leptin we want is decreased, and the ghrelin we don't want is increased—the perfect setup for weight gain.

I thought back to the last time I indulged in potato chips and candy bars. Sure enough, it was when I had fewer than six hours sleep the night before. I wish I could say, "The ghrelin made me do it." But the truth was that I had unwittingly set myself up for defeat the night before. Later in the chapter, we will learn some sleep hacks that, instead, set us up for victory.

Quality sleep also plays a big role in regulating metabolism. Metabolism is the process of trillions of chemical reactions in the human body per second that convert food into energy and support bodily functions. These interactions include regulating blood sugar. If our blood sugar rises above its healthy range, it is easy to gain weight. That's because elevated blood sugar levels trigger the release of insulin, a fat-storing hormone. The complex cause-and-effect sequence is mind-boggling. But the simple way to say it is: Since sleep affects the regulation of blood sugar, sleep, therefore, can affect body-fat composition.

By consciously prioritizing a good night's sleep, we help our hormones support a healthier weight.

This relationship can never be overstated. At the time of our accident, I was carrying excess weight, which correlated with accumulated sleep deprivation over the preceding months. My "beauty sleep" had been lacking, evident by the bags under my eyes, and my work-related stress levels were elevated. That combination of excess weight, elevated stress, and sleep deprivation set me up for bodymind failure. Millions do this to their bodies every day. One way or the other, we pay the price.

Studying the science has convinced me to rearrange my lifestyle habits so I can prioritize a good night's sleep to avoid suffering those consequences ever again.

I wasn't surprised when I found a 2017 study on older British adults that showed a direct correlation between cortisol, the stress hormone, and obesity.[259] Then, what a relief to find that restorative sleep is the medicine that reduces the production of cortisol, leading to fewer cravings, making weight loss easier.[260]

This cause-and-effect sequence followed a pattern similar to many other cause-and-effect sequences we've mentioned in previous chapters. The pattern goes like this: there is a symptom. That symptom is the effect of contributing causes. Those contributing causes are the effect of previous causes, ultimately going back to the root cause: deficiencies in one or more of the FULL POWER principles—in this case, "Rest Up."

SLEEPING YOUR WAY TO BEAUTY

Popular actor and singer Jennifer Lopez said that getting enough sleep, seven to nine hours, is her most important beauty secret. "We don't value sleep," she said. "We value grinding and working hard—and admittedly, nobody gets caught up in that rat race more than me. I've found, however, that sleep to me is the most underrated beauty secret out there."[261]

It's not just Lopez. The Royal Society found that sleep-deprived people were perceived as less attractive, less healthy, with the result being that others were less likely to want to get to know those people.[262] Clearly, beauty sleep is real, and we can take advantage of it.

THE PERILS OF SLEEP DEPRIVATION

Sleep deprivation exacts a devastatingly high cost to our personal health and vitality. A host of studies have linked insufficient sleep to an increased risk of everything from depression and obesity to Type 2 diabetes, cardiovascular disease, cancer, and Alzheimer's disease.

Sean Kerklaan, the former CEO of Fatigue Science in Vancouver, Canada, provides a thought-provoking list of how sleep deprivation affects us. I also divided his list into the three areas of vitality:

Physical Effects of Sleep Deprivation

1. increases diabetes
2. increases heart conditions
3. increases blood pressure
4. weakens the immune system
5. slows reaction time
6. increases mortality

Mental Effects of Sleep Deprivation

1. contributes to poor memory
2. diminishes decision-making abilities
3. reduces productivity

Emotional Effects of Sleep Deprivation

1. contributes to poor mood
2. increases stress
3. reduces motivation
4. exacerbates depression and anxiety[263]

That's a depressing list. One item especially caught my attention: sleep deprivation reduces motivation. I certainly had been experiencing that effect. I noticed that when I went to bed later than usual, it had an effect on my emotions and behavior the next day, which had a domino effect into other areas of life and work.

For example, it was harder to motivate myself to work out the next morning, even if I had the time. It was easier to skip my walk or run, saying "I'll do it tomorrow." That excuse increased my sitting time, making me feel lazy, which was depressing. I felt like I was missing out on the zest for life—all because I didn't get enough sleep. But the more rested I felt, the more productivity I enjoyed during the day—which meant I would burn off that many more calories. Double bonus.

Going to bed late also diminished my mental sharpness at the office. It turns out "that sleep-deprived people had less blood flow to the frontal lobe."[264] That's a problem because the frontal lobe is where complex decision-making happens. With less fuel going to my frontal lobe, I was at a disadvantage when analyzing important issues at a board meeting. That haze, in turn, eroded my sense of integrity as I felt I hadn't given my best.

Imagine how sleep deprivation could affect other situations as well—for example, deciding on whether to make a big purchase, adopt a child, start a new relationship, or move to a new city. With suboptimal decision-making powers, we risk poorer decisions and possible regret.

On the flipside, sleep deprivation overactivated my amygdala, which is where emotions are processed and where stress and fear trigger the fight-or-flight response. If the amygdala is overactivated, it can hijack the rational part of the brain that regulates emotions.

Therefore, knowing that sleep deprivation leads to an overactivated amygdala, I could anticipate at least two tendencies throughout my day:

1. an increased likelihood of using tactless words in my interactions with colleagues, friends, family (impatience), and
2. emotional eating (intemperance).[265]

Because of an overactivated amygdala, a sleep-deprived person will focus more on immediate gratification both in social interactions and food choices, demanding low-maintenance relationships and high-calorie substances.

A good night's sleep, on the other hand, strengthens our self-control over our word choices as well as our food choices. Both create a more pleasant existence.

But here's the most sobering statistic: U.S. businesses lose over $400 billion a year due to sleep deprivation—largely due to reduced workplace productivity and lost work time adding up to an equivalent of 1.23 million absent or "sick" days.[266] The loss of productivity and net revenue for companies and organizations around the world is a real and measurable loss. It is a powerful blow to a nation's vitality because the economy, in turn, impacts the individuals who live within it.

Many sleep experts recommend 7-9 hours of sleep each night for good health. The younger you are, the more sleep you need. Teens need 8-10 hours. School-age children need 9-12 hours. Preschool children need 10-13 hours. Toddlers need 11-14 hours. Infants need 12-16 hours. Newborns need 14-17 hours.[267] Nap time can be counted if taken before 3:00 p.m.[268]

For adults, anything under or over the range of the 7-9 hours is associated with negative health risks.

Sleep deficits become particularly concerning when considering the widespread effects of sleep on the population. The profound implications of sleep deprivation are further underscored when examining the biggest sleep experiment in the world. It takes place twice a year in approximately 70 countries. It's called Daylight Saving Time (DST).

In North America, the start of DST is the day the clocks skip ahead by one hour in March, depriving many of (the effect of) one hour of sleep; the return to Standard Time is the day clocks are put back one hour in November, giving many (the effect of) one extra hour of sleep. The change affects 1.6 billion people, approximately 22% of the world's population.

Researchers made a surprising observation. By studying hospital records, they discovered a 24% increase in heart attacks the Monday after the spring time change when one hour of sleep is lost. When the one hour of sleep is gained back in autumn, heart attacks drop by 21% the following Tuesday (presumably because Monday was a day off). Wow! What an amazing correlation. Several other studies show a similar connection between sleep loss and heart attacks immediately after the spring time shifts.[269]

What's more amazing is that the number of traffic accidents follows the same pattern. Traffic accidents increase following the spring time change and decrease following the fall time change. The neural activity in the brain is as sensitive to sleep deprivation as is the heart.[270] The slowed reaction time of a fatigued driver can be so impaired that he is as dangerous as a drunken driver. Actually, more so: Drinking while driving slows reaction time; sleeping while driving eliminates reaction time altogether.

My drowsy driving made me more dangerous than a drunk driver.

THE BODY'S OVERNIGHT REPAIR SHOP

As we have already suggested, quality sleep is vital for the brain, contributing to enhanced mental alertness and emotional stability. As we sleep, our body goes into nightly maintenance on memory consolidation, emotional regulation, and overall cognitive function.

Here's how it works. Throughout the day, our brain takes in an abundance of fact-based information through the five senses. This new information finds its way into the short-term memory—the hippocampus—but like a sponge, it can only soak up so much information before it needs to be cleaned out. That cleanup work mostly happens at night, during deep, non-dream sleep, when the day's information is transferred to the long-term memory in the cortex. The transfer and storage of information is part of learning and is associated with intelligence, memory, and the cognitive functionality of healthy human beings.

Clearing out debris is essential for optimal bodymind vitality. During waking hours, neuronal activity releases a by-product, a sticky toxic protein called beta-amyloid. If beta-amyloid is not cleared away, it starts to "strangle and kill nerve cells—particularly the memory regions of the brain."[271] The excess accumulation leads to cognitive decline, memory impairment, and an increased risk of Alzheimer's disease as well as a host of other cognitive unpleasantries. Quality sleep clears that toxic waste away. When we wake up after a good night's sleep, we start the day with a "brand-new sponge" prepared to soak up new information and memories of the new day.

The body's repair shop can only do its job of restoration when our body and nervous system is in a restful state. When we live in constant overdrive, our bodies enter a heightened stress response, hindering the healing process. Research suggests that chronic stress and sleep deprivation impair the body's ability to recover fully, diminishing the potential benefits for healing and repair. Consequently, it is more difficult to lose excess weight when we are constantly living with stress.

SLEEP YOUR WAY TO CREATIVITY

When our sleep is restorative, our brain switches back and forth between deep sleep and dream sleep. During deep sleep, information is transferred to the long-term memory storage. But it's during dream sleep, after the new information has been transferred, that it is integrated with other memories that have been long stored there.[272]

That assimilation of new information can generate wonderful new insights of creativity. It's how Paul McCartney came up with the record-breaking song, "Yesterday," how James Watson came up with the paradigm-shifting double-helix structure of DNA, and how Mary Shelley came up with the ground-breaking social commentary, Frankenstein. If we want to wake up with a solution or original idea, giving our brain a chance to do its creative work might be the key.

SLEEP HACKS TO MAXIMIZE YOUR ZZZS

Getting a good night's sleep can be challenging. Whether you're a young parent dealing with a colicky child, working night shifts as a nurse or doctor, grappling with anxiety or chronic pain, taking medications that disrupt sleep, or experiencing the effects of menopause, various factors can make it difficult to achieve restorative rest.

Don't give up. Read the following tips and do what you are able. Even if you are not able to achieve the optimal hours, any effort to get even a little more sleep or deeper sleep will benefit.

1. **Create a relaxing sleep environment.**
    a) **Sleep in a comfortable bed**. We spend a third of our life in it, and our quality of life depends on it. A quality mattress that gives comfort is worth the investment.

    b) **Darken your room.** Before lying down, dim the lights to create a calming mood. This helps create an environment more conducive to the production of melatonin, a hormone that regulates sleep. Darken the room as much as possible. Wear an eye mask if needed.

    c) **Cool your room.** According to the National Sleep Foundation, 60-68 degrees Fahrenheit (15.6 to 20 degrees Celsius) is the optimal range for sleeping.[273] Coolness during sleep sends signals to the body to reduce its metabolic rate and prepare for rest and recovery. As the body temperature drops, it triggers the release of melatonin, which signals to the body it is time to sleep. Cooler temperatures also promote deeper stages of sleep and the release of the growth hormone that plays an important role in tissue repair, muscle growth, and bone density.

    d) **Create quietness**. While some people may be able to sleep through noise due to constant exposure over time, most individuals require a quiet environment to achieve a good quality and restful sleep. Noise can be disruptive to the sleep cycle. Noise sends an alert to the brain to be on guard for threat. A hypervigilant brain doesn't sleep well, stay asleep, or achieve the deeper stages of sleep that are necessary for rest and recovery.

        Noise can also cause sleep fragmentation, a phenomenon where the sleep cycle is disrupted by brief awakenings. Broken sleep can result in daytime sleepiness, fatigue, and irritability. If needed, use earplugs or use white-noise machines.

2. **Establish nighttime routines.**

The brain thrives on routine because it can work at its best with things it can predict. Regular winding down routines for sleep can help the body maintain a healthy circadian rhythm, which in turn promotes better sleep and overall health.

Start to wind down at least 60 minutes before bedtime. When following a consistent pre-sleep routine, the brain associates specific activities with the upcoming sleep period and begins to prepare the body for less activity that leads to more restorative and quality sleep.

Here are ideas for routines:

a. Turn off electronic screens one hour before going to bed. This allows the body to produce melatonin, a hormone that aids sleep. Studies have shown that exposure to bright electric "blue" light between dusk and bedtime can suppress hormones that make us sleepy.274

Evening use of light-emitting e-readers negatively affects sleep, circadian timing, and next-morning alertness.[275] Such devices include smartphones, tablets, and TVs.

b. **Do low-stress activities** that calm the body down, such as light reading, meditation, journaling, and other quiet activities. These can be supportive in winding down the mind and the body.

c. **Stretch and release tension** in the body through gentle stretching and releasing exercise.

d. **Take a warm bath**, which can be helpful, particularly when combined with Epsom salt baths. The water should be warm enough to promote relaxation without causing discomfort or overheating. Epsom salt, which contains magnesium sulfate, is known to have muscle-relaxing properties. The warm water and the magnesium sulfate in Epsom salt can help relax the muscles, relieve tension, and promote a deeper sense of relaxation. Individual experiences may vary.

3. **Establish a consistent sleep schedule.**

Keep a consistent sleep schedule even on weekends because a consistent schedule helps to regulate the body's internal clock and promote natural sleep. Studies show that regular bedtimes promote health benefits, such as protecting your heart. An NPJ Digital Medicine study found that when college students go to bed 30 minutes later than their usual time, their resting heart rate increased during sleep and remained high the following day. As a matter of fact, the later their heads hit the pillow, the higher their heart rate the next day.[276]

An increase in resting heart rate increases cardiovascular risk. Interestingly, the study also found the resting heart rate likewise went up when the students went to bed more than 30 minutes early.[277] Consistency is key. Go to sleep the same time every night for optimal health. It's better to set the alarm for bedtime than for wake time.

One scientist claimed that if we need an alarm clock to wake up in the morning, it is a sign we are not getting enough sleep, and it is a shock to the system to be consistently woken from sleep when we press the snooze button multiple times before we finally rise.

4. **Avoid work in the bedroom**.

Using our bed as a makeshift office turns it into a stimulus for wakefulness, blurring the line between work and rest. By designating our bed solely for sleep and intimacy, we create a powerful cue for the brain to transition into a state of relaxation and readiness for rest.

5. **Exercise before evening**.

Exercise increases alertness levels that can be hard to dissipate in time for sleep. In that the effects of exercise vary with each individual, experiment to see what works for you. But on the flip side, if we don't get enough physical activity during the day, it can make falling asleep harder at night because the body might not be sufficiently tired.

Exercise, especially outdoor exercise early in the day, helps with the body's circadian rhythm and the sleep-wake cycles. It also promotes the body's natural temperature dip that occurs in the evening. Exercise also decreases stress and increases the feel-good neurotransmitter, serotonin. The combination of reduced stress and increased serotonin has been found to induce better sleep.

6. **Be cautious about caffeine.**

A review of epidemiological studies and randomized controlled trials published in Sleep Medicine Reviews reported that caffeine, the world's most widely used (and abused) psychoactive drug, typically delays the onset of sleep, reduces sleep time, and sleep quality.[278]

Just one dose of caffeine (i.e., one cup of coffee) in the evening decreases the sleep quality by 20%.

Caffeine intake may be one place to look for those wishing to improve sleep.

7. **Use deep-breathing exercises.**
    If you're struggling to sleep, try deep breathing. Breath in through your nose and hold your breath for a count of eight. Purse your lips and blow out until your lungs feel empty. Repeat until you feel relaxed.

8. **Understand the effects of alcohol on sleep.**
    Alcohol is often used as a sedative to help people fall asleep. Unfortunately, sedation is not equivalent to sleep. Sedation can induce relaxation and drowsiness, but it does not allow the brain to perform the restorative functions we discussed above.

    Also, alcohol immobilizes the prefrontal cortex, the part of our brain that helps control our impulses.[279]

    Using alcohol to induce sleep fails us in at least two ways:

    a. The liver metabolizes alcohol later in the night, increasing the number of times we wake up and causing fragmented sleep.
    b. Alcohol often suppresses REM sleep, which plays a crucial role in sustaining long-term memory, emotional regulation, and creativity.

    While some older research suggested that moderate drinking may have health benefits, such as reduced risk of heart disease, a 2018 global study published in The Lancet contradicts that claim. By doing a broader study looking at more systems of the body, the researchers found that any level of alcohol consumption increases the risk of health problems, including cancer, injuries, and infectious diseases. The study analyzed data from nearly 700 studies and concluded that "there is no safe level of alcohol consumption."[280]

Perhaps the best way to explain it is this: Any potential health benefits of alcohol are outweighed by its harms.

9. **Understand the effects of sleeping pills.**
    Sleeping pills are known to work in the same area of the brain as does alcohol.[281] While sedation may get someone over a temporary hump, both substances are not a natural or a healthy, sustainable solution.

    The difference between a sedation and natural sleep is in what happens in the brain. Healthy sleep is a time when the brain does its wonderful work of restoration. Sedation is like shutting down the repair shop. We suffer the consequences of sleep deprivation even though we thought we were sleeping.

10. **Clear your conscience**.
    Guilt is an emotional stressor impacting various aspects of our well-being. Going to bed with the stress of a guilty conscience increases cortisol levels. This reduces sleep quality leading to many of the consequences mentioned above. Making amends or asking for forgiveness can alleviate this stress and lead to not only psychological benefits, but also physiological benefits within our bodies. In many cases making amends can be a breakthrough for physical healing and emotional restoration.

INTEGRATING MORE REST IN YOUR LIFE

When it comes to restorative rest, it's not just about nightly sleep. We also need daily, weekly, monthly, and yearly periods of rest and rejuvenation for our bodies and minds. Incorporating regular periods of rest throughout the year is a way to stock up on serotonin, the serenity hormone, and cut down on cortisol, the stress hormone.

Tiffany Shlain, a filmmaker and author of Brain Power: From Neurons to Networks, advocates going on a weekly "Technology Sabbath" to infuse restoration into your life. She walks away from all technology, including smartphones, computers, and TV and engages in activities like playing with children, gardening, riding a bike, writing, or reading. The list is endless.[282]

Tech Sabbaths are catching on. Hollywood producer Devon Franklin doesn't take calls on the Sabbath. He said, "The Sabbath has been the key to my success. Why? Because I'm able to take time to rest… You want your career, your life, your relationships to go to the next level? Take time out and watch what happens."[283]

As a guide for what might be restorative for you, consider doing the opposite of what you do for work. For example, if you are a sedentary office worker, do physical things outdoors. If you are a physical worker during the week, do relaxing activities like stretching classes or reading. Balance is the key.

Whether daily, weekly, monthly, quarterly, or yearly, when we insert periods of restorative rest into our life's journey, both the mind and body surge with strength to accomplish our highest purposes. Bill Gates, Microsoft founder, took a "think week" twice a year alone in a cabin in the woods to do nothing but read papers and proposals written by employees. The game-changing Internet Explorer 1995 was the creative result of one of those weeks.[284]

Here are some restorative things to do while unplugged. Many of them calm down the parasympathetic nervous system. This system is responsible for the "rest and digest" response in the body—slowing down heart rate, decreasing blood pressure, and promoting relaxation. While some of these activities increase blood pressure in the short term, they still have the long-term effect of lowering blood pressure and promoting relaxation.

1. Walk in nature.
2. Ride a bike.
3. Read a book.
4. Play with friends.
5. Work in the garden.
6. Spend a day at the beach.
7. Climb a mountain.
8. Climb a tree.
9. Call an old friend.
10. Visit with family.
11. Write a letter.
12. Forgive an old debt.
13. Paint a picture.
14. Surprise someone with an act of kindness.
15. Cook a special meal.
16. Do something spiritual.
17. Do something that would boost the other FULL POWER principles.
18. Help a neighbor.
19. Get together with friends to help a neighbor.
20. Take a stretching class.
21. Take a cold shower (feels great when you're done).
22. Practice mindfulness (Chapter 5).
23. Take a week-long retreat.
24. Take a holiday.

We know our rejuvenation time is working when we feel both relaxed and strong at the same time. Experiment and see what works for you.

Restorative rest is the final ingredient in nature's formula for optimal body-mind vitality. When we tap into its power, all the faculties of body and mind are revitalized. It enables us to stay fully awake, and fully alive, as we travel the highways of life.

Complete the checklist below to gauge how you are doing on resting up.

Our next endeavor is to integrate restorative rest, along with the other principles of FULL POWER, into an action plan.

PART 1 focused on restructuring the habits of the mind. PART 2 focused on restructuring the habits of the body.

In PART 3, we'll put it all together in a complete FULL POWER plan for optimal bodymind vitality.

CHECKLIST FOR

"REST UP"

	To what degree am I getting restorative rest? On a scale of 0-10, answer these questions, based on the last seven days. The cumulative sum of all nine end-of-chapter checklists will result in a total out of 100.	
1	I slept 7-9 hours each night.	
2	I kept to a consistent sleep schedule.	
3	I turned off technology 60-90 minutes before bedtime.	
4	I practiced a nighttime routine that prepared my mind for sleep each night.	
5	I made sure my bedroom was totally dark, cool, and quiet for sleep each night.	
6	I allowed at least a four-hour gap between my final meal and bedtime.	
7	I exposed my eyes to the morning light to set my circadian rhythm each morning.	
8	I didn't drink coffee or alcohol before going to bed.	
9	I took a weekly day off for rejuvenation.	
10	I scheduled yearly vacation time.	
	Total out of 100	
	Divide by 10 for average out of 10	

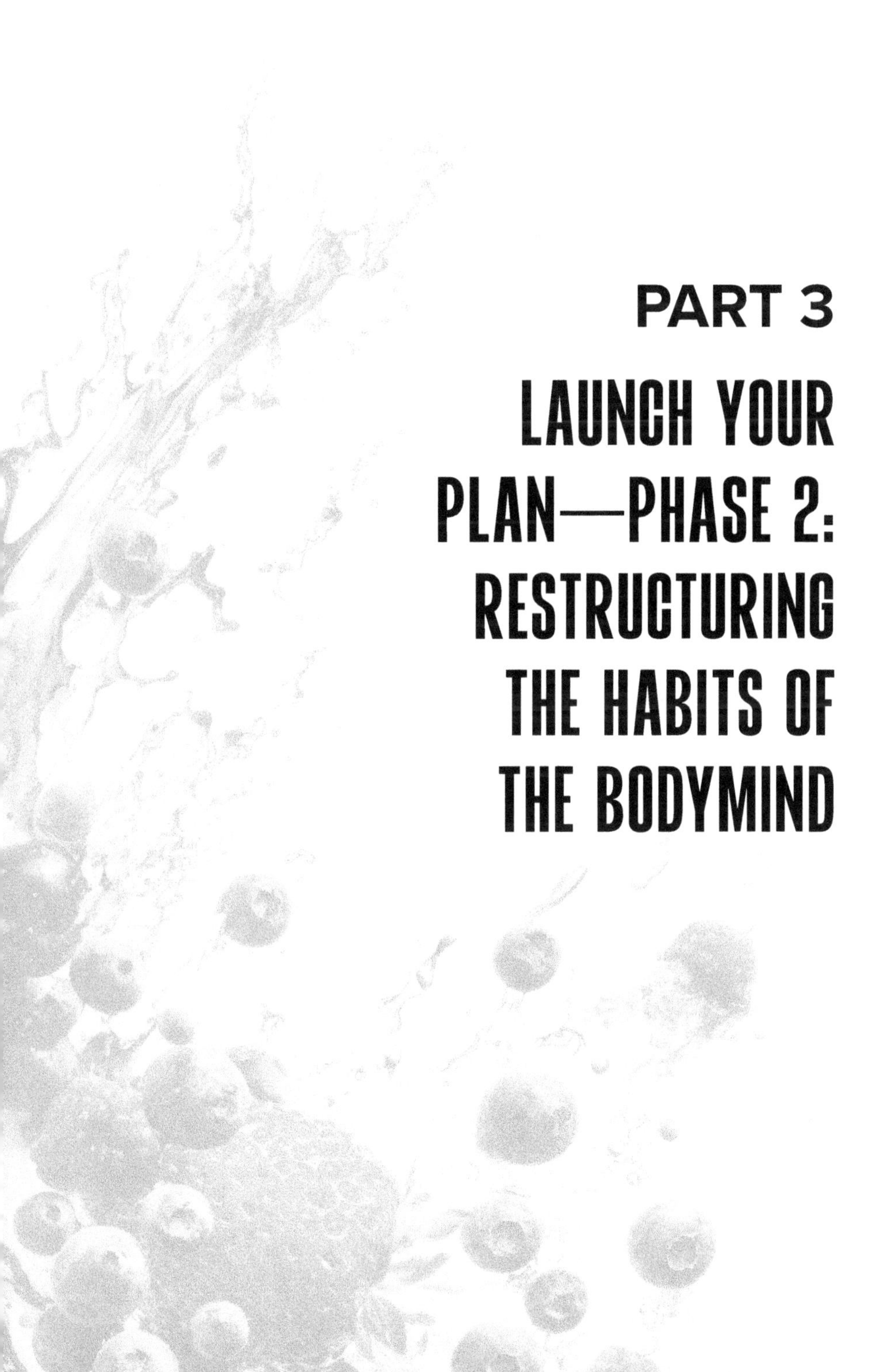

PART 3

LAUNCH YOUR PLAN—PHASE 2: RESTRUCTURING THE HABITS OF THE BODYMIND

CHAPTER 13

ACTIVATING THE FULL POWER PLAN—THE BIG PICTURE

In the opening chapter, we proposed that by harnessing the potential of the bodymind we can achieve unparalleled levels of life satisfaction. Then we laid out nature's formula for accomplishing this through the FULL POWER principles. In this section, PART 3, we will set that potential in motion by transforming the FULL POWER principles into a practical action plan for optimal bodymind vitality—essentially creating our personal makeover plan.

Let's start with the big picture.

THE BIG PICTURE – STRATEGY IS POETRY

Think of achieving your goal of optimal bodymind vitality as a journey of steps from Point A to Point B. When you input your destination (Point B) into the navigation system of your car, it uses the three nearest satellites to determine your current position (Point A). Then, it calculates the route to guide you to your destination—from Point A to Point B. You'll know you're on the right track when the digital map matches your actual surroundings.

These are the steps we'll use to guide us through the implementation phase of the FULL POWER Plan. I've put these steps into a simple rhyme so you can easily recall them. I call it The Strategy Poem.

The Strategy Poem
Where am I now?
Where do I go?
How will I get there?
How will I know?

Over the years, I've used this simple rhyme for leadership and strategic planning. It can be used by any organization, group, or committee wanting to implement change. Here, we will use the strategy poem to propel you to the peak of your potential—optimal bodymind vitality. Start with Step 1.

Step 1: Where am I now?

All journeys have a starting point. We need to set benchmarks against which to measure our progress. They may be in the form of an assessment score, weight measurement, cholesterol level, or other biomarkers.

Step 2: Where do I go?

All journeys have a destination. This is about what, where, and who we can be. It's the vision of our future self. For us, it's optimal bodymind vitality.

Tom Bilyeu, entrepreneur and YouTube host of Impact Theory, said, "It doesn't matter who you are today. It matters who you want to become, and the price you're willing to pay to get there."[285]

Step 3: How will I get there?

All journeys have a route. It's the action plan that takes us from where we are now to where we want to go. It's our "system"—the FULL POWER Plan. It involves implementing a set of habits grounded in the principles of FULL POWER.

Step 4: How will I know?

All journeys have signposts or markers to tell us the distance we've traveled. Passing a marker is how we know we're making progress. That's part of the fun. Markers can take various forms, such as achieving an interim weight goal, reaching a specific waist measurement, receiving a favorable cholesterol reading, completing a phase of a project, finishing a chapter of a book, completing a certain number of push-ups, logging miles on a track, or steps on a trail. Or it could be as simple as finishing the questions in the "Guiding Questions for Finding Your Superpower and Fulfilling Your Purpose" in Chapter 2.

Many habits in the end-of-chapter checklists can be turned into markers to measure. For example: "How many times was I in a state of flow?" or "How many social connections did I make this week?" or "How many cups of water did I drink?" As we pass each marker, we can celebrate the strides we've made. When we pass the last marker—our desired weight, for example—we know we've reached our final goal ("Point B"). It's time to celebrate big time.

To gauge progress, compare your new measurements to your old measurements.

Now that we have a big-picture mentality, it's time to choose our option plan and see how the strategy poem helps us master the plan.

FOUR OPTION PLANS

When it comes to implementing the principles of FULL POWER, there are four options, depending on your needs:

A. the Unstructured Plan
B. the Principle-per-Month Plan
C. the One Habit-per-Principle-per-Month Plan
D. the Focused and Structured 28-Day FULL POWER Action Plan (Chapter 14)

Plan A: The Unstructured Plan

The unstructured plan suits those who prefer a laid-back, casual approach. I include this plan here to contrast it with the more systematic alternatives. You may have informally experimented with some of the suggestions in the book, which means you have been applying the unstructured plan already.

The following simple steps can help bring focus to the casual approach.

Step 1: Where am I now?

Assess your vitality level by completing the Vitality Self-Assessment to set a benchmark against which to measure your progress (see Appendix). It's a quick self-diagnosis of your current state of health—both mental and physical. Like a doctor giving a diagnosis, the Vitality Self-Assessment gives a self-diagnosis.[286]

Step 2: Where do I go?

Destination: optimal bodymind vitality.

Step 3: How will I get there?

Read the chapters looking for actions to implement that best meet your current health situation.

Step 4: How will I know?

After a month, reassess your vitality level by retaking your Vitality Self-Assessment and check your progress.

Plan B: The Principle-per-Month Plan

The principle-per-month plan suits those who want to focus on one principle, or set of lifestyle practices, at a time. This option is for those whose personality, life commitments, or health status require new habits to be gradually implemented. The rewards come from the steadily improving assessment scores and biomarkers.

Step 1: Where am I now?

Assess your vitality level by completing the Vitality Self-Assessment to set a benchmark against which to measure your progress (see Appendix).

Step 2: Where do I go?

Destination: optimal bodymind vitality.

Step 3: How will I get there?

Commit to implementing one principle per month from the FULL POWER formula. As a reminder, here is the FULL POWER formula:

F - Find Your Superpower
U - Unleash Healthy Spirituality
L - Lovify Your Life
L - Launch Your Plan

P - Prioritize High-Octane Fuel
O - Omit What Is Harmful

W - Water Up
E - Exercise Outdoors
R -Rest Up

Focus on the recommendations in the chapter that explains the principle you choose to implement.

For example, in the first month devote all your efforts to finding your superpower (Chapter 2). In the second month, focus on the habits of positive spirituality (Chapter 3). In the third month, focus on increasing the quality of your relationships. Continue until you've completed each principle of FULL POWER.

Maximize the compounding effect of habit-building by carrying over your newly established habits into the next month when you relaunch a fresh set of habits based on the next principle.

Step 4: How will I know?

Retake your Vitality Self-Assessment after each month and celebrate your progress.

Plan C: The One Habit-per-Principle-per-Month Plan

The one habit-per-principle-per-month plan suits those who want to experience something from all nine principles at once but focus on just one habit from each principle. Since there are 10 habits per principle, it would take 10 months. But remember, it's progress we're looking for, not overnight perfection.

Step 1: Where am I now?

Assess your vitality level by completing the Vitality Self-Assessment to set a benchmark against which to measure your progress.

Step 2: Where do I go?

Destination: optimal bodymind vitality.

Step 3: How will I get there?

Commit to at least one new behavior from each of the end-of-chapter checklists. That strategy adds up to nine new behaviors per month.

Here is an example of one behavior from each category that can become a habit:

F - Find Your Superpower:	Using a particular talent
U - Unleash Healthy Spirituality:	Meditating on wisdom quotes
L - Lovify Your Life:	Being more intentional on connecting with people
L - Launch Your Plan:	Monitoring habits
P - Prioritize High-Octane Fuel:	Eating four vegetables daily
O - Omit What Is Harmful:	Avoiding fatty foods
W - Water Up:	Drinking adequate water
E - Exercise Outdoors:	Going for a walk
R - Rest Up:	Darkening bedroom

Imagine practicing these nine behaviors for the first month. Ultimately, we can work toward accomplishing all 10 behaviors in each category. To get the momentum going, start with the easy ones.

Step 4: How will I know?

Retake your Vitality Self-Assessment after each month and celebrate your progress.

We've introduced the Strategy Poem and saw how it applies to the first three option plans. But if you need results fast, and are committed to doing whatever it takes, you'll want a more comprehensive personal makeover plan. Turn to the next chapter for "The Focused and Structured 28-Day FULL POWER Action Plan."

THE FOCUSED AND STRUCTURED 28-DAY FULL POWER ACTION PLAN

This comprehensive plan is Plan D. It's for those have the need and time to go all-out. Plan D suits the type of person who enjoys or needs the motivational power that comes from receiving big rewards fast. Such individuals implement many things at once to achieve the biggest improvement in the shortest amount of time. It's the quintessential lifestyle intervention.

The ones more likely to choose this option are those who have a sense of urgency. Often, it's the ones who can't stop after eating one cookie or one potato chip. For them, one bite is a ticket down the slippery slope to self-sabotage. Simply "cutting back" is not a sustainable option. They must "cut out." Plan D is for those who want to be systematic about turning this intention into a 28-day program.

As before, let's follow the four steps of our strategy poem. But this time, we get to see those steps depicted in graphic form on the FULL POWER Dashboard.

THE FULL POWER DASHBOARD

The FULL POWER dashboard is the central organizing tool for the Focused and Structured 28-Day FULL POWER Action Plan. It pictorializes and tracks your makeover strategy. For a colored version, download it at fullpower1.com.

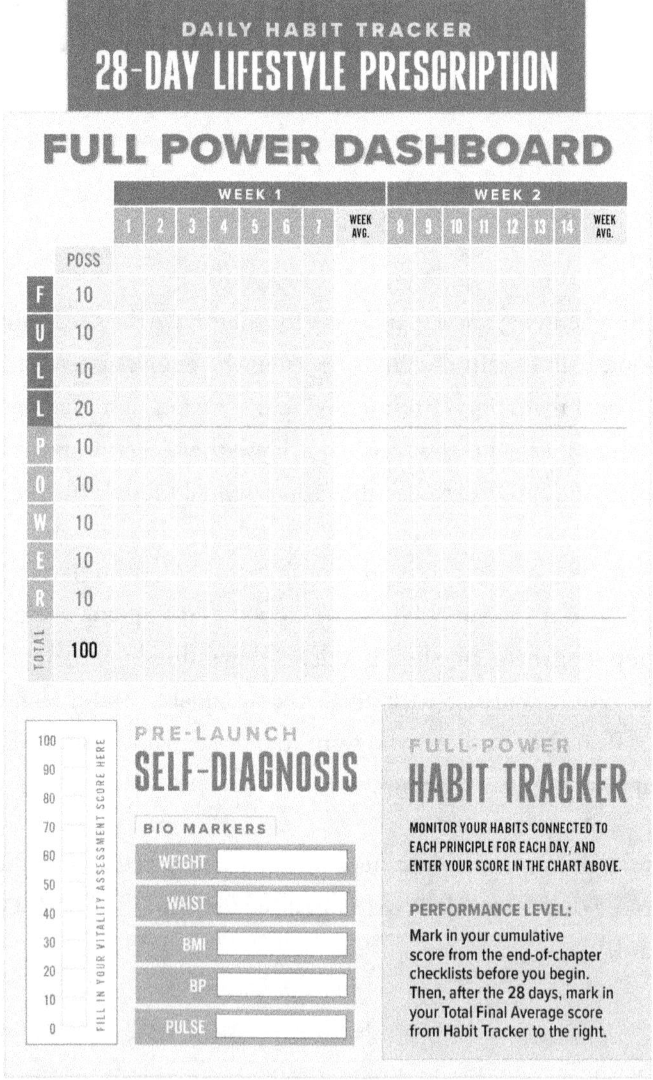

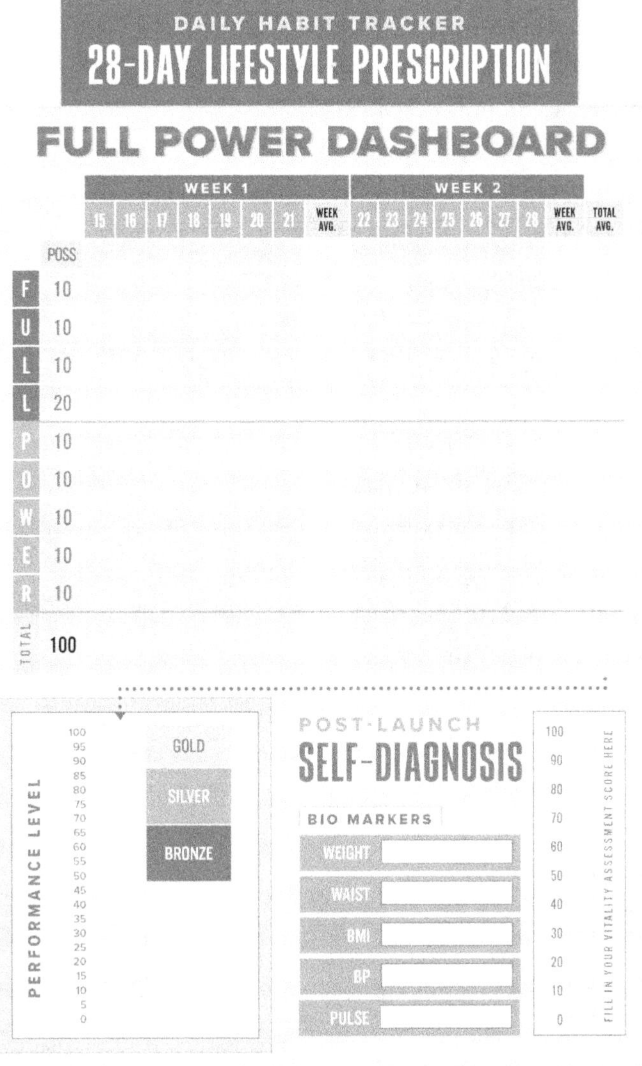

FIGURE 1 - The FULL POWER Dashboard[287]

The dashboard is divided into three major sections. The pink sections on the right and left represent the first two questions in the strategy poem: 1. Where am I now? 2. Where do I go?

The green section in the middle represents the two last questions in the strategy poem: 3. How will I get there? 4. How will I know? Notice that each letter of FULL POWER has its own track. Each track consists of 28 boxes, one box to fill in for each day.

The two pink sections on either side are about how we feel. The green section in the middle is about what we do. We improve how we feel by improving what we do.

As a reminder, here's what each letter of the FULL POWER formula represents:

FULL POWER Principles

F - Find Your Superpower
U - Unleash Healthy Spirituality
L - Lovify Your Life
L - Launch Your Plan

P - Prioritize High-Octane Fuel
O - Omit What Is Harmful
W - Water Up
E - Exercise Outdoors
R - Rest Up

The green horizontal bar graph at the bottom is where you can mark your "before" and "after" habit performance scores.

Let's start at the beginning.

1. **Where am I now?**
   Establish the benchmarks before Launch Day—one benchmark for "How are you feeling?" and the other for "What are you doing?"

The First Benchmark: "How are you feeling?"

Complete everything in the pink "Self-Diagnosis" section on the left side of the dashboard. It represents our "before" picture. This section uses a vertical thermometer-like bar graph for recording and coloring in your Vitality Self-Assessment level. Giving yourself a low score on the Vitality Self-Assessment is like giving yourself a poor diagnosis. It is a non-standardized subjective test. If you have a serious condition, obtain a doctor's diagnosis.

The five boxes in the pink section are to record biomarkers like weight, waist, body mass index (BMI), blood pressure, and resting pulse. These are standardized objective measurements.

1. Assess your vitality level by completing the Vitality Self-Assessment (see Appendix).
2. Complete the checklists at the end of each chapter and add up the scores out of 100. The Vitality Self-Assessment shows how we're feeling; the checklists show what we're doing.
3. Measure your starting weight, waist, blood pressure, and BMI.
4. You can go further, if you wish, by seeing your doctor to get blood work done. Check for biomarkers of vitality such as triglycerides, cortisol, blood sugar, cholesterol, and whatever else your doctor requires to make a full assessment of your current condition.

Mark your score (your "temperature") of your Vitality Self-Assessment on the vertical thermometer-like bar in the pink section at the left of the dashboard. Draw a horizontal line at your score number and color in the thermometer up to that line. This is the number to beat in 28 days.

The objective measurements of weight, waist, blood pressure, resting pulse, BMI (only good for non-muscular adults) are also the numbers to beat in 28 days.

Blood Work (Optional)

Blood work is optional but useful in assessing our current situation. It is not displayed on the dashboard. Your doctor might check for a wide range of biomarkers.

While your doctor can be more specific according to your unique needs, here are some of the general biomarkers that tell the doctor about the health of your organs, such as heart, kidneys, and liver. The results give information about blood glucose, calcium, and electrolytes. It can also be a scan for possible health issues that may be developing. Inform your doctor of your 28-day plan and request assistance with the measurements. It would be ideal if your doctor could take measurements before and after the 28-day program. Here are some of the things that can be measured:

a. **Triglycerides.** Elevated triglyceride levels have been associated with an increased risk of cardiovascular disease and stroke.

b. **Cholesterol.** Elevated cholesterol levels have been associated with an increased risk of cardiovascular diseases, including stroke and hypertension.

c. **Fasting blood glucose**. Elevated fasting blood glucose levels (usually taken in the morning before breakfast) have been associated with an increased risk of diabetes.

d. **Cortisol.** Elevated cortisol levels have been associated with stress. Chronic elevated cortisol levels have been associated with mental health issues, which can trigger or intensify a host of problems, draining vitality.

e. **C-reactive protein (CRP).** This protein is produced by the liver in response to inflammation. Elevated CRP levels have been associated with infection, some autoimmune diseases, some types of cancer, and an increased risk of cardiovascular disease, as well as other chronic conditions such as diabetes and rheumatoid arthritis. CRP can also be used to monitor the effectiveness of treatments for these conditions.

It is valuable to take these measurements before and after a lifestyle-intervention program such as FULL POWER. In this way, you can be scientific about the impact of the program.

The Second Benchmark: "What are you doing?"

Enter the cumulative total of the nine end-of-chapter checklists in the horizontal Performance Scale bar graph at the bottom of the middle section. (Note: Each of the checklists scores up to 10 points, but the "Launch Your Plan" checklist scores up to 20 points because you need to put emphasis on monitoring your new system until it becomes routine.) Draw a vertical line in the Performance Scale bar at your score number marker and color it in up to that line. This is the number to beat.

Prepare for Launch Day

Launch Day is an important day to prepare for. It's like preparing for a race or the first day of school. Reading this book mentally prepares us for Launch Day. It shows what is possible and gives ideas.

Now is the time to write "Launch Day" in your calendar. My wife and I set the first day of the month to be our Launch Day. For example, May 1 on the calendar matched Day 1 of our program. We took the last week in April to prepare for Launch Day. You aren't tied to waiting until the beginning of the new month, though. Start anytime that works best for you.

Here is a sample of 12 tips to prepare for Launch Day:

1. **See a medical doctor** for blood work, measurements, and clearance, if needed.

2. **Cleanse the kitchen** of refined foods.

3. **Stock the kitchen** with whole plant-based foods (fruits, vegetables, legumes, grains, nuts, and seeds).

4. **Talk to friends** and/or family to let them know what you are doing and why. Ask for their support.

5. **List books** you will read to support your new habits and schedule time to read them. For example, you could choose a book from one of the following categories:
    a. finding and living out your purpose
    b. spirituality
    c. relationships
    d. organization and productivity
    e. nutrition
    f. recipe books for unprocessed or minimally processed meals
    g. addictions
    h. self-discipline
    i. exercise routine, including muscle-building, cardio, and stretching
    j. rest

6. **Plan outdoor exercise time** to boost motivation, be inspired, enjoy nature, and breathe fresh air.

7. **Plan what you will do when you're tempted to stray** from the plan. Have trigger protocols in place (see Chapter 8 for tips). List your triggers (i.e., social events, ads, weekends, aromas, locations, tempting situations) and strategies for blocking them. Identify situations that may tempt you to go backwards, then plan to:

   a. connect with others—both in giving and receiving. It's not just about getting support. It's also about giving support to others on a similar journey.

   b. identify the positive behavior that will replace the harmful behavior. Turn that positive behavior into a protocol (sequence of actions) which gets initiated when triggered by a temptation.

   c. identify the strategies for coping with stress—both immediate and preventative.

   d. commit to ongoing support—Facebook group, meetup group, monthly supper clubs.

   e. start a weekly or monthly support club of like-minded people where each person brings a healthy dish and, while eating, discuss a health principle. Use this book as a discussion guide. If the club continues beyond 28 days, all the better.

8. **Practice your new identity** by imagining yourself living with optimal vitality. Study people healthier than you and imagine yourself living with the same vitality. List the emotional, social, physical, financial, spiritual, and professional benefits you plan to receive. Envision the increased energy, enthusiasm, confidence, strength, alertness, and weight loss.

9. **Put a reminder on the fridge**, bathroom mirror, etc., to cue you to take action.

10. **Plan your healthy reward** for each weekly milestone. For example, purchase a new piece of clothing, enjoy a day at the spa, or go on a date.

11. **Set a time to watch** supportive YouTube videos or listen to podcasts.

    Here are some samples from the Resource List (see Appendix):

    a) Hans Diehl videos
    b) Caldwell Esselstyn talks about reversing heart disease on YouTube
    c) Neil Bernard talks about nutrition on YouTube
    d) Nutrition.org videos from Dr. Michael Greger
    e) Miranda Esmonde-White "Essentrics" stretching videos on YouTube
    f) Matthew Walker talks and interviews about sleep on YouTube

EXAMPLE OF A COUNTDOWN TO LAUNCH DAY

Here is what a countdown to Launch Day may look like if you scored low on, for example, "Omit What Is Harmful" on the corresponding end-of-chapter checklist:

7 Days Until Launch

Collect recipes for WFPB (Whole Foods Plant-Based) meals. Plan your menu for the first week. See the "Menu for Life" planner in Appendix.

6 Days Until Launch

Clear kitchen cupboards of foods that contain sugar, fat, oil, salt, white flour—basically all refined foods. (Yes, this is radical, but you are shooting for radical results.)

5 Days Until Launch

Talk to family and friends about your health goals and ask them for support. For example, talk to them about needing 15 minutes of downtime in the morning. Request they give you privacy for that time or ask them to watch the little children, if needed.

4 Days Until Launch

Whenever you see tasty toxins, say to yourself, "That's not my food."[288]

3 Days Until Launch

Shop for healthy food and relevant cooking tools.

2 Days Until Launch

Buy a stainless steel water bottle, a journal, a tape measure, and a weigh scale.

1 Day Until Launch

Lay out the things needed for tomorrow and be in bed on time to prepare for the big day. Visualize your plans for tomorrow.

Welcome to Launch Day. "Launch" means to blast off. Picture a rocket blasting off at Cape Canaveral, Florida. That's you. You are starting your new habits and building a new identity. Your heart, circulation, brain, muscles, lungs, cells, and skin begin their restoration process on this day. Post to your private social media group, "Today Is My Launch Day." Then post what happens.

2. **Where do I go?**

Destination: optimal bodymind vitality. Envision yourself living with purpose, a sleek physique, more energy, and fewer aches and pains. Or maybe just getting a normal reading on your blood report would be huge.

Your destination is represented by the "New Self-Diagnosis" in the pink section at the right side of the dashboard. It's your "after" picture, where you record your new and improved vitality and biomarker scores after 28 days.

3. **How will I get there?**

We get there by using the "28-Day Lifestyle Prescription" in the green section in the middle of the dashboard. This is a fun way to hold yourself accountable for the lifestyle changes you want to make. It's like monitoring how well you're doing on "taking your medicine" —except that it's lifestyle medicine.

Give yourself points for each habit practiced. Video game players receive a dopamine hit for each point they earn. That's why video games can be so addictive. By gamifying your personal makeover plan, you tap into your dopamine system. It's fun to see improvements and celebrate wins along the way.

The "28-Day Lifestyle Prescription" is the system, or plan, you use to improve your diagnosis. It includes a Habit Tracker Summary and a "Performance Scale" bar graph.

The goal is to complete one column per day in the Habit Tracker Summary, starting on Launch Day and finishing on Day 28.

There are nine boxes in the column, one box for each principle. Complete the column by entering a number in each box that aligns with your habit performance on that day for that principle. Then fill in the total score at the bottom.

The fastest way to do this is to write down the number you feel best represents how well you did on that day for that principle. But a more accurate way is to use the Habit Trackers. See below under "Optional Monitoring Tools."

"PERFORMANCE SCALE" BAR GRAPH

Beneath the Habit Tracker Summary on the dashboard is the horizontal "Performance Scale" bar graph. It condenses all our monitored habits into one overall score. The Performance Scale at the bottom of the dashboard can show the "before" and "after" scores: one for marking the pre-launch assessment of habits from the end-of-chapter checklists; the other for marking the 28-day score from the Habits Tracker Summary. Both the "before" and "after" markers are on the same bar graph.

The goal is to see how far we can "slide the marker to the right" in 28 days, hopefully into metal category—bronze, silver, or gold. Reaching 50 points on the Performance Scale gives you the bronze metal. Reaching 70 points gives you the silver level. Reaching 85 points gives you gold.

But it's not about the final score, though. It's about how much progress you've made between Day 1 and Day 28. If, for example, you scored 40 in your pre-launch week (cumulative total from our chapter checklists), draw a vertical line at 40 and color in the bar up to the 40 mark. If, 28 days later, you recorded 60, mark it and measure the difference. This provides a visual of your progress. Your percentage increase is 50%: ((60 − 40)/40).

THE 28-DAY TIMEFRAME

The 28-day timeframe has three advantages:

1. It's long enough to make a measurable difference, but short enough to be manageable.
2. It easily divides into four weeks—psychologically digestible time periods.
3. It gives enough data to help evaluate what worked and what needs tweaking.

The ultimate goal, however, goes far beyond 28 days. It's to live the FULL POWER lifestyle for the rest of your life.

TAKE DAILY ACTION

Monitor actions each day for 28 days. This is "working the plan."

When we get off track, we can ask: "Am I or am I not on a journey toward a worthy purpose?" If so, climb back on the bridge and try again. If not, read Chapter 2 to infuse yourself with the power of purpose.

For me, I often stumble when I don't read books on exercise, vision, business, and health. Motivation "leaks." So, I need the constant flow of reminders and encouragement to keep me motivated. Also, I make sure to align most of my reading and listening habits to my higher purpose.

By focusing on turning daily actions into habits, we build new pathways in the brain in support of short-term goals that lead to long-term purposes. In time, we reach our goals and have the opportunity to set exciting new ones. Keeping up with this process, we see improved health, strength, confidence, mood, energy, memory, a feeling of belonging, and alertness. Our body, personality, character, and discernment grow stronger.

Don't look for a perfect score; let progress be your perfection. That way you can celebrate progress along the way. Making progress toward a purpose is a vital part of happiness.

OPTIONAL MONITORING TOOLS

Besides the main dashboard, Vitality Self-Assessment, and End-of-Chapter Checklists (Performance Assessments), there are two optional monitoring tools that can help you create the big picture of your transformation journey. They are the Daily Habit Trackers and the Habit Performance Display (see Appendix or go to fullpower1.com).

The Daily Habit Trackers

This tool provides a list of 10 questions for each principle, making it very thorough. The nine sets of Daily Habit Trackers are for those who want to monitor themselves more closely by answering 10 questions for each principle for each evening. Each set corresponds to the nine principles in FULL POWER. With 90 questions in total, the tracker can be time-consuming, but very revealing.

The 10 questions in each set of Daily Habit Trackers are a rewording of the questions on the end-of-chapter checklists. Here's the difference between the two: The end-of-chapter checklists assess our habits at the time we read the chapter. The Daily Habit Trackers monitor those same habits during the 28-day program.

Sometimes we use the word "habit" when we really mean actions that we plan to turn into habits.

Habit Performance Display

This graphic displays the checklist score and the habit tracker summary score—very helpful if you are a visual person. Take Tom, for example. Before Launch Day, Tom had a cumulative score of 52 out of 100 on his end-of-chapter checklists. Now he knows the number to beat, 52, and he's anxious to beat it.

FIGURE 2 - Habit Performance Display[289]

But Tom wants to see what his habit performance looks like in graphic form. He also wants to see a comparison of his "before" and "after" scores. The Habit Performance Display (see above) helps him do it. It shows nine vertical cylinders, each represented by a principle of FULL POWER. The level to which each cylinder is filled is determined by his score on the corresponding end-of-chapter checklist. Much like cylinders in a vehicle engine, the performance of each relies on being in their best state (in our case, full). The bottom part of the graphic displays two horizontal bar graphs—one bar to represent the "before" picture and one bar to represent the "after" picture.

To get a visual of his performance for the "before" picture, Tom colors in each cylinder corresponding to each end-of-chapter checklist. Since his cumulative score is 52, he colors in the first horizontal bar to the 52 mark.

Now Tom wants to get a visual of his performance for the "after" picture 28 days later. But since the cylinders are already colored in from 28 days before, Tom draws a second line in the cylinder at the level corresponding to the new scores from the Habit Tracker Summary on the dashboard. Then, he colors in the second horizontal bar past the 52 mark to his new score. Now, he can see the difference in habit scores before and after the 28 days.

HOW WILL I KNOW?

Measure your success by looking at the numbers.

After your 28 days (four weeks), you will have "Weekly Ave" (Average) scores on your Dashboard Habit Tracker Summary, one for each week in each category. For example, on the "W" track for "Water Up," add up each of the four weekly scores, horizontally, to get an average performance score for the cumulative four weeks in that category. Do the same for the other eight categories.

Then, enter the grand total for the final averages in the bottom right (shaded) box of the Dashboard Habit Tracker Summary. Calculate the difference between your pre-launch performance score and the 28-day performance score. That's progress.

Take the Vitality Self-Assessment again and enter your score in the "thermometer" in the pink section on the right of the FULL POWER Dashboard. Compare this new score to your pre-launch score at the left. As with the "Performance Scale," calculate the percentage change by subtracting the first score from the second score and divide the answer by your first score.

For example, if your benchmark first score was 25, and your final second score was 75, do this: 75 – 25 = 50; 50 divided by 25 = 2. To get your percentage increase, multiply by 100%. So, 2 X 100% = 200%, which represents a 200% improvement.

Time to celebrate (not with chocolate cake ☺).

WHAT'S YOUR SCORE?

Here are the scores for a life champion operating at full power in all areas:

Principle		Top Score
F	Fulfill Your Purpose	10
U	Unleash Healthy Spirituality	10
L	Lovify Your Life	10
L	Launch Your Plan	20*
P	Prioritize High-Octane Fuel	10
O	Omit What Is Harmful	10
W	Water Up	10
E	Exercise Outdoors	10
R	Rest Up	10
Total FULL POWER Score:		**100**

* Launch Your Plan is weighted at 20 points because it encompasses all the other actions.

This assessment is a subjective test measured only against your own potential. A score of 100 out of 100 is what Superman would get on a good day.

Calculating your 28-day score is a big deal. Anyone who has completed a 28-day lifestyle-intervention is among the top 2% because they have done what the other 98% didn't do. Post a picture of your score on your social media celebrating your new bodymind.

CONSIDER WHETHER TO RELAUNCH TO NEXT LEVEL

If you still have habits you'd like to change, or if you want to continue building on your progress, relaunch the program for another 28 days. Each cycle builds on the last, and over time, you'll see significant changes in overall health. Many have reversed heart disease, obesity, and diabetes using this kind of program.

With many exceptions, it takes an average of 66 days (not the 21 days you may have heard about) to turn a behavior into a habit depending on the complexity of the habit.[290] A habit is something we practice without using up willpower (see more in Chapters 7 and 8 on "Omit What Is Harmful"). For some, incorporating the action of drinking water into their daily routine is a more manageable habit to develop than adding 20 push-ups. For some others, it may be the other way around.

USING THE FULL POWER DASHBOARD FOR TROUBLESHOOTING

Let's take a look at Jasmine, who feels kind of dull and despondent. Her weight is increasing. Her cravings rule what she eats. Her cell phone controls her focus—hopping from Facebook posts to TikTok, to Instagram, and news that springs forth from everywhere in the world. She feels like she jumped into a river and let the current swoosh her any way it wants to go.

Jasmine asked herself, "What's going on with me?" She checks her FULL POWER dashboard.

Her "Unleash Positive Spirituality" and "Fulfill Your Purpose" scores are low. She realizes she stopped reading from an inspirational book every morning. She investigated why she didn't keep up the practice.

The answer: She woke up later in the morning and had no time for anything except to head straight for work.

But why did she do that?

She stayed up late the night before watching a movie.

Why did she do that?

She had been stressed at work.

She noticed her "Rest Up" scale was low. She hadn't disciplined herself to take time in the day for herself and had not kept a regular bedtime. This neglect affected her entire next day, inducing more stress.

The poorer sleep decreased her willpower, so she gave into processed food more often and binge-watched more movies. Using her FULL POWER Dashboard, Jasmine was able to trace backwards from her dull feelings to her poor sleep hygiene, to her not having time for inspirational reading to help her counter her work stress. She clearly saw a domino effect in action.

To use an axe metaphor, she was like an axe wielder who forgot to sharpen her axe, and it made her dull.

The axe metaphor was introduced to me in the form of an old story of a young lumberjack who bragged about how hard he worked but refused to sharpen his axe. His motto: "Only weaklings waste time sharpening their axes."

Eventually, he became less and less productive and was fired. He complained, saying that he was putting in more effort than the others and shouldn't have been let go.

But the boss said, "I measure you based on your results, not your efforts."

Cutting trees with a dull axe wears us out and makes us give up sooner. Living life with a weak bodymind wears us out and makes us give up sooner.

FULL POWER habits and routines sharpen the axe.

RESTRICTING VERSUS RESTRUCTURING

Often when I tell people that I have cut out sugar, oil, salt, white flour, meat, dairy, coffee, tea, soft drinks, and alcohol to stay healthy, they see my behaviors as restrictive. They are right—if they look at things from a short-term perspective. But it often comes down to short-term pleasures versus long-term vitality.

Seeing the big picture requires a change in mindset.

So, think of it this way: We aren't restricting ourselves; we're restructuring ourselves.

Restrictions are about what we aren't allowed to do. Purpose-driven restructuring liberates us to do what we were born to do.

The new habits become part of our new identity, inspired by our values. They lead to principles and guidelines. Those guidelines lead to goals. Working to achieve our goals determines where we spend our time and money. Ultimately, our habits shape our destiny.

After starting a new lifestyle, some people use a journal to reflect what's going well and what isn't.

The difference between those who achieve their goals and those who don't is that champions build habits based on a set of principles that take them through tough times and make them stronger. The FULL POWER plan will have you reaching the top of your game.

Before long, the mirror will show you your new "you"—the one that took action to switch life to FULL POWER. Optimal bodymind vitality is within your grasp. Claim it.

More power to you!

CONCLUSION

In these pages we have outlined the FULL POWER Plan, a treasure trove of gems designed by nature to create a better life and, ultimately, a better world. It is my hope that you have found something of value for your journey toward optimal bodymind vitality.

May the closing of this book be the opening of the most exciting chapter of your life—one filled with a glorious purpose, empowering spirituality, a loving community, and a practical plan, all energized by high-octane fuel, self-mastery, refreshing water, movement in the great outdoors, and restorative rest.

If you'd like to share a story about how these principles helped you experience optimal vitality, please email me at ejbrake@fullpower1.com. I may include it in a future publication.

Downloads and more insights related to the principles in this book are at fullpower1.com. Sign up to receive small power-packed weekly doses of motivation and information to inspire you on your journey.

Stay tuned for a FULL POWER sequel where we go deeper into the new science of psycho-spiritual contributors to optimal vitality. I'll share more of my transformation journey, adding new dimensions to the principles in this book and addressing unanswered questions that may have arisen during your reading.

May you experience all the vitality of body and mind that nature's formula has to offer.

I am rooting for you.

APPENDICES

VITALITY SELF-ASSESSMENT

The Vitality Self-Assessment is a snapshot of where you are today. It's asking the question, "How are you feeling?" in 25 different ways. This is a self-diagnosis, subjective for you alone at this moment. As you continue on your journey to vitality, your score will be ever-changing.

Ask yourself: "To what degree on a scale of 0-4 are these statements true about me?" (0 = "This is never true." 4 = "This is always true.")

Insert your score in the box to the left of the question. Add up your score on each question for your total out of 100. Use this score as a benchmark to which you compare your future self. After you implement the FULL POWER principles, take this assessment again to see if your vitality score has increased. Have fun!

	1	I feel joy and satisfaction with the direction my life has taken.
	2	I feel useful.
	3	I feel motivated to be active and pursue meaningful goals.
	4	I have inner peace and confidence.
	5	I have a value system that helps me in making long-term decisions.
	6	I feel inspired.
	7	My stress level is manageable.
	8	I am happy in my most important relationships.
	9	I feel a sense of belonging to a nurturing community without compromising my authentic self.
	10	I feel physically alert throughout the day.

	11	I feel mentally alert throughout the day and have the ability to concentrate.
	12	I am at a healthy weight for my height.
	13	I am satisfied with my physical appearance.
	14	It is easy for me to resist junk food and other harmful substances.
	15	I have healthy-looking skin.
	16	I feel energetic and fully alive.
	17	My body feels free and flexible.
	18	I have the physical strength and agility to lift a 20-pound box from the floor.
	19	I am free of aches and pains.
	20	I have clear eyes without dark circles.
	21	I have a work-rest balance that doesn't drain me.
	22	I feel well rested after I rise from sleep.
	23	I have a medication-free lifestyle.
	24	I have the emotional and mental strength to cope with setbacks.
	25	I frequently get compliments on how young and/or healthy I look.
	TOTAL:	My score on the VITALITY SELF-ASSESSMENT – Can be transferred to the FULL POWER Dashboard

HABIT TRACKERS

DAILY HABIT TRACKER
28-DAY LIFESTYLE PRESCRIPTION

F — FIND MY SUPERPOWER – FULFILL MY PURPOSE

Answer these questions each evening on a scale of 0-10. The average at the bottom goes on the dashboard.

		WEEK 1								WEEK 2						
	1	2	3	4	5	6	7	WEEK AVG.	8	9	10	11	12	13	14	WEEK AVG.
1 Today, my daily activities were driven by a sense of purpose.																
2 Today, I used at least one of my top strengths or talents.																
3 Today, I found myself in a state of flow, completely absorbed in what I was doing.																
4 Today, I minimized distractions so I could focus on what was important.																
5 I used the part of the day I'm at my best for my most important work.																
6 Today, I learned something that helped me, or will help me, accomplish my purpose.																
7 Today, I had a positive impact on at least one person.																
8 Today, my work or activities contributed to life satisfaction.																
9 Today, I had projects to work on that I loved more than eating.																
10 Today, my sense of purpose empowered me to resist harmful habits.																
AVERAGE																

DAILY HABIT TRACKER
28-DAY LIFESTYLE PRESCRIPTION

F FIND MY SUPERPOWER — FULFILL MY PURPOSE

Answer these questions each evening on a scale of 0-10. The average at the bottom goes on the dashboard.

		WEEK 3								WEEK 4							
	15	16	17	18	19	20	21	WEEK AVG.	22	23	24	25	26	27	28	WEEK AVG.	TOTAL AVG.
1 Today, my daily activities were driven by a sense of purpose.																	
2 Today, I used at least one of my top strengths or talents.																	
3 Today, I found myself in a state of flow, completely absorbed in what I was doing.																	
4 Today, I minimized distractions so I could focus on what was important.																	
5 I used the part of the day I'm at my best for my most important work.																	
6 Today, I learned something that helped me, or will help me, accomplish my purpose.																	
7 Today, I had a positive impact on at least one person.																	
8 Today, my work or activities contributed to life satisfaction.																	
9 Today, I had projects to work on that I loved more than eating.																	
10 Today, my sense of purpose empowered me to resist harmful habits.																	
AVERAGE																	

DAILY HABIT TRACKER
28-DAY LIFESTYLE PRESCRIPTION

 UNLEASH HEALTHY SPIRITUALITY

Answer these questions each evening on a scale of 0-10. The average at the bottom goes on the dashboard.

		WEEK 1								WEEK 2						
		1	2	3	4	5	6	7	WEEK AVG.	8	9	10	11	12	13	14	WEEK AVG.
1	Today, I lived my life as if I was part of something greater than myself.															
2	Today, I prioritized compassion and integrity over wealth and popularity.															
3	Today, I followed my conscience and modified it as I received greater wisdom.															
4	Today, I made decisions based on spiritual principles.															
5	Today, I read something inspiring.															
6	This week, I connected with others for spiritual purposes.															
7	Today, I meditated, prayed, or practiced a spiritual activity.															
8	Today, I was out in nature.															
9	Today, I practiced gratitude.															
10	Today, I practiced forgiveness, when needed – for myself and others.															
AVERAGE																

DAILY HABIT TRACKER
28-DAY LIFESTYLE PRESCRIPTION

U UNLEASH HEALTHY SPIRITUALITY

Answer these questions each evening on a scale of 0-10. The average at the bottom goes on the dashboard.

	WEEK 3							WEEK AVG.	WEEK 4							WEEK AVG.	TOTAL AVG.
	15	16	17	18	19	20	21		22	23	24	25	26	27	28		
1 Today, I lived my life as if I was part of something greater than myself.																	
2 Today, I prioritized compassion and integrity over wealth and popularity.																	
3 Today, I followed my conscience and modified it as I received greater wisdom.																	
4 Today, I made decisions based on spiritual principles.																	
5 Today, I read something inspiring.																	
6 This week, I connected with others for spiritual purposes.																	
7 Today, I meditated, prayed, or practiced a spiritual activity.																	
8 Today, I was out in nature.																	
9 Today, I practiced gratitude.																	
10 Today, I practiced forgiveness, when needed – for myself and others.																	
AVERAGE																	

DAILY HABIT TRACKER
28-DAY LIFESTYLE PRESCRIPTION

(L) LOVIFY MY LIFE

Answer these questions each evening on a scale of 0-10. The average at the bottom goes on the dashboard.

		WEEK 1								WEEK 2						
	1	2	3	4	5	6	7	WEEK AVG.	8	9	10	11	12	13	14	WEEK AVG.
1 Today, I maintained a healthy balance of give and take in my social interactions.																
2 Today, I am a part of a community of people who share my core values.																
3 Today, I expressed gratitude to people.																
4 Today, I knew when to say no and how to set boundaries that people respect.																
5 Today, I respected others even though I may have disagreed with them.																
6 Today, I served the people who most need my strengths.																
7 Today, I maintained loving relationships without giving up my authentic self.																
8 Today, I showed humility and confidence when I was with people.																
9 Today, I refrained from forcing or manipulating others to achieve my desires.																
10 Today, I actively listened before I spoke, and didn't interrupt, judge, or give unsolicited advice.																
AVERAGE																

DAILY HABIT TRACKER
28-DAY LIFESTYLE PRESCRIPTION

L LOVIFY MY LIFE

Answer these questions each evening on a scale of 0-10. The average at the bottom goes on the dashboard.

		WEEK 3							WEEK 4							
	15	16	17	18	19	20	21	WEEK AVG.	22	23	24	25	26	27	28	WEEK AVG.	TOTAL AVG.

1. Today, I maintained a healthy balance of give and take in my social interactions.

2. Today, I am a part of a community of people who share my core values.

3. Today, I expressed gratitude to people.

4. Today, I knew when to say no and how to set boundaries that people respect.

5. Today, I respected others even though I may have disagreed with them.

6. Today, I served the people who most need my strengths.

7. Today, I maintained loving relationships without giving up my authentic self.

8. Today, I showed humility and confidence when I was with people.

9. Today, I refrained from forcing or manipulating others to achieve my desires.

10. Today, I actively listened before I spoke, and didn't interrupt, judge, or give unsolicited advice.

AVERAGE

DAILY HABIT TRACKER
28-DAY LIFESTYLE PRESCRIPTION

L2 LAUNCH MY PLAN

Answer these questions each evening on a scale of 0-10. The average at the bottom goes on the dashboard.

	WEEK 1								WEEK 2							
	1	2	3	4	5	6	7	WEEK AVG.	8	9	10	11	12	13	14	WEEK AVG.
1 Today, my habits aligned with a purpose that inspired me.																
2 Today, I tracked my progress in maintaining healthy habits.																
3 Today, I have been intentionally living out a plan for my personal growth and health (vitality plan).																
4 Today, I read, watched, or listened to material that supported my vitality plan.																
5 Today, my environment (physical and relational) supported my vitality plan.																
6 Today, my habits were strong enough to help me overcome self-sabotaging behaviors.																
7 Today, I put knowledge into action.																
8 Today, my habits enhanced my mental health.																
9 Today, my habits enhanced my physical health.																
10 Today, I practiced morning and evening routines that supported my vitality plan.																
AVERAGE																

DAILY HABIT TRACKER
28-DAY LIFESTYLE PRESCRIPTION

L2 LAUNCH MY PLAN

Answer these questions each evening on a scale of 0-10. The average at the bottom goes on the dashboard.

	WEEK 3								WEEK 4								
	15	16	17	18	19	20	21	WEEK AVG.	22	23	24	25	26	27	28	WEEK AVG.	TOTAL AVG.
1 Today, my habits aligned with a purpose that inspired me.																	
2 Today, I tracked my progress in maintaining healthy habits.																	
3 Today, I have been intentionally living out a plan for my personal growth and health (vitality plan).																	
4 Today, I read, watched, or listened to material that supported my vitality plan.																	
5 Today, my environment (physical and relational) supported my vitality plan.																	
6 Today, my habits were strong enough to help me overcome self-sabotaging behaviors.																	
7 Today, I put knowledge into action.																	
8 Today, my habits enhanced my mental health.																	
9 Today, my habits enhanced my physical health.																	
10 Today, I practiced morning and evening routines that supported my vitality plan.																	
AVERAGE																	

DAILY HABIT TRACKER
28-DAY LIFESTYLE PRESCRIPTION

 PRIORITIZE HIGH-OCTANE FUEL

Answer these questions each evening on a scale of 0-10. The average at the bottom goes on the dashboard.

		WEEK 1							WEEK 2						
	1	2	3	4	5	6	7	WEEK AVG.	8	9	10	11	12	13	14	WEEK AVG.
1 Today, I ate a whole food plant-based diet.															
2 Today, I ate four or five fruits, including berries (unless I was fasting).															
3 Today, I ate four or five vegetables, including cruciferous vegetables and greens (unless I was fasting).															
4 Today, I ate a few nuts, including almonds (unless I was fasting).															
5 Today, I ate a few seeds - like pumpkin seeds, sunflower seeds, flaxseeds (unless I was fasting).															
6 Today, I ate whole grains (unless I was fasting).															
7 Today, I ate legumes, unless I was fasting. (For those with sensitive stomachs just starting on a whole foods plant-based eating plan, even one bean counts.)															
8 Today, I had 1-4 bowel movements.															
9 Today, I ate two or three meals.															
10 Today, I ate nothing between meals.															
AVERAGE															

DAILY HABIT TRACKER
28-DAY LIFESTYLE PRESCRIPTION

 **PRIORITIZE HIGH-OCTANE FUEL**

Answer these questions each evening on a scale of 0-10. The average at the bottom goes on the dashboard.

		WEEK 3						WEEK AVG.		WEEK 4						WEEK AVG.	TOTAL AVG.
	15	16	17	18	19	20	21		22	23	24	25	26	27	28		
1 Today, I ate a whole food plant-based diet.																	
2 Today, I ate four or five fruits, including berries (unless I was fasting).																	
3 Today, I ate four or five vegetables, including cruciferous vegetables and greens (unless I was fasting).																	
4 Today, I ate a few nuts, including almonds (unless I was fasting).																	
5 Today, I ate a few seeds - like pumpkin seeds, sunflower seeds, flaxseeds (unless I was fasting).																	
6 Today, I ate whole grains (unless I was fasting).																	
7 Today, I ate legumes, unless I was fasting. (For those with sensitive stomachs just starting on a whole foods plant-based eating plan, even one bean counts.)																	
8 Today, I had 1-4 bowel movements.																	
9 Today, I ate two or three meals.																	
10 Today, I ate nothing between meals.																	
AVERAGE																	

DAILY HABIT TRACKER
28-DAY LIFESTYLE PRESCRIPTION

◎ OMIT WHAT IS HARMFUL

Answer these questions each evening on a scale of 0-10. The average at the bottom goes on the dashboard.

		WEEK 1							WEEK AVG.	WEEK 2							WEEK AVG.
		1	2	3	4	5	6	7		8	9	10	11	12	13	14	
1	Today, I avoided refined food (foods with processed sugar, oil or white flour in the ingredients).																
2	Today, I limited my daily sodium intake to 1/4 teaspoon.																
3	Today, I stopped eating before my stomach felt full.																
4	Today, I avoided alcohol, smoking, and illicit drugs.																
5	Today, I avoided meat consumption.																
6	Today, I avoided dairy consumption.																
7	Today, I resisted distractions (things that take me off a healthy track).																
8	Today, I adhered to a preplanned strategy to stay on course whenever I had a craving for something harmful.																
9	Today, I avoided the non-productive use of screen time.																
10	Today, I considered the long-term effects of my actions and decisions.																
	AVERAGE																

DAILY HABIT TRACKER
28-DAY LIFESTYLE PRESCRIPTION

OMIT WHAT IS HARMFUL

Answer these questions each evening on a scale of 0-10. The average at the bottom goes on the dashboard.

		WEEK 3							WEEK 4							
	15	16	17	18	19	20	21	WEEK AVG.	22	23	24	25	26	27	28	WEEK AVG.	TOTAL AVG.
1	Today, I avoided refined food (foods with processed sugar, oil or white flour in the ingredients).															
2	Today, I limited my daily sodium intake to 1/4 teaspoon.															
3	Today, I stopped eating before my stomach felt full.															
4	Today, I avoided alcohol, smoking, and illicit drugs.															
5	Today, I avoided meat consumption.															
6	Today, I avoided dairy consumption.															
7	Today, I resisted distractions (things that take me off a healthy track).															
8	Today, I adhered to a preplanned strategy to stay on course whenever I had a craving for something harmful.															
9	Today, I avoided the non-productive use of screen time.															
10	Today, I considered the long-term effects of my actions and decisions.															
AVERAGE																

DAILY HABIT TRACKER
28-DAY LIFESTYLE PRESCRIPTION

WATER UP

Answer these questions each evening on a scale of 0-10. The average at the bottom goes on the dashboard.

		WEEK 1								WEEK 2						
	1	2	3	4	5	6	7	WEEK AVG.	8	9	10	11	12	13	14	WEEK AVG.
1 Today, I drank enough water for my weight, activity level, and circumstances.																
2 Today, the water I drank was clean.																
3 Today, I drank water upon arising in the morning.																
4 Today, I drank water up to approximately a half hour before meals.																
5 Today, I started drinking water again about an hour after eating.																
6 Today, my urine was pale yellow.																
7 Today, water was the only thing I drank between meals.																
8 Today, I ended my shower with at least 30 seconds of cold.																
9 Today, I counted the number of cups of water I drank.																
10 Today, I distributed my water intake evenly throughout the day.																
AVERAGE																

DAILY HABIT TRACKER
28-DAY LIFESTYLE PRESCRIPTION

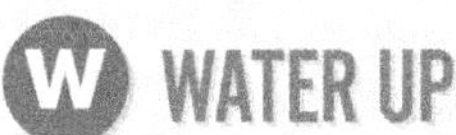

WATER UP

Answer these questions each evening on a scale of 0-10. The average at the bottom goes on the dashboard.

			WEEK 3								WEEK 4						
	15	16	17	18	19	20	21	WEEK AVG.	22	23	24	25	26	27	28	WEEK AVG.	TOTAL AVG.
1 Today, I drank enough water for my weight, activity level, and circumstances.																	
2 Today, the water I drank was clean.																	
3 Today, I drank water upon arising in the morning.																	
4 Today, I drank water up to approximately a half hour before meals.																	
5 Today, I started drinking water again about an hour after eating.																	
6 Today, my urine was pale yellow.																	
7 Today, water was the only thing I drank between meals.																	
8 Today, I ended my shower with at least 30 seconds of cold.																	
9 Today, I counted the number of cups of water I drank.																	
10 Today, I distributed my water intake evenly throughout the day.																	
AVERAGE																	

DAILY HABIT TRACKER
28-DAY LIFESTYLE PRESCRIPTION

E EXERCISE OUTDOORS

Answer these questions each evening on a scale of 0-10. The average at the bottom goes on the dashboard.

		WEEK 1								WEEK 2							
	1	2	3	4	5	6	7	WEEK AVG.	8	9	10	11	12	13	14	WEEK AVG.
1	Today, I completed a strength building routine for my core (buttocks, hip, abdomen) unless I was recovering between workout days.															
2	Today, I completed a strength building routine that built up my upper body unless I was recovering between workout days.															
3	Today, I could rise from a sitting position without using my hands.															
4	Today, I walked at least 1/2 hour.															
5	Today, I rose and moved after each half-hour of sitting.															
6	Today, I stretched for 10-30 minutes.															
7	Today, I performed daily exercises and stretches that enhanced my posture.															
8	Today, I built movement into my daily routines (i.e., taking the stairs, cycling to work).															
9	Today, I spent at least an hour outdoors, ensuring exposure to sunlight and fresh air, and applied healthy sunblock as needed.															
10	Today, I adjusted my exercise intensity according to my fitness level.															
AVERAGE																

DAILY HABIT TRACKER
28-DAY LIFESTYLE PRESCRIPTION

E EXERCISE OUTDOORS

Answer these questions each evening on a scale of 0-10. The average at the bottom goes on the dashboard.

	WEEK 3								WEEK 4								
	15	16	17	18	19	20	21	WEEK AVG.	22	23	24	25	26	27	28	WEEK AVG.	TOTAL AVG.
1 Today, I completed a strength building routine for my core (buttocks, hip, abdomen) unless I was recovering between workout days.																	
2 Today, I completed a strength building routine that built up my upper body unless I was recovering between workout days.																	
3 Today, I could rise from a sitting position without using my hands.																	
4 Today, I walked at least 1/2 hour.																	
5 Today, I rose and moved after each half-hour of sitting.																	
6 Today, I stretched for 10-30 minutes.																	
7 Today, I performed daily exercises and stretches that enhanced my posture.																	
8 Today, I built movement into my daily routines (i.e., taking the stairs, cycling to work).																	
9 Today, I spent at least an hour outdoors, ensuring exposure to sunlight and fresh air, and applied healthy sunblock as needed.																	
10 Today, I adjusted my exercise intensity according to my fitness level.																	
AVERAGE																	

DAILY HABIT TRACKER
28-DAY LIFESTYLE PRESCRIPTION

Answer these questions each evening on a scale of 0-10. The average at the bottom goes on the dashboard.

		WEEK 1								WEEK 2						
	1	2	3	4	5	6	7	WEEK AVG.	8	9	10	11	12	13	14	WEEK AVG.
1	Last night, I slept 7-9 hours.															
2	Last night, I kept to a consistent sleep schedule.															
3	Today, I turned off technology 60-90 minutes before bedtime.															
4	Today, I followed my evening routine to prepare my mind for sleep.															
5	This evening, my bedroom was totally dark, cool, and quiet for sleep.															
6	Today, I allowed at least a four-hour gap between my final meal and bedtime.															
7	Today, I exposed my eyes to the morning light to set my circadian rhythm.															
8	Today, I didn't drink coffee or alcohol.															
9	I take a weekly day off for rejuvenation.															
10	I take yearly vacation time.															
AVERAGE																

DAILY HABIT TRACKER
28-DAY LIFESTYLE PRESCRIPTION

Answer these questions each evening on a scale of 0-10. The average at the bottom goes on the dashboard.

		WEEK 3							WEEK AVG.	WEEK 4							WEEK AVG.	TOTAL AVG.
		15	16	17	18	19	20	21		22	23	24	25	26	27	28		
1	Last night, I slept 7-9 hours.																	
2	Last night, I kept to a consistent sleep schedule.																	
3	Today, I turned off technology 60-90 minutes before bedtime.																	
4	Today, I followed my evening routine to prepare my mind for sleep.																	
5	This evening, my bedroom was totally dark, cool, and quiet for sleep.																	
6	Today, I allowed at least a four-hour gap between my final meal and bedtime.																	
7	Today, I exposed my eyes to the morning light to set my circadian rhythm.																	
8	Today, I didn't drink coffee or alcohol.																	
9	I take a weekly day off for rejuvenation.																	
10	I take yearly vacation time.																	
	AVERAGE																	

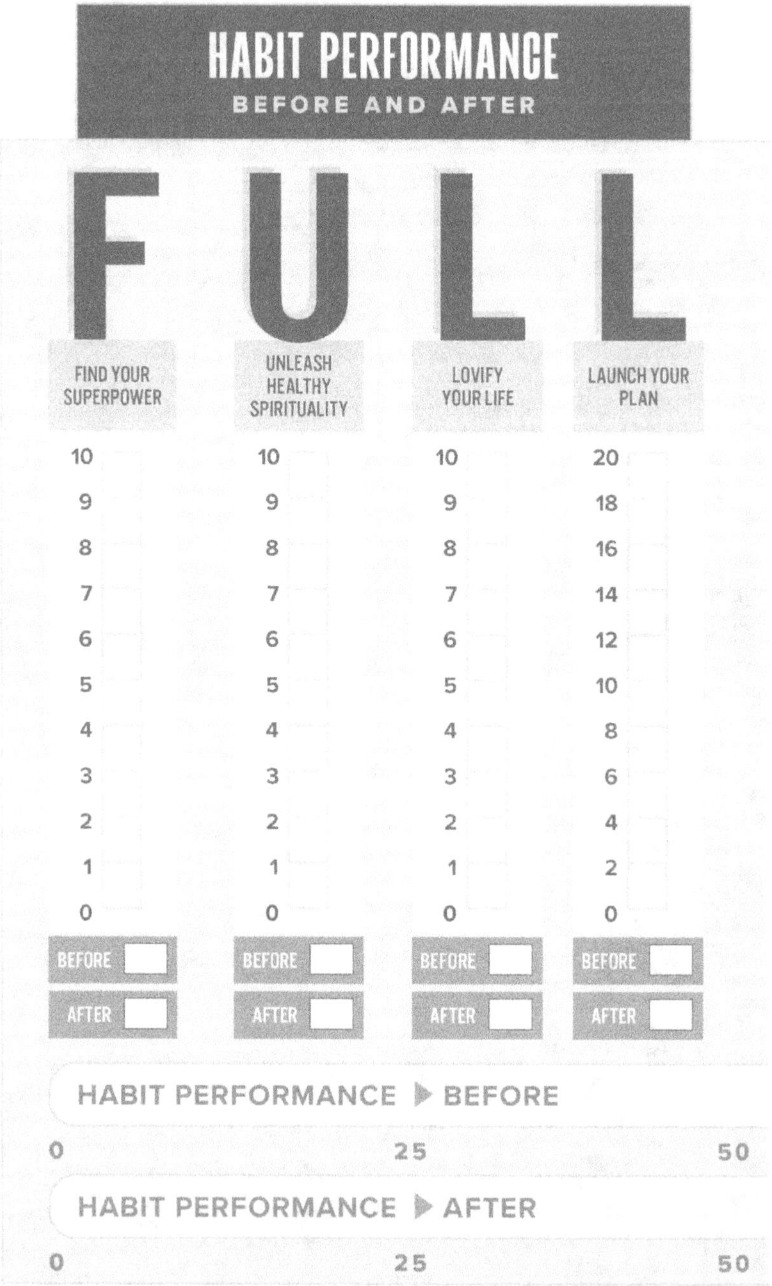

HABIT PERFORMANCE
BEFORE AND AFTER

FULL

FIND YOUR SUPERPOWER	UNLEASH HEALTHY SPIRITUALITY	LOVIFY YOUR LIFE	LAUNCH YOUR PLAN
10	10	10	20
9	9	9	18
8	8	8	16
7	7	7	14
6	6	6	12
5	5	5	10
4	4	4	8
3	3	3	6
2	2	2	4
1	1	1	2
0	0	0	0
BEFORE	BEFORE	BEFORE	BEFORE
AFTER	AFTER	AFTER	AFTER

HABIT PERFORMANCE ▶ BEFORE

0	25	50

HABIT PERFORMANCE ▶ AFTER

0	25	50

HABIT PERFORMANCE
BEFORE AND AFTER

POWER

PRIORITIZE HIGH-OCTANE FUEL	OMIT WHAT IS HARMFUL	WATER UP	EXERCISE OUTDOORS	REST UP	
10	10	10	10	10	
9	9	9	9	9	
8	8	8	8	8	
7	7	7	7	7	
6	6	6	6	6	
5	5	5	5	5	
4	4	4	4	4	
3	3	3	3	3	
2	2	2	2	2	
1	1	1	1	1	
0	0	0	0	0	TOTAL
BEFORE	BEFORE	BEFORE	BEFORE	BEFORE	BEFORE
AFTER	AFTER	AFTER	AFTER	AFTER	AFTER

(USE CUMULATIVE SCORE FROM CHAPTER CHECKLISTS)

75   100

(USE HABIT TRACKERS)

75   100

DAILY HABIT TRACKER
28-DAY LIFESTYLE PRESCRIPTION

FULL POWER DASHBOARD

	POSS	WEEK 1							WEEK AVG.	WEEK 2							WEEK AVG.
		1	2	3	4	5	6	7		8	9	10	11	12	13	14	
F	10																
U	10																
L	10																
L	20																
P	10																
O	10																
W	10																
E	10																
R	10																
TOTAL	100																

PRE-LAUNCH
SELF-DIAGNOSIS

FILL IN YOUR VITALITY ASSESSMENT SCORE HERE

100
90
80
70
60
50
40
30
20
10
0

BIO MARKERS

WEIGHT

WAIST

BMI

BP

PULSE

FULL-POWER
HABIT TRACKER

MONITOR YOUR HABITS CONNECTED TO EACH PRINCIPLE FOR EACH DAY, AND ENTER YOUR SCORE IN THE CHART ABOVE.

PERFORMANCE LEVEL:

Mark in your cumulative score from the end-of-chapter checklists before you begin. Then, after the 28 days, mark in your Total Final Average score from Habit Tracker to the right.

DAILY HABIT TRACKER
28-DAY LIFESTYLE PRESCRIPTION

FULL POWER DASHBOARD

	POSS	WEEK 3								WEEK 4								
		15	16	17	18	19	20	21	WEEK AVG.	22	23	24	25	26	27	28	WEEK AVG.	TOTAL AVG.
F	10																	
U	10																	
L	10																	
L	20																	
P	10																	
O	10																	
W	10																	
E	10																	
R	10																	
TOTAL	100																	

PERFORMANCE LEVEL

100
95
90
85
80
75
70
65
60
55
50
45
40
35
30
25
20
15
10
5
0

GOLD

SILVER

BRONZE

POST-LAUNCH
SELF-DIAGNOSIS

BIO MARKERS

WEIGHT	
WAIST	
BMI	
BP	
PULSE	

FILL IN YOUR VITALITY ASSESSMENT SCORE HERE

100
90
80
70
60
50
40
30
20
10
0

RESOURCE LIST

SOURCES OF BODYMIND VITALITY INSIGHTS

American College of Lifestyle Medicine (ACLM): lifestylemedicine.org

Andrew Huberman (Neuroscience): hubermanlab.com

Blue Zones (Lifestyle Medicine): bluezones.com

Charles Duhigg (Habits): charlesduhigg.com

Cleveland Clinic: my.clevelandclinic.org/health

Dan Beuttner (Blue Zones): danbuettner.com

Dr. Brené Brown (Psychology of Shame): brenebrown.com

Dr. Caldwell Esselstyn (Heart Health): dresselstyn.com/site/

Dr. Douglas Lisle (Addictions): healthpromoting.com

Dr. Gabor Maté (Addictions): drgabormate.com

Dr. Greg Steinke (Lifestyle Medicine Clinic): lifemedclinic.org

Dr. Hans Diehl (CHIP Program): hansdiehl.com

Dr. John McDougall (Lifestyle Medicine): drmcdougall.com

Dr. Lisa Miller (Spirituality): lisamillerphd.com

Dr. Matthew Walker (Sleep): sleepfoundation.org

Dr. Michael Greger (Nutrition): nutritionfacts.org

Dr. Nadine Burk Harris (Adverse Childhood Experiences): burkefoundation.org

Dr. Neil Bernard (Medicine): pcrm.org

Dr. Rangan Chatterjee (Lifestyle Medicine): drchatterjee.com

Dr. Roger Seheult (MedCram): medcram.com

Dr. Susan Peirce Thompson (Weight Loss): susanpeircethompson.com

Dr. T. Colin Campbell (Nutrition): nutritionstudies.org

Happiness: pursuit-of-happiness.org

Harvard Health: health.harvard.edu

James Clear (Habits): jamesclear.com

James Kwik (Memory): jimkwik.com

Mayo Clinic: mayoclinic.org

Miranda Esmonde-White (Stretching): essentrics.com

Shawn Achor (Happiness): shawnachor.com

Silver Hills Bakery (Bread): silverhillsbakery.ca

Silver Hills Guesthouse (Lifestyle Medicine Live-in Center): silverhills.ca

MENU FOR LIFE

WHOLE FOODS PLANT-BASED

Rather than providing a weekly or monthly menu plan, here are principles for choosing your menu plan for life, followed by simple menu guidelines, examples, and recommended cookbooks.

PRINCIPLES

1. Choose your food from fruits, vegetables, whole grains, legumes, and nuts.
2. No oil.
3. No sugar.
4. No refined products.
5. Read ingredients on packaging. Choose foods with the least amount of processing.
6. Be creative.
   For example:
   a. Grains can be made into burgers.
   b. Create baked dishes for breakfast by mixing grains with dates, nuts, and spices, then add nut milk or tofu, etc.
   c. Use your favorite recipes and substitute or omit unwanted ingredients.
7. Adding spices and herbs makes a difference in taste and enjoyment.

MENU GUIDELINE

Breakfast

From the list below, choose three or four fruits, a whole grain or grains, nuts, and seeds.

Second Meal

From the list below, choose three or four vegetables, including a green vegetable. Choose a whole grain or grains or a legume. Make a salad from the vegetable list.

Third Meal

Make the third meal the smallest meal of the day if you have it at all.

CREATE YOUR CUISINE FROM THE HIGH-OCTANE FUEL BELOW

(These lists are not exhaustive)

Fruits

Apples, apricots, avocados, bananas, berries such as blueberries, blackberries, cranberries, cherries, coconuts, dates, durian, figs, grapes, guava, jackfruit, kiwi, kumquat, lemons, limes, mangos, oranges, papaya, pears, peaches, persimmons, pineapple, plums, pomegranates, prunes, raspberries, strawberries, watermelon

Vegetables

Artichokes, arugula, asparagus, beets, brussels sprouts, cabbage, calabash, carrots, cauliflower, celery, chayote, chili, chili peppers, corn, cucumber, edamame, eggplants, fennel, garlic, ginger, jicama, kale, leeks, lettuce, marrow, mushrooms, onion, okra, parsnip, peas, potatoes, pumpkin, radish, rutabaga, shallots, spinach, squash, sweet potatoes, tomatoes, turnip, watercress, yams, zucchini

Whole Grains

Amaranth, barley, black rice, buckwheat, chia seeds, farro, flax meal, flax-seed, freekeh, hemp seeds, oatmeal, pumpkin seeds, quinoa, Red River cereal, sesame seeds, spelt, sunflower seeds, whole rice, whole wheat

Legumes

Adzuki beans, beans, big broad beans, black beans, black-eyed peas, chick-peas (garbanzo), chili beans, green beans, green split peas, kidney beans, lentils, lima beans, mung dal, pinto beans, red calypso beans, Romano beans, scarlet runner beans, soybeans

Nuts

Almonds, Brazil nuts, cashews, chestnuts, hazelnuts, macadamias, peanuts, pecans, pistachios, walnuts

MENU EXAMPLES

Day 1

Breakfast: Cooked grains (i.e., oatmeal, Red River cereal) with almond milk, topped with sliced banana, berries, three prunes, nuts, flax meal, and pumpkin seeds. Multigrain bread with nut & seed butter.

Second Meal: Brown rice bowl with mixed vegetables (carrots, broccoli, bell peppers, and spinach).

Third Meal (Optional): Vegetable soup with whole grain bread and a mixed green salad.

Day 2

Breakfast: Smoothie bowl with blended acai, banana, berries, and topped with sliced almonds, granola, and coconut flakes.

Second Meal: Quinoa and black bean salad with mixed greens, chopped tomato, cucumber, avocado, and a homemade lemon-tahini dressing.

Third Meal (Optional): Grilled portobello mushrooms with roasted sweet potato and mixed vegetables (zucchini, bell peppers, and onions).

Day 3

Breakfast: Buckwheat pancakes with mixed berries and a side of sliced kiwi.

Second Meal: Sweet potato and black bean tacos with salsa and a mixed green salad.

Third Meal (Optional): Spaghetti squash with homemade marinara sauce, pecan tofu balls, and mixed vegetables (eggplant, bell peppers, and mushrooms).

Day 4

Breakfast: Fruit salad with mixed berries, pineapple, mango, and a side of almond butter toast.

Second Meal: Chickpea and vegetable stir-fry with brown rice.

Third Meal (Optional): Baked potato with a mixed green salad and a side of steamed green beans.

Day 5

Breakfast: Chia seed pudding with nut milk, topped with sliced kiwi, banana, mango, and pomegranate seeds.

Second Meal: Lentil and vegetable soup with whole grain bread and a mixed green salad.

Third Meal (Optional): Fruit salad and popcorn.

RECOMMENDED COOKBOOKS

There are many whole food plant-based recipes online. Use search terms such as "unrefined," "unprocessed," "whole food plant-based."

Here are a few cookbooks of varying tastes that largely align with the FULL POWER principles. Some recipes will need to be adjusted to conform with nature's formula.

1. *Brighten Up Breakfast,* Erica Nedley
2. Eat Plants Feel Whole: Harness the Healing Power of Plants and Transform Your Health, George E. Guthrie
3. *Forks Over Knives: The Cookbook,* Del Stroufe
4. *Forks Over Knives: The Plant-Based Way to Health,* edited by Gene Stone
5. *The China Study Cookbook,* Leanne Campbell
6. The China Study Cookbook Revised and Expanded, Leanne Campbell
7. *The Engine 2 Cookbook: More than 130 Lip-Smacking, Rib-Sticking, Body-Slimming Recipes to Live Plant-Strong,* Rip Esselstyn and Jane Esselstyn
8. *The Get Healthy, Go Vegan Cookbook,* Neal Bernard and Robyn Webb
9. *The How Not to Diet Cookbook,* Michael Greger
10. *The Optimal Diet: The Official CHIP Cookbook,* Darlene Blaney and Hans Diehl
11. *The PlantPure Kitchen: 130 Mouthwatering Whole Food Recipes and Tips for a Plant-Based Life,* Kim Campbell
12. *The PlantPure Nation Cookbook,* Kim Campbell

ENDNOTES

1   I was introduced to this term by Dr. Gabor Maté in his book In the Realm of Hungry Ghosts: Close Encounters with Addiction (London: Vermillion, 2018). I'll use this term throughout the book.

2   For more on lifestyle medicine see https://lifestylemedicine.org/overview/ and https://www.health.harvard.edu/blog/lifestyle-medicine-for-all-healthy -food-comes-first-2020092421009.

3   Some characters are composites, and certain names have been altered to safe-guard their privacy.

4   Q with Tom Power, "Matthew Perry Shares His Incredible Story of Survival and Why Fame Wasn't the Answer to His Problems," November 22, 2022, YouTube video, 48:55, https://youtu.be/vrZsyBhmMro?si=DMWBDpAW O10DAQNK.

5   Mihaly Csikszentmihalyi, Flow: The Psychology of Optimal Experience (1990; New York: Harper Perennial, 2008), 49.

6   John Stuart Mill, "Chapter 5: A Crisis in My Mental History. One Stage Onward," in Autobiography, https://www.laits.utexas.edu/poltheory/mill/ auto/auto.c05.html.

7   These life lessons are supported by research from the following source: Emiliana R. Simon-Thomas, "How Strong Is Your Sense of Purpose in Life?" *Greater Good Magazine*, Greater Good Science Center, April 11, 2022, https://greatergood.berkeley.edu/article/item/ how_strong_is_your_sense_of_purpose_in_life.

8   Dan Buettner, "Discovering the Blue Zones Solution: Transform Your Health—And Live Longer" in "Blue Zones: The Science of Living Longer," special issue, National Geographic (2016): 9.

9   CliftonStrengths, "How to Support Your Coaching Clients Effectively: An AMA -- Called to Coach," December 29, 2021, YouTube video, 1:00:44, https://youtu.be/LPCSqFcmtUc?si=t49dPKlkfU3-8cVT.

10 Simon-Thomas, "Your Sense of Purpose."

11 Simon-Thomas, "Your Sense of Purpose."

12 Simon-Thomas, "Your Sense of Purpose."

13 The Blue Zones have been popularized by National Geographic journalist Dan Buettner. They are Ikaria, Greece; Okinawa, Japan; Sardinia, Italy; Nicoya Peninsula, Costa Rica; and Loma Linda, California, USA. Dan Buettner has recently (2023) added Singapore to the list of Blue Zones. Efforts have been made to create Blue Zones in Fort Worth, Texas; Albert Lea, Minnesota; and dozens of other locations throughout the United States.

14 "Big Bang Theory's Mayim Bialik Was Left 'in Tears' by Competitive Moms' Group," Toronto Sun, December 29, 2017, https://torontosun.com/entertainment/celebrity/big-bang-theorys-mayim-bialik-was-left-in-tears-by-competitive-moms-group; Mayim Bialik, "Why Are Moms So Competitive? || Mayim Bialik," December 28, 2017, YouTube video, 5:02, https://youtu.be/K5CiTT-HV9w?si=Y5XleuW_utV8WFqm.

15 Depression, World Health Organization, accessed June 29, 2023, https://www.who.int/health-topics/depression.

16 Lisa Miller, The Awakened Brain: The Psychology of Spirituality (New York: Random House, 2021), 6.

17 Miller, Awakened Brain, 7.

18 Miller, Awakened Brain, 8.

19 Miller, Awakened Brain, 7.

20 Miller, Awakened Brain, 61.

21 Miller, Awakened Brain, 150.

22 Rich Roll, "Lisa Miller, PhD on the Neuroscience Of Spirituality | Rich Roll Podcast," January 10, 2022, YouTube video, 1:57:56, https://youtu.be/BuBDmIRThtk?si=qlin9Ajxz7uDEPXn.

23 Johnaé De Felicis, "The Halo Effect of Sacred Spaces," Blue Zones, accessed February 8, 2024, https://www.bluezones.com/2022/07/the-halo-effect-of-sacred-spaces/.

24 Dan Buettner, The Blue Zones: Lessons for Living Longer from the People Who've Lived the Longest (Washington, DC: National Geographic Society, 2008).

25   De Felicis, "Halo Effect."

26   Building Strength Webinars, "Religion, Spirituality and Health - Dr. Koenig," April 11, 2016, YouTube video, 2:06:03, https://youtu.be/Mlp9l5I ynXI?si=oc9YsaZLyPBEHvqc.

27   Harold G. Koenig and Harvey J. Cohen, eds., The Link between Religion and Health: Psychoneuroimmunology and the Faith Factor (New York: Oxford University Press, 2002).

28   Office of the California Surgeon General, "Understanding ACEs with Dr. Nadine Burke Harris," August 1, 2022, YouTube video, 7:18, https://youtu. be/Hh1idR1XkC4?si=iqVNdY7cfUg8eSsb.

29   Miller, Awakened Brain, 153.

30   Catharine Paddock, "Soil Bacteria Work in Similar Way to Antidepressants," Medical News Today, April 2, 2007, https://www.medicalnewstoday.com/ articles/66840.

31   Angela Duckworth, Grit: The Power of Passion and Perseverance (New York: Scribner, 2016).

32   American physiologist Walter Cannon coined the term "fight or flight" in 1915. But since then, more research has expanded the understanding of the danger response to include fight, flight, freeze, fawn, or faint.

33   "The Stress Response and How It Can Affect You," Center for Integrated Healthcare, July 2013, archived January 17, 2024, at the Wayback Machine, https://web.archive.org/web/20240117085105/https://www.mirecc.va.gov/ cih-visn2/Documents/Patient_Education_Handouts/Stress_Response_and_ How_It_Can_Affect_You_Version_3.pdf.

34   1 Cor. 13:4–8, New International Version (NIV).

35   Liz Mineo, "Good Genes Are Nice, but Joy Is Better," Harvard Gazette, April 11, 2017, https://news.harvard.edu/gazette/story/2017/04/over-nearly-80-years-harvard-study-has-been-showing-how-to-live-a-healthy-and-happy-life/.

36   https://www.thehealthy.com/mental-health/happiness/ how-to-be-happy-the-good-life-dr-waldinger/

37   Robert Waldinger, "What Makes a Good Life? Lessons from the Longest Study on Happiness," filmed November 2015 at TEDxBeaconStreet, TED video, 12:38, https://www.ted.com/talks/robert_waldinger_what_makes_a_ good_life_lessons_from_the_longest_study_on_happiness.

38   Mineo, "Joy Is Better."

39 Shawn Achor, Big Potential: How Transforming the Pursuit of Success Raises Our Achievement, Happiness, and Well-Being (New York: Crown Currency, 2018), 32.

40 Achor, Big Potential, 33.

41 Achor, Big Potential, 33.

42 Achor, Big Potential, 33.

43 Achor, Big Potential, 33.

44 "Social Connection Is the Strongest Protective Factor for Depression," Massachusetts General Hospital, ScienceDaily, August 14, 2020, https://www.sciencedaily.com/releases/2020/08/200814131007.htm.

45 "Depressive Disorder (Depression)," World Health Organization, March 31, 2023, https://www.who.int/news-room/fact-sheets/detail/depression.

46 Bessel van der Kolk, The Body Keeps the Score: Brain, Mind, and Body in the Healing of Trauma (New York: Penguin Books, 2014), 81.

47 Geoffrey Brewer, "Snakes Top List of Americans' Fears," Gallup, March 19, 2001, https://news.gallup.com/poll/1891/snakes-top-list-americans-fears.aspx.

48 Bonnie Betts, "Maintaining Healthy Relationships with Age," Mayo Clinic Health System, April 10, 2023, https://www.mayoclinichealthsystem.org/hometown-health/speaking-of-health/maintaining-healthy-relationships-is-important-as-we-age.

49 Family Action Network, "John and Julie Gottman: Eight Dates: Essential Conversations for a Lifetime of Love (03/13/19)," March 16, 2019, YouTube video, 44:07, https://youtu.be/V8XlHGHP98I?si=Yrj1GlndmWfu0r6a.

50 Prov 15:1 (NIV).

51 James Clear, Atomic Habits: An Easy & Proven Way to Build Good Habits & Break Bad Ones (New York: Avery, 2018), 28.

52 I am indebted to Jack Canfield, coauthor of the Chicken Soup for the Soul series, for this insight.

53 Rafael Badziag, "I Interviewed 21 Self-Made Billionaires About Their Secrets to Wealth and Success—Here's What I Learned," CNBC, June 21, 2019, https://www.cnbc.com/2019/06/21/self-made-billionaires-the-6-habits-of-massive-wealth-and-success.html.

54 Phillippa Lally et al., "How Are Habits Formed: Modelling Habit Formation in the Real World," European Journal of Social Psychology 40, no. 6, 998–1009, https://doi.org/10.1002/ejsp.674.

55 I first heard of this concept from Jim Kwik, author of Limitless: Upgrade Your Brain, Learn Anything Faster, and Unlock Your Exceptional Life.

56 Ananda L. Roy and Richard S. Conroy, "Toward Mapping the Human Body at a Cellular Resolution," Molecular Biology of the Cell 29, no. 15 (2018): 1779–85, https://doi.org/10.1091/mbc.E18-04-0260.

57 T. Alan Jiang, "Health Benefits of Culinary Herbs and Spices," Journal of AOAC INTERNATIONAL 102, no. 2 (2019): 395–411, https://doi.org/10.5740/jaoacint.18-0418.

58 Kathryn Watson, "What Are Flavonoids? Everything You Need to Know," Healthline, last updated July 12, 2023, https://www.healthline.com/health/what-are-flavonoids-everything-you-need-to-know.

59 Kiara Anthony, "Carotenoids: Everything You Need to Know," Healthline, last updated September 18, 2018, https://www.healthline.com/health/carotenoids.

60 Michael Greger and Gene Stone, How Not to Die: Discover the Foods Scientifically Proven to Prevent and Reverse Disease (New York: Flatiron Books, 2015), 70–71.

61 Tom Monte and Ilene Pritikin, Pritikin: The Man Who Healed America's Heart (Emmaus, PA: Rodale Press, 1987), referenced in Greger and Stone, How Not to Die, ix–x.

62 Chef AJ, "How Does Lifestyle Medicine Impact You? | Interview with Dr. Hans Diehl," streamed live on June 3, 2020, YouTube video, 1:10:24, https://www.youtube.com/live/pCLzvYKcTy0?si=G7fsLsU4pYWW7r7m.

63 Chef AJ, "Lifestyle Medicine."

64 Greger and Stone, How Not to Die, 282.

65 "By the Numbers: Diabetes in America," Centers for Disease Control and Prevention, last reviewed October 25, 2022, https://www.cdc.gov/diabetes/health-equity/diabetes-by-the-numbers.html.

66 The late Dr. Hans Diehl, working from his Lifestyle Medicine Institute in Loma Linda, California, published data from over 100,000 CHIP graduates from 1988 to 2012. The compiled data from CHIP programs around the world painted an astounding overall picture of what lifestyle medicine can do. More than 50 papers have been published almost exclusively in peer-reviewed scientific journals. You can find some of the most important ones listed on his website at www.hansdiehl.com/scientific.

67   Darren Morton et al., "The Complete Health Improvement Program (CHIP): History, Evaluation, and Outcomes," *American Journal of Lifestyle Medicine* 10, no. 1 (2016): 64–73, https://doi.org/10.1177/1559827614531391.

68   You can find more information on CHIP at the National Library of Medicine in Morton et al., "The Complete Health Improvement Program (CHIP)." In the report, the American College of Lifestyle Medicine is quoted as saying that CHIP achieved "some of the most impressive clinical outcomes published in the literature."

69   See more at https://www.rebootwithjoe.com/watch-here/.

70   See more at https://www.foodmatters.com/films/hungry-for-change.

71   See more at https://participant.com/film/food-inc.

72   See more at https://www.forksoverknives.com/the-film/.

73   See more at https://www.meatmehalfway.org.

74   See more at https://www.plantpurenation.com/pages/about-us.

75   See more at https://gamechangersmovie.com.

76   See more at https://getvegucated.com/film/.

77   See more at https://www.whatthehealthfilm.com.

78   See more at https://opsociety.org/ops-productions/films/you-are-what-you-eat-a-twin-experiment/.

79   Greger and Stone, *How Not to Die*, 266.

80   Susan Peirce Thompson, *Bright Line Eating: The Science of Living Happy, Thin and Free* (Carlsbad, CA: Hay House, 2017), 62.

81   See more at https://nutritionstudies.org.

82   T. Colin Campbell, "Why Is the Science of Nutrition Ignored in Medicine?," filmed May 2018 at TEDxCornellUniversity, TED video, 16:42.

83   See more at SilverhillsBakery.ca.

84   It's possible that Dr. Ann Vertel, motivational psychologist, originated this saying.

85   Danielle Page, "The Genetic Trait That Makes You Susceptible to Unhealthy Food Cravings," *USA Today*, March 1, 2018, https://www.usatoday.com/story/sponsor-story/bright-line-eating/2018/03/01/sugar-addiction/110965186/.

86 "Harmful Use of Alcohol Kills More Than 3 Million People Each Year, Most of Them Men," World Health Organization, September 21, 2018, https://www.who.int/news/item/21-09-2018-harmful-use-of-alcohol-kills-more-than-3-million-people-each-year--most-of-them-men.

87 Daniel Maté and Gabor Maté, *The Myth of Normal: Trauma, Illness, and Healing in a Toxic Culture* (New York: Avery, 2022), 7.

88 Maté and Maté, Myth of Normal, 7.

89 Diagnostic and Statistical Manual of Mental Disorders, 5th ed. (Arlington, VA: American Psychiatric Association, 2013) 483.

90 Emphasis mine.

91 Diagnostic and Statistical Manual of Mental Disorders, 483–4.

92 Diagnostic and Statistical Manual of Mental Disorders, 481.

93 Diagnostic and Statistical Manual of Mental Disorders, 329.

94 Diagnostic and Statistical Manual of Mental Disorders, 329.

95 Modified summary from "Is There a 12 Step Program for Food Addiction?," 12 Step, accessed May 11, 2022, https://www.12step.com/articles/is-there-a-12-step-program-for-food-addiction.

96 Anna Lembke, Dopamine Nation: Finding Balance in the Age of Indulgence (New York: Dutton, 2021), 109.

97 Peirce Thompson, Bright Line Eating, 57.

98 Ibid.

99 Gabor Maté, In the Realm of Hungry Ghosts: Close Encounters with Addiction (London: Vermillion, 2018), 216.

100 Michael Greger, How Not to Diet: The Groundbreaking Science of Healthy, Permanent Weight Loss (New York: Flatiron Books, 2019), 176.

101 Greger, How Not to Diet, 177.

102 Maté, Hungry Ghosts, 128.

103 "Assessing Your Weight and Health Risk," National Heart, Lung, and Blood Institute, accessed March 14, 2024, https://www.nhlbi.nih.gov/health/educational/lose_wt/risk.htm.

104 "About Adult BMI," Centers for Disease Control and Prevention, last updated June 3, 2022, https://www.cdc.gov/healthyweight/assessing/bmi/adult_bmi/index.html.

105 "Assessing Your Weight and Health Risk."

106 Tyler Wheeler, "What Is Waist to Hip Ratio?," WebMD, July 21, 2023, https://www.webmd.com/fitness-exercise/what-is-waist-to-hip-ratio.

107 Maté, Hungry Ghosts, 357.

108 Maté, Hungry Ghosts, 216.

109 Jordan Fallis, "The 36 Best Natural Ways to Increase Dopamine Levels in the Brain," Optimal Living Dynamics, February 4, 2024, https://www.opti-mallivingdynamics.com/blog/increase-dopamine-naturally.

110 Maté, Hungry Ghosts, 215.

111 Maté, Hungry Ghosts, 143.

112 Maté, Hungry Ghosts, 216.

113 Maté, Hungry Ghosts, 216.

114 John Cawley et al., "Direct Medical Costs of Obesity in the United States and the Most Populous States," Journal of Managed Care & Specialty Pharmacy 27, no. 3 (2021): 354–66, https://doi.org/10.18553/jmcp.2021.20410.

115 "Adult Obesity Facts," Centers for Disease Control and Prevention, last updated May 17, 2022, https://www.cdc.gov/obesity/data/adult.html.

116 "Obesity and Overweight," Centers for Disease Control and Prevention, last updated January 5, 2023, https://www.cdc.gov/nchs/fastats/obesity-overweight.htm.

117 Maté, Hungry Ghosts, 180.

118 Bruce D. Perry and Oprah Winfrey, What Happened to You? Conversations on Trauma, Resilience, and Healing (New York: Flatiron Books, 2021).

119 Dr. Gabor Maté is famous for saying this repeatedly.

120 Maté, Hungry Ghosts, 215.

121 Maté, Hungry Ghosts, 215.

122 Greger, How Not to Diet, 175.

123 For more on the predatory practices of the junk-food industry, read Michael Moss, Salt Sugar Fat: How the Food Giants Hooked Us (New York: Random House, 2013); Michael Moss, Hooked: Food, Free Will, and How the Food Giants Exploit Our Addictions (New York: Random House, 2021).

124 Thompson, Bright Line Eating, 83.

125 Maté, Hungry Ghosts, 360.

126 Daniel Amen, "Change Your Brain, Change Your Life," TEDx Orange Coast, June 7, 2011, YouTube video, 19:09, https://youtu.be/MLKj1puoWCg?si=aybnopQ1wIyHdZZo.

127 R. F. Baumeister et al., "Ego Depletion: Is the Active Self a Limited Resource?," Journal of Personality and Social Psychology 74, no. 5 (1998): 1252–65, https://doi.org/10.1037//0022-3514.74.5.1252.

128 "Habits: How They Form And How To Break Them," NPR, March 5, 2012, https://www.npr.org/2012/03/05/147192599/habits-how-they-form-and-how-to-break-them.

129 Lally et al., "How Are Habits Formed."

130 Clear, Atomic Habits, 95.

131 James Clear, in his Atomic Habits, calls this stacking.

132 Anna Lembke, Dopamine Nation: Finding Balance in an Age of Indulgence (New York: Dutton, 2021), 63.

133 Elizabeth Bacharach, "How Often Do Your Taste Buds Change?," Women's Health, January 17, 2019, https://www.womenshealthmag.com/food/a25838847/how-often-do-your-taste-buds-change/.

134 Lembke, Dopamine Nation, 69.

135 Clear, Atomic Habits, 95.

136 Johann Hari, "Everything You Think You Know About Addiction Is Wrong," filmed June 2015 at TEDGlobalLondon, TED video, 14:33, https://www.ted.com/talks/johann_hari_everything_you_think_you_know_about_addiction_is_wrong.

137 Thompson, Bright Line Eating, 182.

138 Hana Kahleova et al., "Meal Frequency and Timing Are Associated with Changes in Body Mass Index in Adventist Health Study 2," The Journal of Nutrition 147, no. 9 (2017): 1722–28, https://doi.org/10.3945/jn.116.244749.

139 Miller, Awakened Brain, 154.

140 Fallis, "Increase Dopamine Levels."

141 Jon Johnson, "What Causes Food Cravings?," Medical News Today, last updated May 16, 2023, https://www.medicalnewstoday.com/articles/318441

142 Ariana Chao et al., "Food Cravings Mediate the Relationship Between Chronic Stress and Body Mass Index," Journal of Health Psychology, 20, no. 6 (2015): 721–29, https://doi.org/10.1177/1359105315573448.

143 "Dopamine," Cleveland Clinic, last updated March 23, 2022, https://my.clevelandclinic.org/health/articles/22581-dopamine.

144 Achor, Big Potential, 74.

145 Achor, Big Potential, 74.

146 Elizabeth A. Fallon et al., "Prevalence of Diagnosed Arthritis—United States, 2019–2021," Morbidity and Mortality Weekly Report (MMWR) 72, no. 41 (2023): 1101–07, http://dx.doi.org/10.15585/mmwr.mm7241a1, quoted in "National Statistics," Centers for Disease Control and Prevention, last updated October 4, 2023, https://www.cdc.gov/arthritis/data_statistics/national-statistics.html.

147 Ibid.

148 "Why Is Arthritis More Common In Women?," Summit Orthopedics blog, March 23, 2015, https://www.summitortho.com/2015/03/23/ask-dr-rodriguez-arthritis-common-women/

149 "Nutrition and Healthy Eating," Mayo Clinic, accessed March 14, 2024, https://www.mayoclinic.org/healthy-lifestyle/nutrition-and-healthy-eating/in-depth/water/art-20044256.

150 Edmund Hillary, High Adventure: Our Ascent of the Everest (New York: Roli Books, 1955), 209.

151 "Dehydration," Mayo Clinic, accessed March 14, 2024, https://www.mayoclinic.org/diseases-conditions/dehydration/symptoms-causes/syc-20354086.

152 "Best Drinks for Arthritis," Arthritis Foundation, accessed March 14, 2024, https://www.arthritis.org/health-wellness/healthy-living/nutrition/healthy-eating/best-drinks-for-arthritis.

153 MedCram - Medical Lectures Explained CLEARLY, "High Serum Sodium Associated with Mortality and Chronic Disease," January 16, 2023, YouTube video, 13:36, https://youtu.be/dVGEED-i8cc?si=smOCdz0upQmw1vQA.

154 "Water," The Nutrition Source, Harvard T. H. Chan School of Public Health, accessed March 14, 2024, https://www.hsph.harvard.edu/nutritionsource/water/.

155 Dehydration Headache, Cleveland Clinic, last updated December 3, 2021, https://my.clevelandclinic.org/health/diseases/21517-dehydration-headache.

156 "Dehydration," Cleveland Clinic, accessed March 14, 2024, https://my.clevelandclinic.org/health/diseases/9013-dehydration.

157 Matthew Solan, "You Don't Say? The Many Colors of Urine," Harvard Health Publishing, May 1, 2022, https://www.health.harvard.edu/staying-healthy/you-dont-say-the-many-colors-of-urine.

158 "Yes, Drinking More Water May Help You Lose Weight," HUB at Work, Johns Hopkins University, January 15, 2020, https://hub.jhu.edu/at-work/2020/01/15/focus-on-wellness-drinking-more-water/.

159 Steffie Drucker, "Drinking Water May Boost Kids' Mental Sharpness," Discovery, February 12, 2020, https://www.discovery.com/science/drinking-water-may-boost-kids--mental-sharpness.

160 James McIntosh, "Fifteen Benefits of Drinking Water," Medical News Today, last updated December 21, 2023, https://www.medicalnewstoday.com/articles/290814.

161 Brett, "Does Water Therapy Help with Acne?," The Harley Street Dermatology Clinic, August 25, 2021, https://www.theharleystreetderma-tologyclinic.co.uk/does-water-help-with-acne/.

162 "10 Amazing Skin Benefits from Drinking More Water," Manna Hydration, accessed March 14, 2024, https://mannahydration.com/blogs/news/amazing-skin-benefits-from-drinking-water.

163 Lídia Palma et al., "Dietary Water Affects Human Skin Hydration and Biomechanics," Clinical, Cosmetic and Investigational Dermatology 8 (2015): 413–21, https://doi.org/10.2147/CCID.S86822. For example, drinking water makes us less vulnerable to premature wrinkling. McIntosh, "Fifteen Benefits of Drinking Water."

164 D. S. Michaud et al., "Fluid Intake and the Risk of Bladder Cancer in Men," The New England Journal of Medicine 340, no. 18 (1999): 1390–97, https://doi.org/10.1056/NEJM199905063401803.

165 Michael Greger, "How Much Water Should We Drink Every Day?," NutritionFacts.org, last updated August 30, 2017, https://nutritionfacts.org/blog/how-much-water-should-we-drink-every-day/.

166 Susan M. Kleiner, "Water: An Essential but Overlooked Nutrient," Journal of the American Dietetic Association 99, no. 2 (1999): 200–206, https://doi.org/10.1016/S0002-8223(99)00048-6.

167 Mallika Marshall, "The Big Benefits of Plain Water," Harvard Health Publishing, May 26, 2016, https://www.health.harvard.edu/blog/big-benefits-plain-water-201605269675.

168 Greger, How Not to Diet, 437.

169 Lisa, personal interview with the author, spring 2023.

170 "Dehydration," Cleveland Clinic, accessed March 14, 2024, https://my.clevelandclinic.org/health/diseases/9013-dehydration.

171 "Staying Hydrated Boosts Brain Power," Women's Brain Health Initiative, November 2023, https://womensbrainhealth.org/think-tank/brain-buzz/staying-hydrated-boosts-brain-power.

172 Jim Kwik, "Brain Foods That Are Good for You | Jim Kwik & Dr. Lisa Mosconi," December 14, 2018, YouTube video, 39:21, https://youtu.be/qxiAmJllp4I?si=M4X6Y2rfWH-R6Z8z.

173 McIntosh, "Fifteen Benefits of Drinking Water."

174 Greger and Stone, How Not to Die, 381.

175 Ibid.

176 Agatha M. Thrash, "Water," Uchee Pines, September 17, 2013, archived September 5, 2020, at the Wayback Machine, https://web.archive.org/web/20200905222622/https://www.ucheepines.org/water/.

177 Arlene Semeco, "What Happens if You Drink Too Much Water?," Medical News Today, last updated December 19, 2023, https://www.medicalnewstoday.com/articles/318619.

178 "Drinking-Water," World Health Organization, September 13, 2023, https://www.who.int/news-room/fact-sheets/detail/drinking-water.

179 Tatum Pied, "Bottled Water: The Human Health Consequences of Drinking from Plastic," Clean Water Action, July 29, 2020, https://cleanwater.org/2020/07/29/bottled-water-human-health-consequences-drinking-plastic.

180 David Common and Eric Szeto, "Microplastics Found in 93% of Bottled Water Tested in Global Study," CBC, March 14, 2018, https://www.cbc.ca/news/science/bottled-water-microplastics-1.4575045.

181 Charlie Lai, "Microplastics in Water: Threats and Solutions," Earth.org, July 20, 2022, https://earth.org/microplastics-in-water/.

182 Cameron Johnston, "The Joy Will Return," in Wake Up . . . Live the Life You Love: Finding Life's Passion, edited by Lee Beard and Steven E. (Wake Up Inc, 2006), 73–74.

183 Peter Bongiorno, A Cold Splash—Hydrotherapy for Depression and Anxiety, Psychology Today, July 6, 2014, https://www.psychologytoday.com/us/blog/inner-source/201407/cold-splash-hydrotherapy-depression-and-anxiety.

184 Nikolai A Shevchuk, "Adapted Cold Shower as a Potential Treatment for Depression," Medical Hypotheses 70, no. 5 (2008): 995–1001, https://doi.org/10.1016/j.mehy.2007.04.052.

185 Christa Orecchio, "11 Ways to Heal and Nourish the Nervous System," Christa Orecchio, accessed March 14, 2024, https://www.christaorecchio.com/blog/nervous-system-healing-tips.

186 Orecchio, "Heal and Nourish the Nervous System."

187 "How to Activate Parasympathetic Nervous System (14 Ways), LB Health & Lifestyle (blog), March 29, 2023, https://lbhealthandlifestyle.com/ vagus-nerve-exercises-12-ways-to-improve-health/.

188 Geert A. Buijze, "The Effect of Cold Showering on Health and Work: A Randomized Controlled Trial," PLOS ONE 13, no. 8 (2018): e0201978, https://doi.org/10.1371/journal.pone.0201978.

189 Jessica Caporuscio, "What Are the Benefits of Cold and Hot Showers?," Medical News Today, updated March 29, 2023, https://www.medicalnews-today.com/articles/327461.

190 "Risks of Physical Inactivity," Johns Hopkins Medicine, accessed August 9, 2022, https://www.hopkinsmedicine.org/health/conditions-and-diseases/ risks-of-physical-inactivity.

191 Edward R. Laskowski, M.D., "What Are the Risks of Sitting Too Much?," May Clinic, accessed August 21, 2022, https://www.mayoclinic.org/ healthy-lifestyle/adult-health/expert-answers/sitting/faq-20058005.

192 Meredith Chandler, "Sitting Disease: The Terrifying Facts of Prolonged Sitting," Ergonomics Health Association, accessed August 21, 2022, https:// ergonomicshealth.com/sitting-disease.

193 Chandler, "Sitting Disease."

194 Tom Rath, Eat, Move, Sleep: How Small Choices Lead to Big Changes (Missionday, 2013), 48.

195 The region of the brain that creates new memories is called the medial temporal lobe (MTL). A healthy MTL is flush with many neurons and neuro connections, allowing for the free flow of thought. A weak MTL is thin and sparse, with fewer neurons and neuro connections. According to Harvard Health, "MTL thinning can be a precursor to cognitive de-cline and dementia." Matthew Solan, "The Worst Habits for Your Brain," Harvard Health Publishing, April 1, 2022, https://www.health.harvard.edu/ mind-and-mood/the-worst-habits-for-your-brain.

196 Solan, "Worst Habits."

197 Laskowski, "Sitting Too Much."

198 "Risks of Physical Inactivity."

199 Fallis, "Increase Dopamine Levels."

200 Stephen Ilardi, "Depression Is a Disease of Civilization," TEDx Emory, June 7, 2011, YouTube video, 22:20, https://youtu.be/drv3BP0Fdi8?si=wBGNH Yh1N8zPTwLu.

201 The term "Blue Zones" was coined by National Geographic journalist Dan Buettner. The original Blue Zones were Ikaria, Greece; Okinawa, Japan; Sardinia, Italy; Nicoya Peninsula, Costa Rica; and Loma Linda, California, USA. Dan Buettner has recently added Singapore and dozens of other locations to the list.

202 Wendy Suzuki, "Healthy Brain Happy Life," TEDxBayArea, December 22, 2014, YouTube video, 16:15, https://youtu.be/0cJ5pVtvbZA?si=3rthF3R2_QS-5u2a.

203 Wendy Suzuki. Healthy Brain, Happy Life: A Personal Program to Activate Your Brain and Do Everything Better (New York: William Morrow, 2015), 116.

204 Laskowski, "Sitting Too Much."

205 "Arthritis National Statistics," Centers for Disease Control and Prevention, last updated October 4, 2023, https://www.cdc.gov/arthritis/data_statistics/national-statistics.html.

206 "Exercise and Stress: Get Moving to Manage Stress," Mayo Clinic, accessed August 10, 2022, https://www.mayoclinic.org/healthy-lifestyle/stress-management/in-depth/exercise-and-stress/art-20044469.

207 "How Exercise Affects Your Sleep," Cleveland Clinic, November 10, 2020, https://health.clevelandclinic.org/how-exercise-affects-your-sleep/.

208 "Episode 9: Move for a Better Brain," Science of Prevention, video, 35:55, https://scienceofprevention.com/alz/exercise-alzheimers/.

209 Suzuki, "Healthy Brain Happy Life."

210 Wendy Suzuki, "The Brain-Changing Benefits of Exercise," filmed November 2017 at TEDWomen 2017, TED video, 12:54. https://www.ted.com/talks/wendy_suzuki_the_brain_changing_benefits_of_exercise.

211 Suzuki, "Benefits of Exercise."

212 Suzuki, "Benefits of Exercise."

213 Fallis, "Increase Dopamine Levels."

214 Kirk I. Erickson, "Exercise Training Increases Size of Hippocampus and Improves Memory," Proceedings of the National Academy of Sciences of the United States of America 108, no. 7 (2011): 3017–22, https://doi.org/10.1073/pnas.1015950108.

215 "How Exercise Affects Your Sleep."

216 "Shore Up Your Core," Harvard Health Publishing, May 1, 2020, https://www.health.harvard.edu/staying-healthy/shore-up-your-core).

217 Myrna Oliver, "Hulda Crooks, 101; Oldest Woman to Scale Mt. Whitney," Los Angeles Times, November 26, 1997, https://www.latimes.com/archives/la-xpm-1997-nov-26-mn-57923-story.html.

218 Áine Kelly, "Exercise May Reduce Brain Inflammation, Reducing the Risk of Alzheimer's," Neuroscience News, November 28, 2021, https://neurosciencenews.com/exercise-inflammation-alzheimers-19712/.

219 "12 Benefits of Walking," Arthritis Foundation, accessed March 15, 2024, https://www.arthritis.org/health-wellness/healthy-living/physical-activity/walking/12-benefits-of-walking.

220 Chandler, "Sitting Disease."

221 Classical Stretch by Essentrics, "Aging Backwards No.3 Soothe Your Joints | Essentrics," June 14, 2017, YouTube video, 10:56, https://youtu.be/DM5kbmA7LtY?si=ZKDGF5at__q7HVYL.

222 Larry Swanson, "The Definitive Guide to Actual Famous Standing Desk Users," Larry Swanson, June 21, 2016, https://www.larryswanson.com/famous-standing-desk-users/.

223 Qing Li, " 'Forest Bathing' Is Great for Your Health. Here's How to Do It," TIME, May 1, 2018, https://time.com/5259602/japanese-forest-bathing/.

224 Vinh Van Tran, Duckshin Park, and Young-Chul Lee, "Indoor Air Pollution, Related Human Diseases, and Recent Trends in the Control and Improvement of Indoor Air Quality," International Journal of Environmental Research and Public Health 17, no. 8 (2020): 2927, https://doi.org/10.3390/ijerph17082927.

225 Danielle Dresden, "What to Know About the Health Benefits of Sunlight," Medical News Today, November 4, 2020, https://www.medicalnewstoday.com/articles/benefits-of-sunlight.

226 For more information, read Dr. Qing Li's book, Forest Bathing: How Trees Can Help You Find Health and Happiness (New York: Viking, 2018).

227 Q. Li et al., "Forest Bathing Enhances Human Natural Killer Activity and Expression of Anti-Cancer Proteins," International Journal of Immunopathology and Pharmacology 20, 2 Suppl 2 (2007): 3–8, https://doi.org/10.1177/03946320070200S202.

228 Li et al., "Forest Bathing."

229 Marc G. Berman et al., "Interacting with Nature Improves Cognition and Affect for Individuals with Depression," Journal of Affective Disorders 140, no. 3 (2012): 300–305, https://doi.org/10.1016/j.jad.2012.03.012.

230 " 'Depression: Let's Talk' Says WHO, as Depression Tops List of Causes of Ill Health," World Health Organization, March 30, 2017, https://www.who.int/news/item/30-03-2017--depression-let-s-talk-says-who-as-depression-tops-list-of-causes-of-ill-health.

231 MedCram - Medical Lectures Explained CLEARLY, "Sunlight: Optimize Health and Immunity (Light Therapy and Melatonin)," January 21, 2022, YouTube video, 1:56:09, https://youtu.be/5YV_iKnzDRg?si=djCbWhNQz0MKqEm8.

232 Berman, "Interacting with Nature."

233 Kirsten Weir, "Nurtured by Nature," Monitor on Psychology 51, no. 3 (2020): 50, https://www.apa.org/monitor/2020/04/nurtured-nature.

234 Ming Kuo, Michael Barnes, and Catherine Jordan, "Do Experiences with Nature Promote Learning? Converging Evidence of a Cause-and-Effect Relationship," Frontiers in Psychology 10 (2019), https://doi.org/10.3389/fpsyg.2019.00305.

235 Cynthia Aranow, "Vitamin D and the Immune System," Journal of Investigative Medicine: The Official Publication of the American Federation for Clinical Research 59, no. 6 (2011): 881–86, https://doi.org/10.2310/JIM.0b013e31821b8755.

236 NEWSTART, "Sunny Side: Sunlight | NEWSTART Now | Episode 4," August 1, 2022, YouTube video, 38:32, https://youtu.be/6xfJp30zvig?si=xAwI0EmFk_3-9flo.

237 Dresden, "Health Benefits of Sunlight"; H. J. van der Rhee, E. de Vries, and J. W. Coebergh, "Regular Sun Exposure Benefits Health," Medical Hypotheses 97 (2016): 34–37, https://doi.org/10.1016/j.mehy.2016.10.011.

238 Greger and Stone, How Not to Die, x.

239 Richard B. Weller, "Sunlight Has Cardiovascular Benefits Independently of Vitamin D," Blood Purification 41, no. 1–3 (2016): 130–34, https://doi.org/10.1159/000441266.

240 NEWSTART, "Sunny Side: Sunlight."

241 NEWSTART, "Sunny Side: Sunlight."

242 NEWSTART, "Sunny Side: Sunlight."

243 Ryan Raman, "How to Safely Get Vitamin D From Sunlight," Healthline, last updated April 4, 2023, https://www.healthline.com/nutrition/vitamin-d-from-sun.

244 NEWSTART, "Sunny Side: Sunlight."

245 "Surprising Health Benefits of Getting Fresh Air," Long Island Weight Loss Institute, May 28, 2020, https://liwli.com/surprising-health-benefits-of-fresh-air/.

246 "Surprising Health Benefits."

247 David Shukman, "Coronavirus: Fresh Air 'Forgotten Weapon' in Fight," BBC, December 24, 2020, https://www.bbc.com/news/health-55435914.

248 "Surprising Health Benefits."

249 Joseph M Seguel et al., "Indoor Air Quality," American Journal of Lifestyle Medicine 11, no. 4 (2016): 284–95, https://doi.org/10.1177/1559827616653343.

250 Darryl Edwards, "Why Working Out Isn't Working Out," filmed January 2019 at TEDxRoyalTunbridgeWells, TED video, 17:17, https://www.ted.com/talks/darryl_edwards_why_working_out_isn_t_working_out_jan_2019.

251 Michelle Arthurs-Brennan, "Why Cycling is Great for Your Legs, Lungs, Immune System and Mind, Plus 11 Other Great Benefits of Life on Two Wheels!," Cycling Weekly, last updated November 18 2022, https://www.cyclingweekly.com/news/latest-news/benefits-of-cycling-334144.

252 Daniel Preiato, "Is Walking After Eating Good for You?," Healthline, July 13, 2020, https://www.healthline.com/nutrition/walking-after-eating.

253 "Drivers are Falling Asleep Behind the Wheel," National Safety Council, accessed March 15, 2024, https://www.nsc.org/road/safety-topics/fatigued-driver.

254 Matthew Walker, Why We Sleep: Unlocking the Power of Sleep and Dreams (Scribner, New York, 2017), 134.

255 "The State of Sleep Health in America 2023," American Sleep Apnea Association, https://www.sleephealth.org/sleep-health/the-state-of-sleephealth-in-america/.

256 "State of Sleep Health."

257 Walker, Why We Sleep, 107.

258 Dr Chatterjee Clips, "The OPTIMAL Sleep Conditions To Improve SLEEP QUALITY | Matthew Walker," January 19, 2023, YouTube video, 14:45, https://youtu.be/ncJ8PciMiOs?si=wFWBZBKbUHtVojTf.

259 Sarah E. Jackson, Clemens Kirschbaum, and Andrew Steptoe, "Hair Cortisol and Adiposity in a Population-Based Sample of 2,527 Men and Women Aged 54 to 87 Years," Obesity 25, no. 3 (2017): 539–44, https://doi.org/10.1002/oby.21733.

260 Jackson, Kirschbaum, and Steptoe, "Hair Cortisol and Adiposity."

261 Angeline Jane Bernabe, "Jennifer Lopez Says Sleep Is Her Biggest Beauty Secret," Good Morning America, May 22, 2022, https://www.goodmorningamerica.com/style/story/jennifer-lopez-sleep-biggest-beauty-secret-84902292.

262 Tina Sundelin et al., "Negative Effects of Restricted Sleep on Facial Appearance and Social Appeal," Royal Society Open Science 4 (2017): 160918, https://doi.org/10.1098/rsos.160918.

263 Gail Johnson, "Sleep Deprivation Can be a Nightmare: The True Cost of Fatigue," Alive, updated January 18, 2017, https://www.alive.com/health/sleep-deprivation-can-be-a-nightmare/.

264 "Sleep Habits Affect Your Food Habits," PositiveChoices.com, September 5, 2013, https://www.positivechoices.com/positivetip/sleep-habits-affect-your-food-habits/.

265 "Figure 1: Neural Consequences of Sleep Deprivation on Food Desirability" in Stephanie M. Greer, Andrea N. Goldstein, and Matthew P. Walker, "The Impact of Sleep Deprivation on Food Desire in the Human Brain," Nature Communications 4, no. 2259 (2013): https://doi.org/10.1038/ncomms3259.

266 Marco Hafner et al., Why Sleep Matters—the Economic Costs of Insufficient Sleep: A Cross-country Comparative Analysis (Santa Monica, CA: RAND Corporation, 2016), https://www.rand.org/pubs/research_reports/RR1791.html.

267 "How Much Sleep Do I Need?," Centers for Disease Control and Prevention, last reviewed September 14, 2022, https://www.cdc.gov/sleep/about_sleep/how_much_sleep.html.

268 Walker, Why We Sleep, 342.

269 R. Manfredini et al., "Daylight Saving Time and Myocardial Infarction: Should We Be Worried? A Review of the Evidence," European Review for Medical and Pharmacological Sciences 22, no. 3 (2018): 750–55, https://doi.org/10.26355/eurrev_201802_14306.

270 Walker, Why We Sleep, 169.

271 Alice Park, "'A Rinsing of the Brain.' New Research Shows How Sleep Could Ward Off Alzheimer's Disease," TIME, August 6, 2020, https://time.com/5876612/sleep-alzheimers-disease-2/.

272 Walker, Why We Sleep, 75.

273 Danielle Pacheco and Dr. David Rosen, "Best Temperature for Sleep," Sleep Foundation, updated March 4, 2024, https://www.sleepfoundation.org/bedroom-environment/best-temperature-for-sleep.

274 Anne-Marie Chang et al., "Evening Use of Light-Emitting eReaders Negatively Affects Sleep, Circadian Timing, and Next-morning Alertness," Proceedings of the National Academy of Sciences 112, no. 4 (2015): 1232–37, https://doi.org/10.1073/pnas.1418490112.

275 Chang et al., "Evening Use of Light-Emitting eReaders."

276 Louis Faust et al., "Deviations from Normal Bedtimes Are Associated with Short-term Increases in Resting Heart Rate," Nature 3, no. 39 (2020), https://doi.org/10.1038/s41746-020-0250-6.

277 Faust et at., "Deviations."

278 Ian Clark and Hans Peter Landolt, "Coffee, Caffeine, and Sleep: A Systematic Review of Epidemiological Studies and Randomized Controlled Trials," Sleep Medicine Reviews 31 (2017): 70–78, https://doi.org/10.1016/j.smrv.2016.01.006.

279 Walker, Why We Sleep, 271.

280 Robyn Burton and Nick Sheron, "No Level of Alcohol Consumption Improves Health," The Lancet 392, no. 10152 (2018): P987–88, https://doi.org/10.1016/S0140-6736(18)31571-X.

281 Walker, Why We Sleep, 283.

282 Tiffany Shlain, "Tech's Best Feature: The Off Switch," Harvard Business Review, March 1, 2013, https://hbr.org/2013/03/techs-best-feature-the-off-swi.

283 Moments Channel, "DeVon Franklin: Sabbath Rest (A Moment of Insight)," October 24, 2014, YouTube video, 1:30, https://youtu.be/K5zmXjvj8mY?si=at8ENGiZ5AMKywNF.

284 Catherine Clifford, "Bill Gates Took Solo 'Think Weeks' in a Cabin in the Woods—Why It's a Great Strategy," CNBC, July 28, 2019, https://www.cnbc.com/2019/07/26/bill-gates-took-solo-think-weeks-in-a-cabin-in-the-woods.html.

285 Tom Bilyeu, "The 1% DO THIS To Achieve Anything They Want! (START DOING THIS) | Patrick Bet David," June 4, 2019, YouTube video, 40:13, https://youtu.be/Mj8kr-wZqlM?si=0QjNGqfypE6H9w1d.

286 This does not replace a doctor's formal diagnosis.

287 Downloadable at fullpower1.com.

288 This idea came from Susan Peirce Thompson, Bright Line Eating.

289 Downloadable at fullpower1.com.

290 Benjamin Gardner, Phillippa Lally, and Jane Wardle, "Making Health Habitual: The Psychology of 'Habit-Formation' and General Practice," The British Journal of General Practice: The Journal of the Royal College of General Practitioners 62, no. 605 (2012): 664–66, https://doi.org/10.3399/bjgp12X659466.